Lecture Notes in Computer Science   12900

More information about this subseries at http://www.springer.com/series/7410

Robert Krimmer · Melanie Volkamer ·
David Duenas-Cid · Oksana Kulyk ·
Peter Rønne · Mihkel Solvak ·
Micha Germann (Eds.)

Electronic Voting

6th International Joint Conference, E-Vote-ID 2021
Virtual Event, October 5–8, 2021
Proceedings

 Springer

Editors
Robert Krimmer (iD)
University of Tartu
Tartu, Estonia

David Duenas-Cid (iD)
Kozminski University
Warsaw, Poland

University of Tartu
Tartu, Estonia

Peter Rønne (iD)
University of Luxembourg
Esch-sur-Alzette, Luxembourg

Micha Germann (iD)
University of Bath
Bath, UK

Melanie Volkamer (iD)
Karlsruhe Institute of Technology
Karlsruhe, Germany

Oksana Kulyk
University of Copenhagen
København, Denmark

Mihkel Solvak
University of Tartu
Tartu, Estonia

ISSN 0302-9743   ISSN 1611-3349 (electronic)
Lecture Notes in Computer Science
ISBN 978-3-030-86941-0   ISBN 978-3-030-86942-7 (eBook)
https://doi.org/10.1007/978-3-030-86942-7

LNCS Sublibrary: SL4 – Security and Cryptology

This Springer imprint is published by the registered company Springer Nature Switzerland AG
The registered company address is: Gewerbestrasse 11, 6330 Cham, Switzerland

Preface

This volume contains the papers presented at E-Vote-ID 2021, the Sixth International Joint Conference on Electronic Voting, held during October 5–8, 2021. Due to the extraordinary situation brought about by the COVID-19, the conference was held online for the second consecutive edition, instead of in the traditional venue in Bregenz, Austria. The E-Vote-ID conference is the result of the merger of the EVOTE and Vote-ID conferences, with first EVOTE conference taking place 17 years ago in Austria. Since that conference in 2004, over 1000 experts have attended the venue, including scholars, practitioners, authorities, electoral managers, vendors, and PhD students. The conference focuses on the most relevant debates on the development of electronic voting, from aspects relating to security and usability through to practical experiences and applications of voting systems, also including legal, social, or political aspects, amongst others, and has turned out to be an important global referent in relation to this issue.

This year, the conference featured the following:

- Security, Usability, and Technical Issues Track
- Administrative, Legal, Political, and Social Issues Track
- Election and Practical Experiences Track
- PhD Colloquium
- Poster and Demo Session.

E-Vote-ID 2021 received 49 submissions and each paper was reviewed by three to five Program Committee members using a double blind review process. As a result, 11 papers were accepted for this volume, representing 22% of the submitted proposals. The selected papers cover a wide range of topics connected with electronic voting, including experiences and revisions of real-world uses of e-voting systems and corresponding processes in elections.

We would like to thank the German Informatics Society (Gesellschaft für Informatik) with its ECOM working group and KASTEL for their partnership over many years. Further, we would like to thank the Swiss Federal Chancellery and the Regional Government of Vorarlberg for their kind support. E-Vote-ID 2021 was kindly supported through the European Union's Horizon 2020 projects ECEPS (grant agreement 857622) and mGov4EU (grant agreement 959072). Special thanks go to the members of the international Program Committee for their hard work in reviewing, discussing, and shepherding papers. They ensured the high quality of these proceedings with their knowledge and experience.

October 2021

Robert Krimmer
Melanie Volkamer
David Duenas-Cid
Oksana Kulyk
Peter Rønne
Mihkel Solvak
Micha Germann

Organization

General Chairs

Robert Krimmer   University of Tartu, Estonia
Melanie Volkamer   Karlsruher Institut für Technologie, Germany
David Duenas-Cid   Kozminski University, Poland, and University of Tartu, Estonia

Program Track Chairs

Mihkel Solvak   University of Tartu, Estonia
Micha Germann   University of Bath, UK
Oksana Kulyk   IT University of Copenhagen, Denmark
Peter Roenne   University of Luxembourg, Luxembourg

Program Committee

Marta Aranyossy   Corvinus University of Budapest, Hungary
Roberto Araujo   Universidade Federal do Pará, Brazil
Jordi Barrat i Esteve   eVoting Legal Lab, Spain
Bernhard Beckert   Karlsruhe Institute of Technology, Germany
Josh Benaloh   Microsoft, USA
Matthew Bernhard   University of Michigan, USA
Enka Blanchard   Université de Lorraine, France
Stephen Boyce   IFES, USA
Jurlind Budurushi   Cloudical Deutschland GmbH, Germany
Jeremy Clark   Concordia University, Canada
Veronique Cortier   CNRS, Loria, France
Régis Dandoy   Universidad San Francisco de Quito, Equador
Staffan Darnolf   IFES, USA
Constantin Catalin Dragan   University of Surrey, UK
David Duenas-Cid   Kozminski University, Poland, and University of Tartu, Estonia
Helen Eenmaa   University of Tartu, Estonia
Aleksander Essex   University of Western Ontario, Canada
Micha Germann   University of Bath, UK
J Paul Gibson   Institut Mines-Télécom, France
Rosario Giustolisi   IT University of Copenhagen, Denmark
Kristian Gjøsteen   Norwegian University of Science and Technology, Norway
Nicole Goodman   University of Toronto, Canada
Rajeev Gore   The Australian National University, Australia

Contents

Provably Improving Election Verifiability in Belenios

Sevdenur Baloglu[1]([⊠]) [iD], Sergiu Bursuc[1] [iD], Sjouke Mauw[2] [iD], and Jun Pang[2] [iD]

[1] SnT, University of Luxembourg, Esch-sur-Alzette, Luxembourg
{sevdenur.baloglu,sergiu.bursuc}@uni.lu
[2] DCS, University of Luxembourg, Esch-sur-Alzette, Luxembourg
{sjouke.mauw,jun.pang}@uni.lu

Abstract. Belenios is an online voting system that provides a strong notion of election verifiability, where no single party has to be trusted, and security holds as soon as either the voting registrar or the voting server is honest. It was formally proved to be secure, making the assumption that no further ballots are cast on the bulletin board after voters verified their ballots. In practice, however, revoting is allowed and voters can verify their ballots anytime. This gap between formal proofs and use in practice leaves open space for attacks, as has been shown recently. In this paper we make two simple additions to Belenios and we formally prove that the new version satisfies the expected verifiability properties. Our proofs are automatically performed with the Tamarin prover, under the assumption that voters are allowed to vote at most four times.

Keywords: Electronic voting · Formal verification · Verifiability

1 Introduction

Election verifiability aims to ensure that the outcome of an election, relying on a given electronic voting protocol, correctly reflects the votes of eligible voters. One of its important features is that it should be software independent and end-to-end: even if an adversary corrupts (the software on) voting platforms, election authorities, or voting servers, the public information published on the bulletin board should be sufficient to verify that the election outcome correctly reflects voter choices. This verification is performed by honest parties, which are typically a subset of voters and election auditors. Especially for voters, the verification procedure should also be easy to use, in order to achieve widespread adoption and security guarantees.

Helios is an internet voting system that targets this notion of end-to-end verifiability [1,6,7]. However, an important assumption is that the voting server is honest. Otherwise it could stuff ballots, allowing the adversary to add illegitimate votes, most easily for voters that have not voted. In general, for usability, *revoting is allowed* and *voters can verify their ballots anytime* after voting. In that case ballot stuffing is possible even for voters that have verified their ballots successfully. For example, the server can let some time elapse after a ballot was

© Springer Nature Switzerland AG 2021
R. Krimmer et al. (Eds.): E-Vote-ID 2021, LNCS 12900, pp. 1–16, 2021.
https://doi.org/10.1007/978-3-030-86942-7_1

cast, and cast a new ballot in the name of the same voter. This looks like revoting to observers and will not be noticed by voters verifying their ballots right after voting. The so-called clash attacks allow ballot stuffing in a more surreptitious way [22, 23, 26]: the adversary gives the same credential to two voters, one single vote is cast for them, and the adversary can cast an additional ballot with no change in the total number of ballots. If revoting is disallowed or ballot verification is after the voting phase, this requires voting platforms to be corrupted, since the adversary needs to supply the same ballot for two voters. Otherwise, it was shown in [9] that corrupting the voting platform is not needed: one voter can verify one ballot and another voter can subsequently verify another ballot for the same credential.

Belenios extends Helios in order to get stronger election verifiability [2, 16]. There is no single party that has to be trusted: verifiability holds as soon as either the voting server *or* the voting registrar is not corrupted. The registrar generates public credentials, publishes them on the bulletin board, and distributes the respective private credentials to each voter. The public credential is the verification key of a fresh signing key pair, while the private credential is the corresponding signing key. Ballots are signed and election authorities can verify on the bulletin board that all ballots have been cast by the expected legitimate party. A second advantage of Belenios is that it was proved to satisfy a formal notion of election verifiability, both in the symbolic model [15] (for a particular variant) and in the computational model [14]. This adds confidence that verifiability is satisfied by the protocol specification. Nonetheless, several problems of Belenios and of verifiability definitions in [14, 15] were shown in [9], leading to weaker guarantees than expected. In the typical scenario when revoting is allowed and voters can verify their ballots anytime, attacks on verifiability are still possible, most damaging in the case when the registrar is corrupted. Even in the ideal case when both the server and the registrar are honest, ballot reordering attacks are possible, breaking individual verifiability. These attacks are outside the scope of proofs in [14, 15], since they do not consider the typical scenario of revoting.

Usability, Everlasting Privacy and Verifiability. There are two main features that, put together, allow these attacks on verifiability in Belenios. The first feature is that, in practice [2], revoting is allowed and voters can verify their ballots anytime. This is important for usability and, eventually, also for coercion-resistance [11, 21]. The second feature is that the voting server does not know the link between the public credentials and the corresponding voter identities. Only at ballot casting time does the voter reveal this link, and the server ensures its consistency, e.g. that the same public credential does not correspond to two different voters. Revealing minimal information about the association between voters and their public credentials is important in order to ensure everlasting privacy: even if an adversary may break the underlying encryption scheme and penetrate the private logs of the server, the connection between voters and the corresponding votes should remain private. A similar pattern underlies all attacks in [9]: a corrupted voter can be used by the adversary to cast a ballot for a public credential corresponding to an honest voter. Even if honest voters successfully verified their ballots, revoting allows the adversary to undetectably replace them with its own ballots (when the registrar is corrupted), or with earlier ballots submitted by the same voters (when the registrar is honest).

Our Contributions. We propose two simple additions to Belenios and we prove that election verifiability of the resulting system, that we call Belenios+, is strictly stronger in all three scenarios that are subject to attacks in [9]. Each scenario is defined by the corruption abilities of the adversary: $\mathcal{A}_1$ - both the server and the registrar are honest; $\mathcal{A}_2$ - the server is corrupt and the registrar honest; $\mathcal{A}_3$ - the server is honest and the registrar corrupt. In all cases, we assume the adversary may corrupt the secret key of the election, any number of voters and the communication network. For voters, the proposed additions do not require any change in the voting and verification procedures, maintaining the same usability as Belenios. We do not communicate any new information to the voting server regarding the link between voter identities and public credentials. We simply enforce the veracity of the information the voter already communicates. This means that our additions should not affect everlasting privacy in Belenios (everlasting privacy has not been formally proved for Belenios, but it is thought to hold when revoting is not allowed [16]). Our security proofs are in the symbolic model, automatically performed with the Tamarin prover [24], although we need to make some further abstractions, as explained below. We use the verifiability definition of [9], which is more general than [14,15], accounting for revoting and different corruption scenarios.

Belenios relies on a zero-knowledge proof in order to verifiably attach a label to each ballot cast. The label is the public credential of the voter who constructs the ballot and the ballot cannot be detached from the intended label. The goal of this construction is to ensure that each ballot is consistently cast for the intended public credential. Our techniques enrich the structure of the label in order to ensure stronger consistency properties. The first problem that we tackle is a ballot reordering attack, which is possible in all three corruption scenarios, i.e. even for the weakest adversary $\mathcal{A}_1$. Omitting some details (presented in Sect. 2.2), the attack is as follows: an honest voter with public credential cr, may submit two successive ballots b_1 and b_2; then, relying on a corrupt voter, the adversary can cast b_2 before b_1, for the same public credential cr. The honest voter may then verify b_2 and expect it to be tallied, whereas b_1 is tallied instead. The solution we propose for this problem is to augment the label in the zero-knowledge proof such that each new ballot can also be verifiably linked to the ballot that was cast just before for a given public credential. This proof is publicly verified on the bulletin board, thus it also helps in the scenario $\mathcal{A}_2$.

The second problem in Belenios relates to the scenario $\mathcal{A}_3$ and is at the root of several attacks in [9]: because the voting server does not know in advance the connection between voter identities and public credentials, an adversary corrupting the registrar and a voter may submit any ballot for any public credential cr, and claim it corresponds to that corrupt voter. In particular, this may be a ballot b constructed by an honest voter that received the public credential cr at registration. This leads to the fact that the honest voter may successfully verify b on the bulletin board, while afterwards the adversary is able to cast its own ballot b_A for the credential cr. The solution we propose for this problem is to further augment the label in the zero-knowledge proof such that the voting server can ensure that the cast ballot is intended for the corresponding voter. However, we need to make sure that only the server can verify the link between a ballot and the voter identity. That is why the label does not directly contain the identity id of the voter, but a commitment to id, for which the server learns the randomness from the voting platform. The randomness can be discarded by the server after reconstructing the commitment and verifying the proof. To hide the identity from an all-powerful adversary against the bulletin board, we can use standard commitment schemes that are perfectly hiding, for example the Pedersen commitment [25].

Abstraction. In practice, the two additions we make do not significantly affect the complexity of running Belenios. However, the fact that we need to recursively link every new ballot with a previously cast ballot significantly affects the running time of Tamarin. To overcome this difficulty, we assume that each voter casts at most four ballots, in effect allowing revoting only thrice (all attacks of [9] occur in scenarios with at most two ballots per voter). We leave as open the problem of formally proving (or disproving) the validity of this assumption. We note that formal results that bound the number of agents or voters for verification have a similar flavour [8,12,13].

Paper Structure. Section 2 contains preliminaries about election verifiability and attacks on Belenios. In Sect. 3 we describe our improvements and in Sect. 4 we describe the protocol specification and automated verification with the Tamarin prover.

2   Preliminaries

We describe Belenios in more detail in Sect. 2.1. The formal notion of election verifiability and the attacks on Belenios are described in Sect. 2.2.

2.1   Introduction to Belenios

Apart from voters (V), the parties in the Belenios protocol [2,16] are:

- *Administrator* (A): determines the list of eligible candidates and the list of eligible voters.
- *Bulletin Board* (BB): public ledger containing election information: the public key, the list of candidates, the list of public credentials for eligible voters, the list of cast ballots, the final outcome and proofs of correctness. We denote specific portions of BB with suffixes. In particular, BBkey contains the public key of the election, BBcast contains the list of ballots cast for each public credential, and BBtally contains the list of ballots chosen for tally. BB can only be changed by writing new information on it; previously written information cannot be changed.

- *Trustees* (T): generate the secret key of the election, publish the corresponding public key on BB, compute the final outcome.
- *Registrar* (VR): for each eligible voter, it creates a fresh signing key pair (vk, skey); vk is the public credential, which is also denoted by cr in the following; it publishes the list of all public credentials on BB.
- *Voting Server* (VS): receives ballots cast by authenticated voters and publishes them on BB; voter authentication is done via passwords.
- *Voting Platform* (VP): constructs ballots for voter choices; authenticates voters with respect to VS and transmits ballots to VS; each ballot contains a ciphertext encrypting the vote, a signature of the ciphertext with respect to skey of the corresponding voter, and zero-knowledge proofs.
- *Election Auditors* (EA): perform audit and verification of proofs on BB. The validity of the ballot is verified by VS at ballot-casting time, and can also be verified by EA at any time afterwards on BBcast.

Setup Phase. A determines the list of eligible voters $id_1, \ldots, id_n$, and sends the list to VR and VS. VR generates the public and private credentials for each voter, while VS generates login passwords. Each voter id receives the tuple $\langle cr, skey, pwd \rangle$ during setup phase and BB is updated by the following:

$$\text{BBkey: pk;} \quad \text{BBcand: } v_1, \ldots, v_k; \quad \text{BBreg: } cr_1, \ldots, cr_n.$$

Voting Phase. In this phase, voters interact with their voting platform VP to construct a ballot b, which is sent together with their public credential cr to VS. Upon authentication of the voter and validity checks with respect to cr, the ballot is published on BBcast.

$$\text{VP: } c = enc(v, pk, r); \quad s = sign(c, skey); \quad pr_R = proof_R(c, r, \langle v_1, \ldots, v_k \rangle);$$
$$pr_L = proof_L(c, r, cr); \quad b = \langle c, s, pr_R, pr_L \rangle;$$
$$\text{VS: authenticates id with pwd; receives b and the public credential cr;}$$
$$\text{verifies } s, pr_R \text{ and } pr_L; \text{ and stores } (id, cr) \text{ in Log;}$$
$$\text{BBcast: } (cr, b).$$

The signature ensures the voter holds the private part of the public credential cr. The zero-knowledge proof pr_R ensures that the ciphertext contains a vote in a valid range $\langle v_1, \ldots, v_k \rangle$. The proof pr_L ensures that the ballot (and the ciphertext) is verifiably linked to the label cr, and cannot be cast for any other credential cr'. In the cryptographic construction, the underlying zero-knowledge proof system takes the arguments of $proof_R$ and $proof_L$ and returns pr_R and pr_L [14, 16]. Moreover, the following consistency property is ensured by VS for the Log storing the association between voter identities and public credentials:

$$(id, cr) \in Log \land (id, cr') \in Log \Rightarrow cr = cr' \quad \text{and}$$
$$(id, cr) \in Log \land (id', cr) \in Log \Rightarrow id = id'.$$

This prevents a corrupt voter to use a public credential already used by an honest voter, and also to cast ballots for more than one public credential. In addition to ensuring basic integrity properties, consistency of the log also prevents ballot copy attacks like in [17]. The individual verification procedure enables voters to check their ballots on BB anytime during the election. Specifically, they should check that the expected ballot b is published next to their public credential cr on BBcast.

Tally Phase. The ballots which will be tallied are selected and marked as input for the tally procedure. Selection typically chooses the last ballot cast by each cr_i and we have BBtally: $(cr_1, b_1), \ldots, (cr_n, b_n)$. $b_i = \bot$ if no ballot was cast for cr_i. Based on the homomorphic properties of ElGamal encryption [18,20], ciphertexts corresponding to non-empty ballots on BBtally are combined into a ciphertext c encoding the total number of votes for each candidate. Then, c is decrypted by trustees to obtain the result of the election.

2.2 Election Verifiability and Attacks on Belenios

We consider the symbolic definition of election verifiability from [9], which is an extension of the symbolic definition introduced in [15]. Election verifiability is modelled as a conjunction of properties $\Phi_{iv}^h \wedge \Phi_{eli} \wedge \Phi_{cl} \wedge \Phi_{res}^\circ$, where:

Individual verifiability: Φ_{iv}^h ensures that if an honest voter successfully verified the last ballot they cast, then the corresponding vote should be part of the final tally.

Eligibility: Φ_{eli} ensures that if a voter successfully verified a ballot, then the corresponding public credential should be recorded at registration on BB. Moreover, any tallied ballot should correspond to a public credential recorded at registration.

No clash: Φ_{cl} ensures that no two voters can successfully verify their ballot for the same public credential.

Result integrity: Φ_{res}° ensures that the adversary can cast a ballot for a given public credential only if the corresponding voter is corrupted or has not performed the individual verification procedure for any of the ballots cast. A stronger notion of result integrity, denoted by $\Phi_{res}^\bullet$, prohibits the adversary to cast a ballot even if the voter has not verified any of the ballots cast.

A violation of Φ_{res} is called ballot stuffing; a violation of Φ_{cl} is a clash attack. Belenios is expected to satisfy election verifiability in the following adversarial scenarios: $\mathcal{A}_1$ - both the server and the registrar are honest; $\mathcal{A}_2$ - the server is corrupt and the registrar honest; $\mathcal{A}_3$ - the server is honest and the registrar corrupt. Security should be ensured by private signing keys - when the registrar is honest, and by private passwords and server logs - when the server is honest. However, [9] shows several attacks resulting from the fact that the server does not know the association between a public credential and the identity of the corresponding voter. A corrupt voter can then cast a ballot for any public credential, as soon as the adversary manages to obtain ballots signed with the corresponding private credential.

Ballot Reordering Attack by $\mathcal{A}_1$, $\mathcal{A}_2$ or $\mathcal{A}_3$. Assume an honest voter id with public credential cr casts ballots b_1 and b_2, in this order, and only verifies b_2. Then b_2 should be counted for the respective public credential. However, the adversary can cause b_1 to be counted instead. The attack scenario is as follows:

V(id, cr): casts b_1 and b_2, which are blocked by $\mathcal{A}$;
     $\mathcal{A}$: casts b_2 for cr (relying on a corrupted voter or voting server);
BBcast: (cr, b_2) is verified by the voter V(id, cr);
     $\mathcal{A}$: casts b_1 for cr;
BBtally: (cr, b_1).

In a normal execution, the reception of b_1 or b_2 from id would link cr to id, thus the adversary cannot cast b_1 after b_2 when the server is honest - unless it corrupts the password of id. The crucial point of the attack by $\mathcal{A}_1$ is that b_2 is cast for the same public credential cr by a distinct corrupted voter.

Ballot Stuffing Attack by $\mathcal{A}_3$. When an honest voter id_1 with cr_1 casts a ballot b, the adversary can block and cast it in the name of a corrupt voter id_2, for the same public credential cr_1. The voter id_1 successfully verifies b. Subsequently, relying on a corrupt registrar, the adversary can cast another ballot $b_{\mathcal{A}}$ for cr_1. This violates result integrity Φ_{res}° and individual verifiability Φ_{iv}, since an adversarial ballot $b_{\mathcal{A}}$ is cast for cr_1, even though the corresponding voter is honest and has successfully verified the ballot b.

     $\mathcal{A}$: corrupts VR and V(id_2) to obtain $\langle cr_1, skey_1, pwd_2 \rangle$;
V(id_1): casts b, which is blocked by $\mathcal{A}$;
     $\mathcal{A}$: casts b with $\langle cr_1, pwd_2 \rangle$, and VS stores ($id_2, cr_1$) in Log;
BBcast: (cr_1, b) is verified by V(id_1);
     $\mathcal{A}$: casts $b_{\mathcal{A}}$ with $\langle cr_1, pwd_2 \rangle$, which is accepted and published;
BBtally: ($cr_1, b_{\mathcal{A}}$).

If the voter id_2 verified the cast ballot b, this also counts as a clash attack in the definition from [9], as it requires resistance to clash attacks even for corrupted voters. A variation of this attack can also lead to a weaker form of ballot stuffing: the adversary can submit $b_{\mathcal{A}}$ before id_1 has a chance to cast a ballot. In that case, the voting server will not accept any further ballot from id_1, since this would break the consistency of the log for cr_1. Formally, this is a violation of $\Phi_{res}^\bullet$. Our techniques in the following protect against (strong) ballot stuffing, ballot reordering, and the clash attack. They do not protect against the weaker form of ballot stuffing, i.e. the violation of $\Phi_{res}^\bullet$.

3   Towards Improved Election Verifiability

In Belenios, the aim of the zero-knowledge proof $pr_L = proof_L(c, r, cr)$ in a ballot $b = \langle c, s, pr_R, pr_L \rangle$ is to verifiably link the ciphertext $c = enc(v, pk, r)$, and therefore the ballot b, to the public credential cr for which b is cast. We denote the corresponding verification procedure by $ver_L(pr_L, c, cr)$. A valid proof can only be constructed by the party who constructs the ciphertext, by proving knowledge of the corresponding randomness r with the label cr. This is called labeled encryption in [14]. The idea is that the ciphertext cannot be detached from the label: the adversary cannot copy c, or create a ciphertext related to the encoded vote, and cast it for a different credential cr′. This is required in order to protect from attacks against privacy like in [17]. Concretely, the labeled encryption in Belenios is based on ElGamal encryption with a Chaum-Pedersen proof of knowledge, where the label cr is part of the input to a hash function (SHA256) that computes the challenge for a non-interactive zero-knowledge proof.

We enrich the structure of the label in order to also protect against the attacks presented in Sect. 2.2. The elements of the new label structure can be given as inputs to the hash function along with cr in the Chaum-Pedersen proof, thus we can rely on the same labeled encryption construction as Belenios. Moreover, we prove in Sect. 4 that no further attacks are possible on election verifiability in the resulting system. We present the new structure of the label stepwise: first a label structure that protects against ballot reordering attacks by $\mathcal{A}_1, \mathcal{A}_2$ or $\mathcal{A}_3$; then a label structure that protects against other attacks by $\mathcal{A}_3$ (in particular ballot stuffing); finally, combining the two labels protects against all attacks by $\mathcal{A}_1, \mathcal{A}_2$ or $\mathcal{A}_3$.

3.1   Protection Against Ballot Reordering

We assume initially there are empty ballots next to eligible public credentials on BB. Moreover, a specific portion of BB is reserved for displaying the last ballot cast for each credential:

$$(\text{Before voting}) \ \mathsf{BBlast} : (\mathsf{cr}_1, \perp), \dots, (\mathsf{cr}_n, \perp)$$
$$(\text{During voting}) \ \mathsf{BBlast} : (\mathsf{cr}_1, \mathsf{b}_1), \dots, (\mathsf{cr}_n, \mathsf{b}_n)$$

When the voting platform VP constructs a new ballot for a voter with public credential cr, it fetches from BBlast the last ballot b′ next to cr. Then, in the construction of the proof pr_L, instead of cr, VP uses the label $\mathsf{h}(\mathsf{cr}, \mathsf{b}')$, where h is a collision-resistant hash function mapping the pair $(\mathsf{cr}, \mathsf{b}')$ into the appropriate domain for labels:

$$\ell = \mathsf{h}(\mathsf{cr}, \mathsf{b}'); \quad \mathsf{pr}_\mathsf{L} = \mathsf{proof}_\mathsf{L}(\mathsf{c}, \mathsf{r}, \ell); \quad \mathsf{b} = \langle \mathsf{c}, \mathsf{s}, \mathsf{pr}_\mathsf{R}, \mathsf{pr}_\mathsf{L}, \ell \rangle.$$

BBcast records all ballots cast for cr, and their order cannot be changed on BB. Election auditors can look at any two consecutive ballots b′ and b cast for a credential cr and verify that

$$\mathsf{ver}_\mathsf{L}(\mathsf{pr}_\mathsf{L}, \mathsf{c}, \mathsf{h}(\mathsf{cr}, \mathsf{b}')) = \mathsf{ok},$$

thereby ensuring that the party constructing b indeed expects it to follow b′. In particular, if an honest voter casts b_2 after b_1, the adversary cannot cast b_2 first, since it would have to generate a proof linking b_2 to an earlier ballot b_0, which is impossible since the adversary does not know the randomness in the ciphertext corresponding to b_2. This label structure ensures election verifiability in corruption scenarios when the registrar is honest, i.e. $\mathcal{A}_1$ and $\mathcal{A}_2$.

3.2 Protection Against a Corrupted Registrar

The main cause of the ballot stuffing and clash attacks, in the scenario with a corrupted registrar, is that the adversary can block a ballot b of an honest voter and cast it under the identity of a corrupt voter, while maintaining the same public credential associated to b. Subsequently, after the honest voter verified b, the adversary can override it with an own ballot $b_{\mathcal{A}}$. In order to prevent this, we enrich the label attached to b so that it includes a commitment to the identity of the voter. More precisely, during ballot casting for a voter id, VP generates a fresh randomness t, constructs the label $\langle cr, com(id, t)\rangle$ and sends t together with the ballot to the voting server VS. Since the label cannot be reconstructed publicly by election auditors, we explicitly include it in the ballot. We have:

VP $: \ell = \langle cr, com(id, t)\rangle; \quad pr_L = proof_L(c, r, \ell); \quad b = \langle c, s, pr_R, pr_L, \ell\rangle,$

VS : receives (cr, b, t) from VP for a given id; $\ell' = \langle cr, com(id, t)\rangle,$
     casts b if and only if $\ell' = \ell$ and $ver_L(pr_L, c, \ell) = ok.$

In the attack scenario described above, the adversary cannot construct a proof pr'_L so that b is cast by VS under the identity of a corrupt voter. Indeed, the ciphertext in b cannot be detached from the identity of the honest voter. More generally, we prove that this structure of the label is sufficient to ensure election verifiability in the corruption scenarios when the server is honest, i.e. $\mathcal{A}_1$ and $\mathcal{A}_3$. Election auditors can still check the proof pr_L on BB, but they are only be able to ensure the ballot is cast for the expected public credential cr and will not have knowledge of the underlying id. Note that we cannot use the id directly in the label, as this would reveal the link between id and cr. Moreover, the commitment scheme should be perfectly hiding, in order to resist an all-powerful, e.g. quantum, adversary.

3.3 Putting the Labels Together

We combine the labels from Sect. 3.1 and Sect. 3.2 as follows:

$$\ell_1 = h(cr, b'); \qquad \ell_2 = com(id, t); \qquad \ell = \langle \ell_1, \ell_2\rangle.$$

We call Belenios$_{tr}$ (from tracking) the variant of Belenios where we augment the label as described in Sect. 3.1, Belenios$_{id}$ the variant where the label is as in Sect. 3.2 and Belenios+ the variant where the label ℓ is as described in this section. For a protocol P, a corruption scenario $\mathcal{A}$ and a property Φ, we denote by $(P, \mathcal{A}) \models \Phi$ the fact that P satisfies Φ in the corruption scenario $\mathcal{A}$. Let Φ°_{E2E} be the election verifiability property $\Phi^h_{iv} \wedge \Phi_{eli} \wedge \Phi_{cl} \wedge \Phi^\circ_{res}$ as described in Sect. 2.2 and in [9]. In the next section, we describe the specification and automated verification with Tamarin. They allow us to derive the following results:

$$\begin{aligned}
(\text{ Belenios}_{tr}, \ \mathcal{A}) &\models \Phi^\circ_{E2E} && \text{for } \mathcal{A} \in \{\mathcal{A}_1, \mathcal{A}_2\}, \\
(\text{ Belenios}_{id}, \ \mathcal{A}) &\models \Phi^\circ_{E2E} && \text{for } \mathcal{A} \in \{\mathcal{A}_1, \mathcal{A}_3\}, \\
(\text{ Belenios+}, \ \mathcal{A}) &\models \Phi^\circ_{E2E} && \text{for } \mathcal{A} \in \{\mathcal{A}_1, \mathcal{A}_2, \mathcal{A}_3\}, \\
\text{while we have } (\text{ Belenios}, \ \mathcal{A}) &\not\models \Phi^\circ_{E2E} && \text{for } \mathcal{A} \in \{\mathcal{A}_1, \mathcal{A}_2, \mathcal{A}_3\}.
\end{aligned}$$

The property $\Phi^\circ_{\mathsf{E2E}}$ corresponds to the standard verifiability notion used in [14,15]. In particular, this notion ensures that, if an honest voter successfully verified a ballot b for a public credential cr, then b is counted in the final tally as the contribution of cr. A stronger notion of verifiability, denoted by $\Phi^\bullet_{\mathsf{E2E}}$, was also proposed in [9]: if a ballot is counted for a public credential corresponding to an honest voter, then it must necessarily have been cast by that voter - independently of the individual verification procedure. In the scenario $\mathcal{A}_3$, an adversary corrupting the registrar and a voter can cast a ballot $b_{\mathcal{A}}$ for any public credential, violating the strong verifiability notion $\Phi^\bullet_{\mathsf{E2E}}$, even in Belenios+. The label $\langle \mathsf{h}(\mathsf{cr}, \mathsf{b}'), \mathsf{com}(\mathsf{id}, \mathsf{t}) \rangle$ does not help here, since the adversary can freely combine the identity of a corrupted voter with any credential, sign the ballot and construct valid zero-knowledge proofs. If the honest voter already submitted and successfully verified a ballot b, then the adversary cannot make VS accept $b_{\mathcal{A}}$ for the same public credential under the identity of a corrupt voter. This is due to the fact that the association between the honest voter and the public credential is recorded by the server in the log upon accepting b. That is why $\Phi^\circ_{\mathsf{E2E}}$ holds for Belenios+.

4   Specification and Verification

4.1   Specifying Protocols in Tamarin

We perform our analysis of Belenios+ using the Tamarin prover, which is based on a multiset rewriting framework. We only illustrate the most relevant features of Tamarin here. For a detailed understanding of Tamarin we refer the reader to [3,24,27]. In Tamarin, messages (or terms) are built from a set of function symbols and properties of cryptographic primitives are modelled by a set of equations. Protocol state information and adversarial knowledge are represented by facts, modelled relying on special fact symbols. Protocol actions are specified by multiset rewriting rules, denoted by $[L] \dashv [\![M]\!] \rightarrow [N]$, in which a set of *premise facts* L allows to derive a set of *conclusion facts* N, while recording certain events in *action facts* M.

Example 1. In a voting protocol, the generation of a secret/public key pair can be modelled by the following multiset rewriting rule, that we denote by $\mathsf{R}_{\mathsf{key}}$:

$$[\; \mathsf{Fr}(\mathsf{k}) \;] \dashv [\![\mathsf{!BBkey}(\mathsf{pk}(\mathsf{k})), \mathsf{Phase}('\mathsf{setup}')]\!] \rightarrow [\; \mathsf{!Sk}(\mathsf{k}), \mathsf{!BBkey}(\mathsf{pk}(\mathsf{k})), \mathsf{Out}(\mathsf{pk}(\mathsf{k})) \;]$$

where $\mathsf{Fr}(\mathsf{k})$ denotes the randomly generated fresh key k as a premise. The conclusion facts $\mathsf{!Sk}(\mathsf{k})$ and $\mathsf{!BBkey}(\mathsf{pk}(\mathsf{k}))$ record the secret and the public key of the election, respectively; the term $\mathsf{pk}(\mathsf{k})$ represents the public key itself, while $\mathsf{!BBkey}(\mathsf{pk}(\mathsf{k}))$ represents the fact that $\mathsf{pk}(\mathsf{k})$ is a public key published on BBkey. If a fact is preceded by !, it means that it can be consumed (i.e. used as premise) any number of times by other protocol rules. Otherwise it can be consumed only once, and it is called a *linear* fact. The fact symbols In and Out are used for communication over the network, controlled by the attacker. The action fact

BBkey(pk(k)) records the event that the public key is published on the bulletin board. The action fact Phase('setup') records that the rule should be executed in the setup phase. The following rules set up candidates v_1 and v_2 and voter identities id:

$$R_{cand} : [\ In(\langle v_1, v_2 \rangle)\ ] \!-\!\!| \, Phase('setup') \, |\!\!\rightarrow [\ !BBcand(v_1), !BBcand(v_2)\ ]$$
$$R_{id} : \qquad [\ In(id)\ ] \!-\!\!| \, Phase('setup') \, |\!\!\rightarrow [\ !Id(id)\ ]$$

To cast a ballot, the voter with identity id makes a choice between the candidates recorded on BBcand and encrypts the vote v using the public key from BBkey together with fresh randomness r. The output including the voter identity id can be sent to the server over the network. To model this action, we define the following rule, where the event Vote(id, v) is recorded as an action fact:

$$R_{vote} : [\ !Id(id), !BBcand(v), !BBkey(pk(k)), Fr(r)\ ]$$
$$-\!\!| \, Vote(id, v), Phase('voting') \, |\!\!\rightarrow [\ Out(\langle id, enc(v, pkey, r) \rangle)\ ]$$

Cryptographic operations are specified by equations. For example, decryption using the private key k is specified by:

$$dec(enc(v, pk(k), r), k) = v$$

where the term $enc(v, pk(k), r)$ represents the encryption of v with public key pk(k) and randomness r. It can be decrypted only if the secret key k is provided.

A *restriction* in Tamarin is a logical formula that constrains the application of protocol rules. For example, the restriction $\forall x, y, i, j.\ BBkey(x)\ @i\ \wedge$ $BBkey(y)\ @j \Rightarrow x = y$ applied to the rule R_{key} in Example 1 means that it is not possible to have two different election keys. The symbol @ refers to the timepoints i and j in the execution trace when the rule R_{key} is applied. We can also express a timepoint ordering or equality. For example, the restriction $\forall i, j.\ Phase('setup')\ @i\ \wedge\ Phase('voting')\ @j \Rightarrow i \prec j$ means that all setup actions should occur before voting actions. A restriction can also encode the equality predicate, enforcing that u and v are equal in any occurrence of the action fact $Eq(u, v) : \forall u, v, i.\ Eq(u, v)\ @i \Rightarrow u = v$.

We note that formal verification with Tamarin does not guarantee full-proof security, as Tamarin itself may have bugs. Recently, there is research aiming to underpin fully automated provers like Tamarin with foundations from interactive theorem provers like Coq [4,10,19].

4.2 Specification and Verification of Belenios+

We define a set of equations used for specifying decryption (1), signature verification (2), verification of a range proof (3), and verification of a proof attaching a label to a ciphertext (4):

(1) $dec(enc(x, pk(y), z), y) = x,$

(2) $ver(sign(x, y), x, pk(y)) = ok,$

(3) $(\forall i)\ ver_R(proof_R(enc(x_i, y, z), z, \langle x_1, \ldots, x_k \rangle), enc(x_i, y, z), y, \langle x_1, \ldots, x_k \rangle) = ok,$

(4) $ver_L(proof_L(enc(x, y, z), z, \ell), enc(x, y, z), \ell) = ok.$

To specify the set of Eqs. (3) in Tamarin, the number of candidates k has to be fixed in advance. We use $k = 2$, but any constant would work. For modelling the actions of participants in the protocol, we define a set of rules and restrictions. For the complete specification, we refer to the Tamarin code online [5]. It is an extension of the code corresponding to Belenios in [9]. In the following, we discuss two of the most important rules in the specification: ballot casting as it happens on the voting platform VP and on the voting server VS. We highlight the difference between Belenios+ and Belenios in red. We use special linear facts in order to track the last ballot cast for each credential: $\mathsf{VPlast}(\mathsf{cr}, \mathsf{b_0})$ - to be used by the voting platform, and $\mathsf{BBlast}(\mathsf{cr}, \mathsf{b_0})$ - to be used by the voting server. The rule for ballot casting on the voting server makes sure these two facts are in sync. For voter credentials, we use special facts $!\mathsf{Reg}(\mathsf{id}, \mathsf{cr}, \mathsf{skey})$ and $!\mathsf{Pwd}(\mathsf{id}, \mathsf{pwd})$ to store credentials received from the registrar and from the server, respectively. Ballot casting by VP is represented by the following rule:

$\mathsf{R^{VP}_{vote}}$: **construct a ballot, authenticate and send it to VS**

> let $\mathsf{c} = \mathsf{enc}(\mathsf{v}, \mathsf{pkey}, \mathsf{r})$; $\mathsf{s} = \mathsf{sign}(\mathsf{c}, \mathsf{skey})$; $\ell = \langle \mathsf{h}(\mathsf{cr}, \mathsf{b_0}), \mathsf{com}(\mathsf{id}, \mathsf{t}) \rangle$;
> $\mathsf{pr_R} = \mathsf{proof_R}(\mathsf{c}, \mathsf{r}, \mathsf{vlist})$; $\mathsf{pr_L} = \mathsf{proof_L}(\mathsf{c}, \mathsf{r}, \ell)$;
> $\mathsf{b} = \langle \mathsf{c}, \mathsf{s}, \mathsf{pr_R}, \mathsf{pr_L}, \ell \rangle$; $\mathsf{a} = \mathsf{h}(\langle \mathsf{id}, \mathsf{pwd}, \mathsf{cr}, \mathsf{b}, \mathsf{t} \rangle)$ in
>
> [$!\mathsf{BBcand}(\mathsf{v})$, $!\mathsf{BBkey}(\mathsf{pkey})$, $\mathsf{Fr}(\mathsf{r})$, $\mathsf{Fr}(\mathsf{t})$, $!\mathsf{Vlist}(\mathsf{vlist})$, $!\mathsf{Reg}(\mathsf{id}, \mathsf{cr}, \mathsf{skey})$,
> $!\mathsf{Pwd}(\mathsf{id}, \mathsf{pwd})$, $\mathsf{VPlast}(\mathsf{cr}, \mathsf{b_0})$]─[$\mathsf{Vote}(\mathsf{id}, \mathsf{cr}, \mathsf{v})$, $\mathsf{VoteB}(\mathsf{id}, \mathsf{cr}, \mathsf{b})$]↦
> [$!\mathsf{Voted}(\mathsf{id}, \mathsf{cr}, \mathsf{v}, \mathsf{b})$, $\mathsf{Out}(\langle \mathsf{id}, \mathsf{cr}, \mathsf{b}, \mathsf{a}, \mathsf{t} \rangle)$]

where we use the Tamarin construction let. . . in for assigning terms to variables. The rule abstracts password-based authentication with the help of a hash function, essentially ensuring that only a party knowing the password can cast a ballot for a given id. In reality, the randomness t used for the commitment should be sent on the same secure channel as the password. However, the secrecy of t is not important for verifiability properties, thus we can send it on the public channel. The rule $\mathsf{R^{VP}_{vote}}$ consumes the linear fact $\mathsf{VPlast}(\mathsf{cr}, \mathsf{b_0})$, thus it can be executed only once for any ballot posted on BB. This mechanism is complemented by the ballot casting rule on the server side:

$\mathsf{R^{VS}_{cast}}$: **authenticate voter, verify and publish ballot**

> let $\ell = \langle \mathsf{h}(\mathsf{cr}, \mathsf{b_0}), \mathsf{com}(\mathsf{id}, \mathsf{t}) \rangle$; $\mathsf{b} = \langle \mathsf{c}, \mathsf{s}, \mathsf{pr_R}, \mathsf{pr_L}, \ell \rangle$;
> $\mathsf{a'} = \mathsf{h}(\langle \mathsf{id}, \mathsf{pwd}, \mathsf{cr}, \mathsf{b}, \mathsf{t} \rangle)$ in
>
> [$\mathsf{In}(\langle \mathsf{id}, \mathsf{cr}, \mathsf{b}, \mathsf{a}, \mathsf{t} \rangle)$, $!\mathsf{BBkey}(\mathsf{pkey})$, $!\mathsf{Vlist}(\mathsf{vlist})$, $!\mathsf{BBreg}(\mathsf{cr})$, $!\mathsf{Pwd}(\mathsf{id}, \mathsf{pwd})$,
> $\mathsf{BBlast}(\mathsf{cr}, \mathsf{b_0})$]─[$\mathsf{a'} = \mathsf{a}$, $\mathsf{ver}(\mathsf{s}, \mathsf{c}, \mathsf{cr}) = \mathsf{ok}$, $\mathsf{ver_R}(\mathsf{pr_R}, \mathsf{c}, \mathsf{pkey}, \mathsf{vlist}) = \mathsf{ok}$,
> $\mathsf{ver_L}(\mathsf{pr_L}, \mathsf{c}, \ell) = \mathsf{ok}$, $\mathsf{Log}(\mathsf{id}, \mathsf{cr})$, $!\mathsf{BBcast}(\mathsf{cr}, \mathsf{b})$]↦
> [$!\mathsf{BBcast}(\mathsf{cr}, \mathsf{b})$, $\mathsf{BBlast}(\mathsf{cr}, \mathsf{b})$, $\mathsf{VPlast}(\mathsf{cr}, \mathsf{b})$]

where we receive a ballot from the voter and perform the corresponding validation steps: verifying the password, the signature and the zero-knowledge proofs. The fact containing the last ballot cast is consumed, and new facts are produced for the new ballot: one to be consumed by the voting platform, and one to be consumed by the server when the next ballot is cast. In order to obtain termination, we have a restriction limiting the number of applications of this rule to at most four for each voter. The following rule and restriction model the individual verification procedure, where the restriction ensures that the voter verifies the last ballot cast:

$$R_{ver}^V : [\, \mathsf{Voted}(id, cr, v, b), \mathsf{BBcast}(cr, b) \,]\!-\!\!\{ \mathsf{Verified}(id, cr, v), \mathsf{VerB}(id, cr, b) \}\!\!\rightarrow\! [\;\,]$$
$$\mathsf{BBcast}(cr, b) \,@i \,\wedge\, \mathsf{BBcast}(cr, b') \,@j \,\wedge\, \mathsf{VerB}(id, cr, b) \,@l \,\wedge\, i \prec l \,\wedge\, j \prec l$$
$$\Rightarrow j \prec i \,\vee\, b = b'$$

Corruption Scenarios. We have three adversary models $\mathcal{A}_1$, $\mathcal{A}_2$ and $\mathcal{A}_3$, as described in Sect. 2.2. Trustees are corrupted by default: we have a rule that takes the secret key as input from the attacker. For other corruption abilities, we have the following rules:

$\mathcal{C}_{corr}^V$: **corrupt voter to reveal credentials**
$$[\, !\mathsf{Reg}(id, cr, skey), !\mathsf{Pwd}(id, pwd) \,]\!-\!\!\{ \mathsf{Corr}(id, cr) \}\!\!\rightarrow\! [\, \mathsf{Out}(\langle id, cr, skey, pwd \rangle) \,]$$

$\mathcal{C}_{pwd}^{VS}$: **corrupt server to determine password**
$$[\, !\mathsf{Id}(id), \mathsf{In}(pwd) \,]\!-\!\{\,\}\!\!\rightarrow\! [\, !\mathsf{Pwd}(id, pwd) \,]$$

$\mathcal{C}_{cast}^{VS}$: **corrupt server to stuff ballots**
$$[\, \mathsf{In}(\langle cr, b \rangle), \mathsf{BBlast}(cr, b_0) \,]\!-\!\{!\mathsf{BBcast}(cr, b) \}\!\!\rightarrow$$
$$[\, !\mathsf{BBcast}(cr, b), \mathsf{BBlast}(cr, b), \mathsf{VPlast}(cr, b) \,]$$

$\mathcal{C}_{reg}^{VR}$: **corrupt registration of public / secret credentials**
$$\text{let } cr = \mathsf{pk}(skey) \text{ in}$$
$$[\, !\mathsf{Id}(id), \mathsf{In}(\langle skey, cr' \rangle) \,]\!-\!\{!\mathsf{BBreg}(cr') \}\!\!\rightarrow\! [\, !\mathsf{Reg}(id, cr, skey), !\mathsf{BBreg}(cr') \,]$$

Moreover, when the server is corrupted, in the rule R_{vote}^{VS} we only keep the verification actions that can be publicly performed by election auditors. Table 1 contains verification results for the corresponding specifications with Tamarin, obtained with the specifications posted online [5]. We can see that the positive results for Belenios+ are the union of the positive results for Belenios$_{tr}$ and Belenios$_{id}$, in each of the corruption cases $\mathcal{A}_1$, $\mathcal{A}_2$ and $\mathcal{A}_3$. In Table 2, we give execution times for the verification of Belenios+ when we bound the number of ballots per voter accordingly. Tamarin does not terminate without such a bound (it takes more than one hour for five ballots per voter).

Table 1. Verifiability analysis of the variants of Belenios.

$\Phi/\mathcal{A}_j$	Belenios*			Belenios$_{tr}$		Belenios$_{id}$		Belenios+		
	$\mathcal{A}_1$	$\mathcal{A}_2$	$\mathcal{A}_3$	$\mathcal{A}_1$	$\mathcal{A}_2$	$\mathcal{A}_1$	$\mathcal{A}_3$	$\mathcal{A}_1$	$\mathcal{A}_2$	$\mathcal{A}_3$
Φ_{iv}^h	✗	✗	✗	✓	✓	✓	✓	✓	✓	✓
Φ_{eli}	✓	✓	✓	✓	✓	✓	✓	✓	✓	✓
Φ_{cl}	✓	✓	✗	✓	✓	✓	✓	✓	✓	✓
$\Phi_{res}^{\bullet}$	✓	✓	✗	✓	✓	✓	✗	✓	✓	✗
Φ_{res}°	✓	✓	✗	✓	✓	✓	✓	✓	✓	✓

∗: Verification results for Belenios as in [9].

Table 2. Execution times for the verification of verifiability of Belenios+.

#b/$\mathcal{A}_j$	Belenios+		
	$\mathcal{A}_1$	$\mathcal{A}_2$	$\mathcal{A}_3$
2 ballots per voter	17 s	8 s	57 s
3 ballots per voter	1 min	33 s	2 min 47 s
4 ballots per voter	12 min 6 s	15 min	15 min 53 s

5   Conclusion and Future Work

We have introduced a simple extension of Belenios and we have proved with the Tamarin prover that the resulting system improves election verifiability in various corruption scenarios. These additions do not affect usability and efficiency of Belenios. We also claim that (everlasting) privacy is not affected, but this has to be formally proved. The bulletin board has the same structure, but the order in which all ballots are cast for a given credential should be clear. Our open problems are related to the formal verification and to the design of electronic voting protocols. Our specification makes certain abstractions that should be lifted or formally justified, for greater confidence in results. The most important abstraction is the one limiting the number of ballots to four for each voter. Concerning the design, our techniques still do not achieve the stronger notion of election verifiability, that prevents the adversary from casting ballots even for honest voters that have not verified their ballots. We also think election verifiability could be achieved in stronger corruption scenarios, e.g. when both the registrar and the server are (partially) corrupted. For example, it could be interesting to achieve public verifiability for the fact that each ballot is associated to an eligible voter, while perfectly hiding the actual identity of the voter. This would limit the corruption abilities of the registrar who generates the public credentials, without relying on the server to perform the verification.

Acknowledgement. This work was supported by the Luxembourg National Research Fund (FNR) and the Research Council of Norway for the joint INTER project SURCVS (No. 11747298).

References

1. Helios - Verifiable online elections. https://heliosvoting.org/
2. Belenios - Verifiable online voting system. https://belenios.org/
3. Tamarin prover. https://tamarin-prover.github.io
4. The Coq proof assistant. https://coq.inria.fr/
5. Tamarin specifications for the variants of Belenios. https://github.com/sbaloglu/tamarin-codes/tree/main/belenios-zkp
6. Adida, B.: Helios: web-based open-audit voting. In: van Oorschot, P.C. (ed.) Proceedings of the 17th USENIX Security Symposium, San Jose, CA, USA, 28 July–1 August 2008, pp. 335–348. USENIX Association (2008). http://www.usenix.org/events/sec08/tech/full_papers/adida/adida.pdf
7. Adida, B., De Marneffe, O., Pereira, O., Quisquater, J.J.: Electing a university president using open-audit voting: analysis of real-world use of Helios. In: 2009 Electronic Voting Technology Workshop/Workshop on Trustworthy Elections. USENIX (2009)
8. Arapinis, M., Cortier, V., Kremer, S.: When are three voters enough for privacy properties? In: Askoxylakis, I., Ioannidis, S., Katsikas, S., Meadows, C. (eds.) ESORICS 2016. LNCS, vol. 9879, pp. 241–260. Springer, Cham (2016). https://doi.org/10.1007/978-3-319-45741-3_13
9. Baloglu, S., Bursuc, S., Mauw, S., Pang, J.: Election verifiability revisited: automated security proofs and attacks on Helios and Belenios. In: 34th IEEE Computer Security Foundations Symposium (2021). https://eprint.iacr.org/2020/982
10. Castéran, P., Bertot, Y.: Interactive Theorem Proving and Program Development. Coq'Art: The Calculus of Inductive Constructions. Texts in Theoretical Computer Science. Springer, Heidelberg (2004). https://hal.archives-ouvertes.fr/hal-00344237
11. Clarkson, M.R., Chong, S., Myers, A.C.: Civitas: toward a secure voting system. In: 2008 IEEE Symposium on Security and Privacy (S&P 2008), Oakland, California, USA, 18–21 May 2008, pp. 354–368 (2008). https://doi.org/10.1109/SP.2008.32
12. Comon-Lundh, H., Cortier, V.: Security properties: two agents are sufficient. In: Degano, P. (ed.) ESOP 2003. LNCS, vol. 2618, pp. 99–113. Springer, Heidelberg (2003). https://doi.org/10.1007/3-540-36575-3_8
13. Cortier, V., Dallon, A., Delaune, S.: Bounding the number of agents, for equivalence too. In: Piessens, F., Viganò, L. (eds.) POST 2016. LNCS, vol. 9635, pp. 211–232. Springer, Heidelberg (2016). https://doi.org/10.1007/978-3-662-49635-0_11
14. Cortier, V., Drăgan, C.C., Dupressoir, F., Warinschi, B.: Machine-checked proofs for electronic voting: privacy and verifiability for Belenios. In: Proceedings of the 31st IEEE Computer Security Foundations Symposium, pp. 298–312. IEEE Computer Society (2018). https://doi.org/10.1109/CSF.2018.00029
15. Cortier, V., Filipiak, A., Lallemand, J.: BeleniosVS: secrecy and verifiability against a corrupted voting device. In: 32nd IEEE Computer Security Foundations Symposium, pp. 367–381 (2019). https://doi.org/10.1109/CSF.2019.00032
16. Cortier, V., Gaudry, P., Glondu, S.: Belenios: a simple private and verifiable electronic voting system. In: Guttman, J.D., Landwehr, C.E., Meseguer, J., Pavlovic, D. (eds.) Foundations of Security, Protocols, and Equational Reasoning. LNCS, vol. 11565, pp. 214–238. Springer, Cham (2019). https://doi.org/10.1007/978-3-030-19052-1_14
17. Cortier, V., Smyth, B.: Attacking and fixing Helios: an analysis of ballot secrecy. J. Comput. Secur. **21**(1), 89–148 (2013). https://doi.org/10.3233/JCS-2012-0458

18. ElGamal, T.: A public key cryptosystem and a signature scheme based on discrete logarithms. In: Blakley, G.R., Chaum, D. (eds.) CRYPTO 1984. LNCS, vol. 196, pp. 10–18. Springer, Heidelberg (1985). https://doi.org/10.1007/3-540-39568-7_2

19. Hess, A.V., Mödersheim, S., Brucker, A.D., Schlichtkrull, A.: Performing security proofs of stateful protocols. In: 34th IEEE Computer Security Foundations Symposium (CSF), vol. 1, pp. 143–158. IEEE (2021). https://doi.org/10.1109/CSF51468.2021.00006. https://www.brucker.ch/bibliography/abstract/hess.ea-performing-2021

20. Hirt, M., Sako, K.: Efficient receipt-free voting based on homomorphic encryption. In: Preneel, B. (ed.) EUROCRYPT 2000. LNCS, vol. 1807, pp. 539–556. Springer, Heidelberg (2000). https://doi.org/10.1007/3-540-45539-6_38

21. Juels, A., Catalano, D., Jakobsson, M.: Coercion-resistant electronic elections. In: Proceedings of the 2005 ACM Workshop on Privacy in the Electronic Society, WPES, pp. 61–70 (2005). https://doi.org/10.1145/1102199.1102213

22. Küsters, R., Truderung, T., Vogt, A.: Verifiability, privacy, and coercion-resistance: new insights from a case study. In: 32nd IEEE Symposium on Security and Privacy, pp. 538–553. IEEE Computer Society (2011). https://doi.org/10.1109/SP.2011.21

23. Küsters, R., Truderung, T., Vogt, A.: Clash attacks on the verifiability of e-voting systems. In: 33rd IEEE Symposium on Security and Privacy, pp. 395–409. IEEE Computer Society (2012). https://doi.org/10.1109/SP.2012.32

24. Meier, S., Schmidt, B., Cremers, C., Basin, D.: The TAMARIN prover for the symbolic analysis of security protocols. In: Sharygina, N., Veith, H. (eds.) CAV 2013. LNCS, vol. 8044, pp. 696–701. Springer, Heidelberg (2013). https://doi.org/10.1007/978-3-642-39799-8_48

25. Pedersen, T.P.: Non-interactive and information-theoretic secure verifiable secret sharing. In: Feigenbaum, J. (ed.) CRYPTO 1991. LNCS, vol. 576, pp. 129–140. Springer, Heidelberg (1992). https://doi.org/10.1007/3-540-46766-1_9

26. Pereira, O., Wallach, D.S.: Clash attacks and the STAR-vote system. In: Krimmer, R., Volkamer, M., Braun Binder, N., Kersting, N., Pereira, O., Schürmann, C. (eds.) E-Vote-ID 2017. LNCS, vol. 10615, pp. 228–247. Springer, Cham (2017). https://doi.org/10.1007/978-3-319-68687-5_14

27. Schmidt, B., Meier, S., Cremers, C.J.F., Basin, D.A.: Automated analysis of Diffie-Hellman protocols and advanced security properties. In: 25th IEEE Computer Security Foundations Symposium, (CSF 2012), pp. 78–94. IEEE Computer Society (2012). https://doi.org/10.1109/CSF.2012.25

Improving the Accuracy of Ballot Scanners Using Supervised Learning

Sameer Barretto, William Chown, David Meyer, Aditya Soni[⊠], Atreya Tata, and J. Alex Halderman

University of Michigan, Ann Arbor, USA
{sambarr,chownwil,davidmey,adisoni,artata,jhalderm}@umich.edu

Abstract. Most U.S. voters cast hand-marked paper ballots that are counted by optical scanners. Deployed ballot scanners typically utilize simplistic mark-detection methods, based on comparing the measured intensity of target areas to preset thresholds, but this technique is known to sometimes misread "marginal" marks that deviate from ballot instructions. We investigate the feasibility of improving scanner accuracy using supervised learning. We train a convolutional neural network to classify various styles of marks extracted from a large corpus of voted ballots. This approach achieves higher accuracy than a naive intensity threshold while requiring far fewer ballots to undergo manual adjudication. It is robust to imperfect feature extraction, as may be experienced in ballots that lack timing marks, and efficient enough to be performed in real time using contemporary central-count scanner hardware.

1 Introduction

Hand-marked paper ballots counted by optical scanners are the most popular voting method in the United States, used by jurisdictions home to about 70% of registered voters [29], and they are becoming even more prominent due to the rapid expansion of postal voting spurred by the COVID-19 pandemic [13]. Despite its importance, optical scan voting faces two significant integrity challenges. First, deployed scanners suffer from a host of well-documented vulnerabilities (e.g., [2,11,14,15,18]). Second, and the focus of this study, even in the absence of an attack, traditional scanning techniques sometimes fail to accurately count some voter marks [12]. In principle, risk-limiting audits can address both problems by ensuring that any fraud or error sufficient to change the outcome of a contest is likely to be detected [17,24], but widespread adoption of RLAs, even for Federal contests, may be a decade or more in the future. Given that many major contests will not be subject to rigorous audits anytime soon, it is important to ensure that scanners themselves count ballots as accurately as practically possible.

Today's ballot scanners typically employ variations of a relatively simplistic technique [12,27]. After creating a digital image of the ballot, they identify the voting targets and calculate the average shading within each target area, s_i. For a predefined threshold α, target i is treated as marked whenever $s_i \geq \alpha$. Some

© Springer Nature Switzerland AG 2021
R. Krimmer et al. (Eds.): E-Vote-ID 2021, LNCS 12900, pp. 17–32, 2021.
https://doi.org/10.1007/978-3-030-86942-7_2

Fig. 1. Voted targets from Humboldt (*top*) and Pueblo (*bottom*) datasets. These scans originate from Hart InterCivic and Dominion scanners, respectively. This difference is reflected in the style of the targets and the quality of the scans.

modern scanners make use of a second threshold, β. If $\beta \leq s_i < \alpha$, the target is treated as an ambiguous or *marginal* mark, and the ballot is set aside for officials to manually determine the voter's intent, in a process known as *adjudication*.

This technique performs well on ballots that have been properly marked, but it sometimes falls short when handling ballots where the voter has not followed the instructions precisely [12], as in many of the samples in Fig. 1. Often, voters disregard ballot instructions and use other marks such as X-marks or check marks to indicate their intent. As discussed in Sect. 3.1, we found that roughly 8.5% of marks in one large corpus of voted ballots were not filled as directed. While humans can easily identify these "marginal" marks and typically interpret them correctly, they may be challenging for current optical scanning systems to process accurately. If marks are not dark enough, they may not meet either threshold will therefore be ignored by current systems. Even in the case where marks fall within the adjudication range, tabulating them imposes increased labor costs for resource-constrained voting jurisdictions.

We investigate the feasibility of improving scanner accuracy and reducing adjudication costs by applying supervised learning techniques. Using real voted ballots, we train a convolutional neural network to classify a variety of mark styles, including both properly marked targets and common marginal marks. Compared to a generic implementation of mark recognition based on intensity thresholds, our model achieves more accurate classification and lower rates of adjudication. We further validate our technique using a second real-world ballot corpus for which we have the results of scanning and adjudication reported in the election, and achieve identical results in every case. These findings suggest that our approach could improve scanner accuracy while reducing election costs.

2   Related Work

The challenging nature of ballot mark recognition has long been recognized and is discussed at length by Jones [12] and Toledo et al. [27].

A number of previous studies have investigated methods for improving ballot scanning. Several groups have approached the problem by combining computer vision for feature extraction with human judgement for checking the interpretation of marks. In 2010, Cordero et al. proposed a method for efficiently verifying the scanner's mark interpretations by having humans review batches of ballot images automatically superimposed on each other [6]. Wang et al. later developed

OpenCount, a system that similarly automated feature extraction and provided interactive tools for classifying voter marks [30]. Although our goal is to improve automatic mark recognition and reduce reliance on operator input, these earlier works could complement our techniques and result in further efficiency gains, if applied to the ballots that our approach determines require manual adjudication.

More closely related to our approach, other prior work has applied supervised learning to mark recognition. In 2009, Xiu et al. briefly investigated a classification approach generally similar to ours, but based on modified quadratic discriminant functions (MQDFs) instead of convolutional neural networks (CNNs) [31]. Although they reported strong performance, their dataset consisted of only a few hundred ballots, making comparisons with real-world scanner performance difficult. A 2015 NIST study further benchmarked several ML-based approaches for categorizing marginal marks [1], but their primary goal was to improve testing of optical scanners rather than to surpass intensity-based mark detection.

3   Methods

In recent years, convolutional neural networks (CNNs) have become the industry standard for image classification [26]. CNNs use a divide and conquer strategy to classify images, attempting to gain a localized understanding of an image's structure to identify key characteristics which are then used to classify the image as a whole. For instance, in classifying marks on a ballot, one feature a CNN might identify is lines at a 45° angle, corresponding to X-marks. We chose to use a two-dimensional CNN, since it allows for the detection of multidimensional structures, in contrast to a one-dimensional fully-connected network which would immediately flatten the image, losing the ability for the network to extract this type of structural feature from the data. Another advantage of CNNs is that they use comparatively fewer parameters than fully connected networks, since they reuse their parameters several times. This means that the model is easier to train because it requires less data to achieve a higher accuracy and takes less time.

We developed our own CNN model and then tested it on ballot scans collected from actual elections, evaluating its performance relative to a simple threshold-based approach. It was not possible to obtain a currently marketed optical scanner to use as a baseline for comparison, so we wrote our own implementation closely modeled on the Dominion ImageCast scanner system, as described in patents and court documents [7,22]. The Dominion system, which is used in parts of 28 states [29], defaults to $\alpha = 35\%$ and $\beta = 12\%$, which we adopted for our implementation. One advantage of using this baseline model rather than an actual optical scanner was that both models used the same extracted features, allowing for a truer comparison of their mark detection methods.

We decided to build a model that would classify individual targets as features rather than examining entire pages. This way our model generalizes well across different contests and page types, so long as the targets are the same shape and size. Since the two datasets we used (described below) had differently shaped targets, we used a separate model for each. Both models used the same CNN architecture, but each was trained on different data.

3.1 Data

The ballot scans we used came from two datasets: the November 2009 election in Humboldt County, California and the November 2020 election in Pueblo County, Colorado [23]. Initially, we used a representative subset of the Humboldt data, consisting of 23,846 out of the 28,383 non-blank pages, which contained 149,394 voting targets. Later, to validate our approach, we used a subset of the Pueblo dataset, which provided ballot scans as well as the official interpretation of each target resulting from the real scanners and adjudication process. This allowed us to directly compare the CNN model's output to real election practice. From the 89,098 Pueblo County ballots, we used a representative subset of 1,719 ballots that contained 147,121 voting targets. Each ballot consisted of multiple contests. Some Humboldt contests allowed for only one vote while others allowed multiple choices to be selected. Additionally, the ballots in both datasets did not have a straight-ticket option, so most contests contained marked targets.

Labeling. To provide ground truth for the Humboldt data, we manually labeled all of the targets in our subset. We started by labeling each ballot page type; for purposes of this study, a page type is defined as a set of scans that contain the same contests in the same relative locations on each page. We then labeled the individual targets in two passes, according to two labeling schemes. In the first pass, we labeled targets by the mark type, and in the second, by perceived voter intent (0 for no vote, 1 for vote). The first schema is presented in Fig. 2, along with a summary of the first pass of labeling. Approximately 69% of targets were unmarked, 29% were properly marked, and 2.7% contained a marginal mark.

We verified our labels by comparing the election results published by Humboldt County [10]. There was near perfect agreement for contests that had been labeled completely, with the maximum difference being 15 out of 6529 votes (or 0.2%). Most contests were either in complete agreement or differed by only 1 or 2 votes. In all the contests where there was a mismatch, our vote totals were less than the official counts. Upon investigation, most of the discrepancies were due to malformed or flipped scans, which we did not label. The small residual disagreement could be due to inaccuracies in the original count or our own human error.

Unlike the Humboldt scans, which were stored as grayscale images, the Pueblo scans were 1-bit black and white. There may have been some faint marginal marks on ballots that were undetected by the optical scanners and were also missed by our manual labeling. In this case, all models would have misclassified this type of mark, since it was lost at the scanning stage rather than the interpretation stage.

Feature Extraction. The ballots in the Humboldt dataset lack timing marks, and we found that the position and orientation of the ballot relative to the scanned image was inconsistent across scans. To overcome this, we created a template for each page type that indicated the location of each voting target relative to the top-left corner of a rectangular printed border that surrounds the ballot. We used OpenCV's contour detection algorithm [3] to obtain the coordinates of the corners of the border in each scan, then aligned the appropriate

Mark Type	Count
No Mark	100,999
Properly Marked	42,165
Marginal Mark:	
X-Marked	1,115
Check-Marked	93
Lightly Marked	1,903
Partially Marked	489
Marked and Crossed Out	316
Bad Scan / Wrong contest	2,242
Other	72
Total	149,394

Fig. 2. Number of marks of different types in Humboldt dataset, as determined by manual classification. 8.5% of the marks in this dataset were marginal marks.

template to extract all of the voting targets. This method accounted for the common case of vertical and horizontal shifts of the ballot within the scans. However, this method is not able to account for other kinds of scanning artifacts, including ballots with nonlinear distortions due to misfeeding.

For the Pueblo dataset, the ballots contained timing marks, which provided four points of reference for each individual target, giving us an extremely accurate position for extraction. For each page type, we used OpenCV to identify the timing marks corresponding to each target and used them to extract the target regions. This was highly resilient to rotations and other scanner distortions.

Partitioning into Training and Test Data. We used a subset of the labeled targets from each dataset for training and the remainder for testing. Of labeled targets from the Humboldt dataset, 54% (corresponding to 12 out of 17 page types) were used for training. For the Pueblo dataset, 75% were used for training. These differing splits were a matter of convenience. Both models exhibited excellent performance, but we note that the larger amount of training data may have benefited the performance of the Pueblo model relative to the Humboldt model.

3.2   Baseline Model

We sought to compare our methods to the commonly used intensity-threshold technique. Since we did not have access to a deployed ballot scanner, we created our own implementation modeled after the Dominion system described in Sect. 2. For each ballot, our baseline model considers all the extracted targets in a given contest and predicts each target as either no vote, vote, or adjudicate. In practice, a single adjudicated mark will result in the entire contest on that ballot being reviewed by humans, so if any mark was predicted as adjudicate, we labeled all the targets in that contest the same way.

Dominion's scanners create 1-bit-per-pixel bitmaps, as shown in Fig. 1. In order to replicate this behavior using the grayscale Humboldt scans, we applied Floyd-Steinberg dithering (a common graphics algorithm provided by the imaging library we used [4]) to reduce the grayscale images to black and white while approximately maintaining the average intensity within local regions.

The next step was to calculate the number of marked pixels inside the target area. However, each feature consisted of not only the voter's mark (inside the target), but also the pre-printed target border and the area immediately outside it. To account for this, we first converted our thresholds into raw pixel counts, leveraging the fact that all targets had the same dimensions. Then we subtracted the average number of black pixels occupied by the unmarked target border.

To allow for imperfect feature extraction, our baseline implementation considered a target area that is somewhat larger than the printed targets. Some fielded scanners are known to do so as well, but to our knowledge the specifics of this behavior are not well documented by any manufacturer. We note this as a limitation of our baseline model. It is possible that real scanners differ in such aspects and so would sometimes produce different results; however, we expect variations based on marks outside the printed target to be uncommon. In our datasets, such marks rarely occurred except in cases where the shading within the printed target alone would have clearly been an intended mark.

3.3   CNN Model

Preprocessing. Before we could train our model, we needed to transform our dataset. In order to decrease computational costs, we resized the cropped target areas to 28×28 pixels with 8-bits-per-pixel of depth. We then stored them in a three-dimensional array, X, parallel to their associated labels, y. Finally, we normalized the pixel values in X to a 0–1 scale.

Our manual classification rubric included "lightly", "partially", and "properly" marked labels, but we later realized that the distinction between these classes varied depending on who was assigning the label. Due to the subjectivity, we merged these classes prior to training. All three labels indicated that the voter intended a mark; we reviewed the entire contest when making these classifications, and in each case the voter's intent was clear.

Finally, we made a second partition of the targets from those that were set aside for training, reserving 85% for training and a standard 15% for validation. This allowed us to train our model using various parameter combinations and determine which were best by examining performance on the validation set. We followed this process for both datasets independently.

Model Structure. The model we chose consisted of a single convolutional layer with 25 filters of kernel size 3×3, stride 1, and no padding. The output was passed through a ReLU nonlinearity, followed by a fully connected layer with ReLU, and finally a second fully connected layer that culminated in seven neurons. We used the softmax function to create a probability distribution from the final layer weights and outputted our prediction as the class with the highest probability.

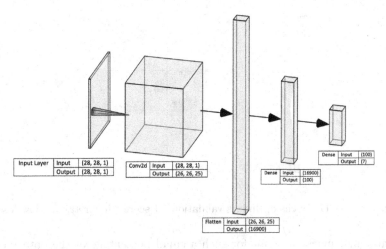

Fig. 3. The CNN architecture we used. Pictured layers appear from left to right in the order they were applied. (*Image generated using* [16].)

A primary consideration while designing the model was the number of convolutional layers. Models today can have upwards of 50 layers [9], but excess layers can cause overfitting. Our dataset was relatively uncomplicated, with X-marks, check marks, and marked and crossed-out marks being the most complicated structures. We wanted a model capable of learning these structures but also general enough to categorize all X-marks, regardless of their shape, size or orientation, as an X-mark. We initially made the assumption that more layers would result in higher accuracy, but in evaluating our model, we noticed that our training loss was significantly lower than testing loss, and our validation accuracy was low, which suggested that the design was overfitting. This led us to use a shallower model, reduced to one convolutional layer and with an increased number of convolutional filters. We observed that this approach reduced overfitting and significantly increased validation accuracy (Fig. 3).

Before trying a shallower model, we experimented with hyperparameter tuning, as well as regularization methods such as dropout. We also attempted to add a pooling layer, to downsample, and to reduce the number of parameters, but found that these features were unnecessary due to the already low spatial size of our images. The shallower model we settled on also had the side benefit of faster training, allowing more iteration in our model development process.

We implemented our model using Keras and TensorFlow. We were able to take advantage of the built-in convolutional and fully-connected layers while having the flexibility to write our own evaluation metrics.

Hyperparameter Selection. One important hyperparameter was the evaluation metric. Our ultimate goal is to produce a vote tally that comes as close as possible to the collective will of the voters, and our model also should be intelligible to voters, allowing people to understand how their votes are counted. With these criteria in mind, accuracy is the most logical evaluation metric. For training the model, however, simply trying to optimize for accuracy has its drawbacks.

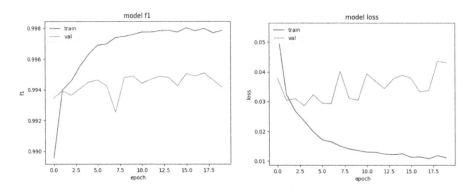

Fig. 4. Using 17 epochs optimizes validation F1 score while retaining low loss.

Since marginal marks account for such a small percentage of the data relative to properly marked and blank marks, a model trained for accuracy would not learn to classify these marks as well as their more prevalent counterparts. To address this, we chose to use a model that optimizes F1 score, the harmonic mean of precision and recall, which puts more weight on correctly classifying these marginal marks. By optimizing for F1 score, we were able to produce a model that had a higher overall accuracy compared to one that optimized for accuracy directly.

The other traditional hyperparameters we selected were batch size and the number of epochs. Based on a number of trial runs, we expect that a fairly wide range of batch sizes would be appropriate; we chose 32. For the number of epochs, we chose 17, which testing determined was past the point of diminishing marginal returns for the F1 score while maintaining low loss, as shown in Fig. 4.

The final important hyperparameter was a threshold for confidence, which we used to apply our trained model to an entire contest rather than individual targets. That is, how confident did we need to be that all the targets in a contest were classified correctly in order to not designate that ballot for adjudication? To utilize this threshold, we first obtained the product of the label probabilities for each of those targets, and then compared that value to the threshold. Similarly to the baseline model, if this value was lower than the threshold then we would send the entire contest for adjudication. We tested several threshold values and obtained the best results with a threshold of 0.95 combined with adjudicating any contest in which the classifier found three or more different types of marks.

3.4 Differences for Pueblo Dataset

Although the model structure for the Pueblo dataset was broadly similar to the Humboldt model, we did not use the baseline model to evaluate it since we had the scanner's actual interpretation as ground truth. Each ballot in the dataset included the officially counted votes (and the results of adjudication, if applicable) as a final page in the scan, a feature that Dominion calls AuditMark [8]. We extracted these results using the Pytesseract optical character recognition library (Fig. 5).

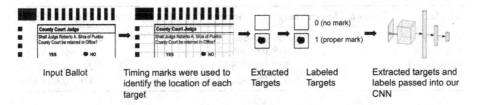

Fig. 5. For Pueblo ballots, we used timing marks to extract targets, manually labeled them, and passed these features to our CNN model.

Through manual and automated inspections of the Pueblo dataset, we established that it contains far fewer marginal marks than the Humboldt data. This may be due in part to Pueblo County acting to protect voter privacy by removing ballots with unusual styles of marks that were flagged for adjudication. For this reason, we used the Pueblo dataset to test how a CNN model would perform compared to current scanning systems under "ideal" ballot conditions—i.e., post adjudication, limited marginal marks, and clear ballot instructions. Our goal was to establish whether a CNN-based system would perform as well as current systems even under the circumstances where current systems are most accurate.

4   Evaluation and Results

To compare ballot scanning models, there are three distinct metrics to consider: classification accuracy, number of ballots that require adjudication, and computational cost. First, it is important that a model is as accurate as possible because it is vital that the tabulated results match the intent of the voters. Second, it is important to minimize ballots that require adjudication. In many states such as Colorado, where the Pueblo dataset originated, ballots that are "kicked" by scanners must be adjudicated by a bipartisan team of election judges who determine how the vote should be counted by a set of criteria [5]. This process is slow and potentially subjective. If a ballot scanner kicks too many ballots, counting will be cost prohibitive. Finally, if the model is too slow, using it in practice (such as in real-time as ballots are scanned) may be difficult.

Before accuracy could be computed, we needed to determine how targets labeled as adjudicated should be handled when calculating accuracy. Our models assigned each target one of three labels—vote, no vote, or adjudicate. By contrast, each target in the dataset was labeled as either a vote or a no vote. When computing accuracy, we assumed all adjudicated ballots would be correctly classified by the adjudication process. We separately evaluated the number of ballots that required adjudication. We show results for these metrics in Fig. 6.

4.1   Baseline Model Performance

The baseline model performed better than we anticipated; however, it still struggled where we expected. First, it sometimes classified targets with small or light

Model	Targets Accurately Classified	Flagged for Adjudication
Baseline	68,540 (99.895%)	2,181 (3.179%)
CNN	68,588 (99.965%)	1,465 (2.135%)
Hybrid #1	68,597 (99.978%)	3,242 (4.725%)
Hybrid #2	68,557 (99.920%)	430 (0.627%)

Fig. 6. Performance of each model on the Humboldt dataset. The CNN misclassifies 67% fewer targets and flags 33% fewer ballots for adjudication versus the baseline.

marks as no votes because these marks did not contain enough dark pixels to pass either threshold and be classified as a vote or flagged for adjudication. Second, the model often classified targets with marks that were filled in and crossed out as votes, because these targets contained a higher percent than the second threshold of dark pixels. Figure 7 shows examples of misclassified targets.

4.2   CNN Model Performance

By comparison, the CNN model outperformed the baseline model in both overall accuracy and number of ballots sent to a human. It had 66.7% fewer misclassifications and 32.8% fewer ballots flagged for adjudication versus the baseline.

The cases where the CNN model produced inaccurate classifications fell into a few categories. First, it appeared to be more sensitive than the baseline model to poor feature extraction and struggled off center targets. Fortunately, there exist more sophisticated techniques for ballot feature extraction than was used in this study [19]. Second, our model struggled with some of the X-marked targets. The CNN model occasionally labeled these targets as empty, causing it to predict no vote where a vote should have been. Figure 7 shows examples where the CNN model failed, but we emphasize that its overall performance was clearly superior to the baseline's when comparing accuracy or adjudications.

Figure 8 shows how each model performed on targets the other classified correctly, incorrectly, or adjudicated. Notably, all marks that the CNN model misclassified were also misclassified or flagged for adjudication by the baseline model.

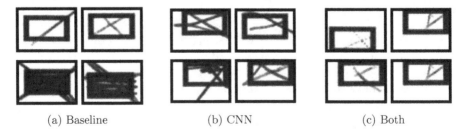

(a) Baseline   (b) CNN   (c) Both

Fig. 7. Examples of misclassified targets from Humboldt ballots. The CNN performed better overall, but it failed in some cases with X marks or off-center targets.

		Baseline		
		Correct	Adjudicate	Incorrect
	Correct	65,355	1,742	26
CNN	Adjudicate	1,004	430	31
	Incorrect	0	9	15

Fig. 8. Overlapping performance of each model on 68,612 Humboldt targets.

4.3   Computational Costs

An additional metric to consider is computational cost. For the CNN, the most computationally expensive step was training the model. However, training need only be done once for each type of scanner hardware and style of voting target.

Ideally, a pre-trained model can predict labels for ballots at least as fast as they are scanned in, ensuring that the model is not a limiting component of the device as a whole. Today, a typical speed rating for a high-speed central-count optical scanner is on the order of 300 ballots per minute [28]. Different ballots contain vastly different numbers of targets, but an upper bound estimate for a traditional-style ballot might be 128 targets per page. With double-sided ballots, the high-speed scanner would need to process 1280 targets per second to keep up. Both the pre-fitted CNN and the baseline model far exceeded this rate, taking less than a second on a mid-line laptop to label the extracted, preprocessed features from the 68,612 targets in our test dataset. (Although feature extraction adds additional costs, these are the same with both models.) This indicates that the CNN approach can outperform the baseline in both accuracy and adjudication frequency while performing fast enough to keep pace with modern scanners.

4.4   Hybrid Models

After examining the results from the baseline and CNN models, we considered additional models that involved combining the two. We optimized the first of these hybrid models for accuracy. In this model, we flagged a contest's targets for adjudication if either the baseline model or the CNN model labeled any of that contest's targets as adjudicate, or if the two models disagreed on their predictions. This hybrid achieved a higher overall accuracy than either model alone. However, it also required adjudicating significantly more targets than either model alone did. Since this model was better than the CNN model by accuracy but worse by number of ballots adjudicated, it is not clearly an improvement. It is also worth noting that similar results might be possible from the CNN alone by increasing the confidence threshold at which the CNN model flags ballots for adjudication.

The second combined model we considered strove to maintain accuracy while reducing the number of ballots adjudicated. In this hybrid, we used the CNN model as a primary classifier, and when the CNN model chose to adjudicate, we used the baseline model to try to classify the target first. By accuracy, this model was still better than the baseline model but not as good as the CNN alone. By number of adjudications, this method was highly effective. It would be interesting to investigate if one could increase the accuracy of this type of hybrid model by increasing the confidence threshold of the CNN. Like the first hybrid model, since this model was better than the CNN in one aspect but worse in the other, we cannot conclude which is decisively better. Figure 6 shows results for both hybrids.

4.5   Optimized Baseline Model

In addition to the performances of combined CNN and baseline models, we also investigated how a baseline model with different thresholds would have performed compared to the CNN. By starting with the Humboldt voting results and working backwards, it was possible to use a brute force approach to calculate which thresholds would produce the optimal results for this specific dataset given either a minimum accuracy or maximum adjudication rate condition.

If we insist that the baseline model achieves a lower adjudication rate than the CNN, $\alpha = 13.2\%$ and $\beta = 8.1\%$ maximized accuracy. This modified baseline achieved an accuracy of 99.862%—worse than even the original baseline model—and an adjudication rate of 2.035%. Likewise, if we modify the baseline model to have an accuracy higher than the CNN model, $\alpha = 99.8\%$ and $\beta = 1.7\%$ minimized adjudication. While this model had an accuracy of 99.968%, it would be virtually pointless as 97.042% of all contests required adjudication. This strongly suggests that there are types of marks, such as those marked and then crossed out, that simply cannot be correctly identified by a model that only looks at the shading of the target area.

4.6   Pueblo Test Results

We used the Pueblo dataset to more directly compare the CNN model to a deployed election system and to address concerns about whether a CNN could sometimes harm results. That is, in elections where current scanners perform well, would a CNN achieve a comparable accuracy? Once we had determined the efficacy of a CNN for the relatively messy Humboldt dataset, we retrained our model on the comparatively clean Pueblo dataset. Retraining was necessary, because the datasets use different styles of voting targets, and the raw scans, which were captured on different types of hardware, have vastly different intensity response characteristics. We used the same model architecture, only changing input/output sizes for the model layers. This model achieved similar training accuracy and loss to the Humboldt CNN model.

The Pueblo CNN model found 36 contests on 24 ballots with an overvote. When combined with 161 targets where feature extraction failed, this amounted to 0.0067% of the targets in the test dataset, and after accounting for the overvotes, the Pueblo model agreed with the post-adjudication ballot interpretations from the real election for every target in the test dataset of about 35,000 targets. This suggests that a CNN can produce accuracy as good as state-of-the-art deployed systems, while potentially requiring fewer ballots to be adjudicated.

Since the Pueblo dataset had extremely few marginal marks, the baseline also had a very high accuracy and made almost no mistakes, leaving little room to improve upon the accuracy. However, our previous experiments showed that on datasets with a larger variety of marks, such as the Humboldt ballots, our CNN approach can achieve significant improvements to accuracy.

5   Discussion

We trained CNN models on the Humboldt dataset and the Pueblo dataset and found that they match or outperform the baseline threshold-intensity approach in terms of the number of correctly labeled targets and the number of ballots that require adjudication by election officials. A similar approach could be implemented in future elections. Scanner manufacturers could each train a model once on ballots that reflect their particular style of voting targets (e.g., ovals or rectangles) and hardware imaging characteristics (e.g., grayscale or one-bit black and white), then implement the model in a software update for their machines. This would potentially benefit future elections in multiple ways.

The benefits to increased labeling accuracy are clear. Better target classifications mean election results will better match voter intent. Demonstrated accuracy improvements may also increase public trust in the election process. Additionally, despite the expert consensus regarding the importance of rigorous post-election audits as a defense against both fraud and error [20], many states still do not require any form of tabulation audit, and very few perform risk-limiting audits [21]. As a result, the outcomes of the vast majority of contests currently depend on the accuracy of ballot scanners. Even when audits or manual recounts are applied, it is important for initial machine counts to be accurate, because if the audit or recount shows different counts, public confidence is likely to be eroded.

One of the biggest benefits of adjudicating fewer ballots is the time saved. When an absentee ballot is sent for review, election officials need to analyze it in the presence of multiple observers, determine voter intent, and then (for manual adjudication processes) copy the voter intent onto a new ballot and scan it. Reducing adjudication will save administrative costs and improve the speed at which election results are tabulated—which may help further increase voter confidence. Moreover, reducing the number of times voter intent needs to be determined by humans will reduce the potential for bias, subjectivity, and disputes.

5.1   Future Work

Our results suggest that application of machine learning techniques can achieve substantial improvements for the ballot scanning process, but we emphasize that far more work is possible. While our model was able classify targets correctly with greater than 99.9% accuracy, outperforming the baseline model, there are numerous improvements that can be made to further enhance the performance of supervised learning techniques and better understand voter intent.

First, although our CNN model matched the performance of an actual scanner for the Pueblo dataset, which had very few marginal marks, further work is needed to more rigorously quantify the gains from CNN techniques against actual deployed scanners when marginal marks are more common. The baseline model we implemented may be more capable towards marginal marks than some currently deployed tabulators, since it considers intensity within a fairly large region around the voting target, and so may underestimate the potential improvements.

Second, performance can very likely be enhanced by improving on the rather basic feature extraction methods that we used in the bulk of our experiments. Most of the mistakes in the Humboldt model originated from our target crops not being centered. A model trained on more structurally uniform, less variable data should better classify targets. In the Pueblo dataset, our feature extraction used timing marks and was more accurate than the Humboldt extraction. However, not all ballots utilize timing marks, and those that do not would benefit from the application of more sophisticated existing target extraction techniques (e.g., [30]).

Third, the performance of the CNN model can likely be greatly improved by training on a larger corpus of marginal marks, particular X-marks, check marks, and marked-and-crossed-out marks. With more data from these classes, models will be even better equipped to correctly classify these less common marks. Election officials could help accelerate this process by making larger and more complete datasets of scanned ballots available for research.

Fourth, more research is needed to investigate how ML techniques might provide even greater flexibility in understanding voter intent, such as by recognizing and processing marks that are not in the voting targets or in the small area around them. We found several examples of voters making marks and even writing in the margins of the ballots. These marks get ignored by both the current system and by our model. Scanners could potentially make better use of these marks for deciphering voter intent, whether by intelligently processing them or merely recognizing when they call for adjudication.

Finally, there is some evidence that demographic disparities exist in the rate of voter error when using existing ballot scanners [25, p. 19]. Since CNN models perform better when interpreting marginal marks, they might help reduce this bias. Research is needed to fully understand the causes and extent of bias in existing systems and to test how adopting a CNN model would affect it.

6   Conclusion

Marginal marks are a common feature on hand marked paper ballots, and current ballot scanning systems do not adequately account for them. In one dataset, we found that 8.5% of marked targets were not filled in completely, but rather consisted of X-marks, check marks, lightly filled targets, partially filled targets, and various forms of crossed-out targets. While traditional intensity-threshold methods are often able to classify such marginal marks correctly, we identified numerous cases where they either fail or require unnecessary human intervention.

By accounting for different kinds of marks and using a CNN trained to identify them, we were able to make ballot scanning more accurate. Compared to the baseline, we found that our model correctly classifies more targets and reduces the number of ballots sent to humans for review. While additional work is needed, our research indicates that supervised learning has the potential to make ballot scanning smarter by counting ballots both faster and more accurately.

Acknowledgments. The authors thank Marilyn Marks and Harvie Branscomb for assistance acquiring ballot images and the students of EECS 498.5: Election Cybersecurity (Fall 2020) for their suggestions and feedback. We thank the Humboldt County Election Transparency Project and Pueblo County Elections for making ballot images available. We also thank our anonymous reviewers and our shepherd, Catalin Dragan. This material is based upon work supported by the Andrew Carnegie Fellowship, the U.S. National Science Foundation under grant number CNS-1518888, and a gift from Microsoft.

References

1. Bajcsy, A., Li-Baboud, Y.-S., Brady, M.: Systematic measurement of marginal mark types on voting ballots. Technical report (2015). https://nvlpubs.nist.gov/nistpubs/ir/2015/NIST.IR.8069.pdf. NIST
2. Bowen, D.: Top-to-Bottom Review of voting machines certified for use in California. Technical report (2007). https://www.sos.ca.gov/elections/voting-systems/oversight/top-bottom-review/. California Secretary of State
3. Bradski, G.: The OpenCV library. Dr. Dobb's J. Softw. Tools (2000)
4. Clark, A.: Pillow (PIL Fork) Documentation (2015). https://buildmedia.readthedocs.org/media/pdf/pillow/latest/pillow.pdf
5. Colorado Secretary of State Elections Division: Voter Intent: Determination of Voter Intent for Colorado Elections (2013). https://www.broomfield.org/DocumentCenter/View/11702/Voter-Intent-Guide
6. Cordero, A., Ji, T., Tsai, A., Mowery, K., Wagner, D.: Efficient user-guided ballot image verification. In: Electronic Voting Technology/Workshop on Trustworthy Elections. EVT/WOTE (2010)
7. Curling v. Raffensperger, Civil Action No. 1:17-cv-2989-AT (N.D. Ga. Oct. 11, 2020)
8. Dominion Voting Systems: AuditMark. https://www.dominionvoting.com/democracy-suite-ems/
9. He, K., Zhang, X., Ren, S., Sun, J.: Deep Residual Learning for Image Recognition. CoRR abs/1512.03385 (2015). arXiv:1512.03385
10. Humboldt County: November 3, 2009 UDEL Election: Official Canvass Precinct Report. https://humboldtgov.org/DocumentCenter/View/3941/November-3-2009-UDEL-Election-Official-Canvass-Precinct-Report-PDF
11. Hursti, H.: Critical Security Issues with Diebold Optical Scan Design, The Black Box Report (2005)
12. Jones, D.W.: On optical mark-sense scanning. In: Chaum, D., et al. (eds.) Towards Trustworthy Elections. LNCS, vol. 6000, pp. 175–190. Springer, Heidelberg (2010). https://doi.org/10.1007/978-3-642-12980-3_10

13. Kamarck, E., Ibreak, Y., Powers, A., Stewart, C.: Voting by mail in a pandemic: a state-by-state scorecard, Brookings Institution (2020). https://www.brookings.edu/research/voting-by-mail-in-a-pandemic-a-state-by-state-scorecard/
14. Kiayias, A., Michel, L., Russell, A., Shvartsman, A.: Security assessment of the Diebold optical scan voting terminal (2006). https://voter.engr.uconn.edu/voter/wp-content/uploads/uconnreport-os.pdf
15. Kiayias, A., Michel, L., Russell, A., Shashidhar, N., See, A., Shvartsman, A.: An authentication and ballot layout attack against an optical scan voting terminal. In: USENIX/ACCURATE Electronic Voting Technology Workshop (EVT) (2007)
16. LeNail, A.: NN-SVG: publication-ready neural network architecture schematics. J. Open Source Softw. **4**(33), 747 (2019). https://doi.org/10.21105/joss.00747
17. Lindeman, M., Stark, P.: A gentle introduction to risk-limiting audits. IEEE Secur. Priv. **10**, 42–49 (2012)
18. McDaniel, P., Blaze, M., Vigna, G.: EVEREST: evaluation and validation of election-related equipment, standards and testing. Technical report (2007). http://siis.cse.psu.edu/everest.html. Ohio Secretary of State
19. Nagy, G., Lopresti, D., Smith, E.H.B., Wu, Z.: Characterizing challenged Minnesota ballots. In: 18th Document Recognition and Retrieval Conference (2011)
20. National Academies of Sciences, Engineering, and Medicine: Securing the Vote: Protecting American Democracy. The National Academies Press, Washington, DC (2018). https://www.nap.edu/catalog/25120/securing-the-vote-protecting-american-democracy
21. National Conference of State Legislatures: Post-Election Audits (2019). http://www.ncsl.org/research/elections-and-campaigns/post-election-audits635926066.aspx
22. Poulos, J., Hoover, J., Ikonomakis, N., Obradovic, G.: Marginal Marks with Pixel Count, U.S. Patent 9,710,988 B2 (2012)
23. Pueblo County Elections: Ballot Images, November 2020 Election. https://county.pueblo.org/clerk-and-recorder/ballot-images
24. Rivest, R.: On the notion of 'software independence' in voting systems. Phil. Trans. R. Soc. A **366**(1881), 3759–3767 (2008)
25. State of Georgia: Report of The 21st Century Voting Commission, (2001). https://voterga.files.wordpress.com/2014/11/21st_century_report.pdf
26. Sultana, F., Sufian, A., Dutta, P.: Advancements in image classification using convolutional neural network. ICRCICN (2018). https://doi.org/10.1109/icrcicn.2018.8718718
27. Toledo, J.I., Cucurull, J., Puiggalí, J., Fornés, A., Lladós, J.: Document analysis techniques for automatic electoral document processing: a survey. In: Haenni, R., Koenig, R.E., Wikström, D. (eds.) VOTELID 2015. LNCS, vol. 9269, pp. 129–141. Springer, Cham (2015). https://doi.org/10.1007/978-3-319-22270-7_8
28. U.S. Election Assistance Commission: Central Count Optical Scan Ballots (2008). https://www.eac.gov/sites/default/files/documentlibrary/files/Quick_Start_Guide_-_Central_Count_Optical_Scan_Ballots.pdf
29. Verified Voting: The Verifier: Polling Place Equipment (2021). https://www.verifiedvoting.org/verifier/
30. Wang, K., Kim, E., Carlini, N., Motyashov, I., Nguyen, D., Wagner, D.: Operator-assisted tabulation of optical scan ballots. In: Electronic Voting Technology/Workshop on Trustworthy Elections. EVT/WOTE (2012)
31. Xiu, P., Lopresti, D., Baird, H., Nagy, G., Smith, E.B.: Style-based ballot mark recognition. In: 10th International Conference on Document Analysis and Recognition (2009)

STROBE-Voting: Send Two, Receive One Ballot Encoding

Josh Benaloh[(✉)]

Microsoft Research, Redmond, WA, USA
benaloh@microsoft.com

Abstract. Numerous designs for end-to-end verifiable voting systems have been proposed in recent years to accommodate in-person voting scenarios and Internet voting scenarios, but very few have been offered to support vote-by-mail and none that are practical with current equipment and processes. This work describes a simple approach to end-to-end verifiable vote-by-mail that can be implemented with little change to existing processes. A specific architecture is described in this work, but the basic technique can also be used to enable many existing end-to-end verifiable systems to support vote-by-mail.

Since most election jurisdictions utilize some combination of in-person voting and vote-by-mail, there is great value in an approach which allows both modes to be unified into an end-to-end verifiable system that produces a single verifiable tally.

1 Introduction

Vote-by-mail (VbM) is becoming an increasingly popular mode of voting, and the importance of VbM is drastically magnified in a time of pandemic when in-person voting creates potential health risks. However, it is difficult to ensure the integrity of VbM systems, and while expert assurances can be given, there is no direct evidence provided to voters that their votes have been correctly recorded and counted.

End-to-end (E2E) verifiability is an existing technology that allows voters to confirm for themselves that their votes have, indeed, been correctly recorded and counted. Specifically, in an E2E-verifiable election, two properties are achieved.

1. Voters can confirm that their own votes have been correctly recorded.
2. Any observer can confirm that all recorded votes have been correctly tallied.

Many end-to-end (E2E) verifiable election systems include an interactive step in which voters have an opportunity to make a choice to confirm the accurate recording of their votes. While such an interaction can be instantiated in-person or even via Internet voting, such opportunities are generally not available for voters who cannot interact directly with a voting system.

The lack of support for vote-by-mail not only limits the assurances that can be offered to mail-in voters, it also poses significant challenges for many practical environments which offer an assortment of modes. Many jurisdictions do not

© Springer Nature Switzerland AG 2021
R. Krimmer et al. (Eds.): E-Vote-ID 2021, LNCS 12900, pp. 33–46, 2021.
https://doi.org/10.1007/978-3-030-86942-7_3

wish to report tallies separately for in-person voters and mail voters. However, E2E-verifiability requires the publication of a public tally to be verified. Thus, if only in-person votes are verifiable, the in-person and mail-in vote tallies must be reported separately. This can make many E2E-verifiable systems incompatible with the basic requirements of many jurisdictions.

The techniques of STROBE-Voting bridge that gap by allowing the same verifiable system to be used for both in-person and mail-in voters. STROBE-Voting is described herein as a companion to a class of E2E-verifiable voting systems following the approach of Benaloh in [4]. Such systems include Helios [1], STAR-Vote [3], and ElectionGuard [11]. However the techniques of STROBE-Voting can also be applied to pre-printed ballot designs like Scantegrity [7] and Prêt à Voter [9].

With STROBE-Voting, mail-in voters can simply hand-mark paper ballots as they do with traditional mail-in ballots. The blank ballots can be delivered by post or downloaded over the Internet. Voters who choose to do so can retain information that enables verification and then check the retained data against election artifacts posted by election administrators—usually after the close of voting.

Comparison to Remotegrity

Like STROBE-Voting, Remotegrity [15] is a design which can be applied to multiple E2E-verifiable systems to enable mail-in voting. However, Remotegrity requires code voting and scratch-off labels and only applies to pre-printed ballot systems. STROBE-Voting is much simpler—requiring no special effort on the part of voters—and is applicable to a much wider array of E2E-verifiable systems.

Limitations

STROBE-Voting is not a voting system unto itself but rather a heuristic technique that can be applied within a wide variety of systems. As such, it is not appropriate to include proofs of effectiveness outside of the context of individual systems. However, to better explain how STROBE-Voting can be used, a more detailed example is included to demonstrate how STROBE-Voting might be applied.

As with Remotegrity, a simplifying assumption is made herein that centralized ballot printers will not compromise privacy by retaining secret info about ballots they print. This is an important limitation which will be discussed in greater detail subsequently in this work. One use case eliminates this assumption by utilizing electronic ballot delivery in which secret data that could compromise voter privacy is generated on voter devices and never exposed.

2   Sample Methodology

A STROBE-Voting ballot can look almost identical to a traditional vote-by-mail paper ballot. The only additions are a very short code beside every selectable option (e.g., two letters or three digits) and a larger (32-byte) hash code at the bottom of the ballot. Voters need do nothing more than fill in ovals (or make other marks) corresponding to their selections. Any additional voter actions are completely optional.

A randomized encryption is produced for each selectable option on each ballot (the encryption changes for each new ballot). These encryptions are retained but **not** printed on ballots. Instead, the encryptions are locked by being hashed together, and this hash of all encryptions on a ballot is printed at the bottom of the ballot. Other than the ballot hash, the only vestiges of the encryptions that appear on ballots are short codes that are deterministically derived from each encryption and printed beside the corresponding options. The short *selection codes* are entirely locked by the larger *ballot code* and serve simply as identifiers for each selection. The only restriction on selection codes is that they must be unique within each contest on a ballot. If the internal randomness used to produce a ballot and ultimately the long ballot code results in duplicate short selection codes, then all or part of that randomness is replaced until all short selection codes within a ballot are unique (within each contest). **It is important to recognize that even though the selection codes are very short, there is no way to search for or deduce the selections to which they correspond without breaking the corresponding encryptions. The ease with which one can find other encryptions which produce identical short selection codes is not a security threat since the encryptions are fully locked by each ballot's long ballot code.**

The randomness used for each encryption can be generated independently, so if a short selection code collides with another for the same contest, the randomness used in that encryption can be changed. This can be repeated as necessary to ensure that all short selection codes within any contest are unique. In theory, a single-byte short selection code can accommodate as many as 256 selections per contest. However, the time to generate suitable encryptions would slow significantly as the number of options approaches 256. Of course, the code can be lengthened as desired to accommodate larger numbers of selections, for computational efficiency, for usability in a large ballot if it is desired to have all short codes be distinct across the entire ballot, or if (as may be desirable for some scenarios) all of the randomness on a ballot is to be generated deterministically from a singe seed.

As with Helios, STAR-Vote, ElectionGuard, and related systems, every selectable option is encoded with exponential ElGamal [12] which facilitates easy distributed key generation and homomorphic tallying. To preview the more detailed description given below, a vector of encryptions is prepared for each selectable option in which the encryption corresponding to the selected option is an encryption of one and the remaining values are encryptions of zero. The encryption of each selection is hashed with SHA-256 and then truncated to a single byte to form the short selection code for that selection.[1] The byte can be

---

[1] A hash isn't strictly necessary here. Any deterministic function of the encryption vector would suffice. One could even just use the last byte of the last encryption of the vector. The selection code merely serves as a convenient means of identifying which of the encryptions (published elsewhere and locked by the 32-byte ballot code) has been selected.

represented in human readable form in a variety of ways including a two-letter code, a three-digit code, a letter followed by a digit, or the common form of two hexadecimal characters.

As described above, if two of the selections within any one contest yield the same short selection code, some of the randomness used for encryption is changed to ensure that all selection codes within any single contest are distinct. Finally, all of the full encryptions used to produce all of the short selection codes are hashed together to form the 32-byte ballot hash code. As will be detailed below, within each contest, the encryptions are sorted before being hashed to avoid revealing the association between the encryptions and the individual selections to which they correspond.

Every set of STROBE-Voting encryptions is paired with an independently-generated twin set of encryptions. Each voter receives both twins and makes selections using either one of the two encryptions sets.

In its simplest presentation, each voter receives (either by post or by download) two blank STROBE-Voting ballots with the instructions that only one should be returned and the other may be used as a spare in case of errors. However, it will be described later how STROBE-Voting can be accomplished by providing only a single ballot to each voter.

After receipt of a STROBE-Voting ballot, an election jurisdiction publishes the following.

- All of the encryptions, short selection codes, and the long ballot code on each of the received ballot and its twin[2] (note that this step could be performed on all ballots prior to receipt)
- Non-interactive zero-knowledge (NZIK) proofs that every encryption is either an encryption of zero or an encryption of one, that exactly one element in each vector is an encryption of one, and that every position has exactly one encryption of one across all of the vectors for a contest
- All of the short selection codes corresponding to selections the voter made on the received ballot
- Decryptions and randomness used to generate all encryptions on the ballot that is the twin to the ballot received.

This information allows voters and observers to check that all ballots are well-formed. Because a voter could have cast either one of the two twin ballots, evidence of the correctness of the cast ballot (the encryptions correctly match the printed options) is indirectly provided by the demonstration of the correctness of its uncast twin ballot.

In effect, the published NIZKs prove to all observers that each ballot is well-formed and does not carry more (or fewer) votes than allowed. The twin ballot provides evidence to the voter that the selection codes recorded for that voter correctly match the selections made by the voter.

---

[2] Within each contest, the encryptions should be sorted alphanumerically according to their short selection codes to avoid revealing the association between the encryptions and the selections.

The well-formedness of any ballots in the published record can be confirmed by independent election verifiers. So a diligent voter need only check that the correct short codes are listed for the returned ballot (identified by its ballot hash code) and that the hash code of the twin is listed an unsealed ballot and has matching short codes. A convenient way of displaying uncast twin ballots to voters is to publish an image of each blank twin ballot. This enables a diligent voter to easily compare this published image with the physical ballot (which remains in the voter's possession) and confirm that the short codes match. This allows for a clean division of responsibilities wherein those voters who choose to do so can verify the correct recording of their selections by simply comparing ballots and codes—without having to perform any mathematical operations. Verification of ballot correctness can be combined with verification of election results—which can be done by any interested parties (including voters) by writing and/or executing independent election verification applications.

3   Undervotes

To accommodate the possibility that some voters may choose to not vote in some contests, each contest also has a blank or did-not-vote option and associated short selection code. This did-not-vote option is treated like any other selection, and its short selection code is derived from a vector of encryptions of zero for all ordinary options and an encryption of one associated with the did-not-vote option. If the voter does not select any of the contest options, the short selection code associated with the did-not-vote option is published for that contest as part of the information associated with the returned ballot. This prevents the published information from revealing which contests were voted on any given ballot.

In some elections, there are contests in which a voter is permitted to select more than one option. In such cases, the short selection code for each selected option will be published. Multiple did-not-vote selection codes will be provided for that contest—enough to accommodate the number of selections a voter may make for that contest. For example, in a "select up to three" contest, three did-not-vote selection codes are prepared and shown on the ballot. If a voter makes three selections in that contest, the three corresponding selection codes are published. If the voter makes only two selections, the two corresponding selection codes are published together with one of the three did-not-vote selection codes. One selection requires the publication of the one selected short code together with two of the did-not-vote selection codes, and no selections requires the publication of all three did-not-vote selection codes.

4   A Detailed Example

To better describe the approach, a small example is included below. It is assumed that a single public encryption key has been produced by combining (using a threshold key distribution) ElGamal public keys generated independently by a pre-determined set of election trustees.[3] Encryption using public key is denoted by $\mathcal{E}$.

Suppose that an election is to be conducted with a single "vote for one" contest featuring candidates Alice, Bob, and Carol. To accommodate the possibility that a voter might not choose any candidates, a fourth pseudo-candidate *did-not-vote* is added and treated just like any actual candidate.

The structure of the encryptions of the votes in is shown in the following table.

Candidate voted for	Vote (vector of encryptions)	Sample selection code
Alice	$\langle \mathcal{E}(1), \mathcal{E}(0), \mathcal{E}(0), \mathcal{E}(0) \rangle$	Q4
Bob	$\langle \mathcal{E}(0), \mathcal{E}(1), \mathcal{E}(0), \mathcal{E}(0) \rangle$	D6
Carol	$\langle \mathcal{E}(0), \mathcal{E}(0), \mathcal{E}(1), \mathcal{E}(0) \rangle$	L7
did-not-vote	$\langle \mathcal{E}(0), \mathcal{E}(0), \mathcal{E}(0), \mathcal{E}(1) \rangle$	R9

The selection codes are generated as one-byte truncations of SHA-256 hashes of each associated vector of encryptions. The short selection code for each vote is printed beside the oval used by the voter to select a candidate. Other than the inclusion of a single long ballot code on each printed ballot (described further below), the addition of a short selection code beside each oval is the only observable change to a physical ballot.

The associated physical ballot may look something like the following.

$$\begin{array}{rcl} \text{Alice} & \bigcirc & \text{Q4} \\ \text{Bob} & \bigcirc & \text{D6} \\ \text{Carol} & \bigcirc & \text{L7} \\ \text{none} & & \text{R9} \end{array}$$

Ballot code: `XC3K0-A21BM-8WP8Q-MWQ6E-UYW9Y-ZPBL5-93LRE-M3J62-MJ1W7-87DYF`

The encryptions associated with each ballot are made public as part of the election. However, they are re-ordered (sorted according to their short selection codes—which are guaranteed to be distinct) to avoid revealing which encryption corresponds to which candidate.

The public information associated with a ballot is shown below.

Vote (vector of encryptions)	Sample selection code
$\langle \mathcal{E}(0), \mathcal{E}(1), \mathcal{E}(0), \mathcal{E}(0) \rangle$	D6
$\langle \mathcal{E}(0), \mathcal{E}(0), \mathcal{E}(1), \mathcal{E}(0) \rangle$	L7
$\langle \mathcal{E}(1), \mathcal{E}(0), \mathcal{E}(0), \mathcal{E}(0) \rangle$	Q4
$\langle \mathcal{E}(0), \mathcal{E}(0), \mathcal{E}(0), \mathcal{E}(1) \rangle$	R9

---

[3] There is nothing novel about the generation and sharing of exponential ElGamal keys to produce a single ElGamal key for which threshold decryption is possible. This is done in STAR-Vote, ElectionGuard, and (without the threshold decryption capability) Helios. Since the details are not relevant, they are not included herein.

Ballot code: `XC3K0-A21BM-8WP8Q-MWQ6E-UYW9Y-ZPBL5-93LRE-M3J62-MJ1W7-87DYF`

The published information associated with each ballot also includes the following non-interactive zero-knowledge proofs (using the Fiat-Shamir heuristic [13]).

- Every encryption is an encryption of either zero or one (Cramer-Damgård-Schoenmakers disjunctive technique [10] applied to Chaum-Pedersen proofs [8] of encryption of zero and encryption of one).
- Every row is shown to have exactly one encryption of one (Chaum-Pedersen proof that the product of the encryptions in each row is an encryption of one).
- Every column is shown to have exactly one encryption of one (Chaum-Pedersen proof that the product of the encryptions in each column is an encryption of one).

All of the encryptions for this contest are then hashed in the sorted order shown here using SHA-256 to produce the long ballot code that is printed on the ballot. (In a ballot with multiple contests, the encryptions of each contest are hashed together in this way—preserving contest order—to form a single ballot code).

The long ballot code serves to lock all of the encryptions on the ballot. Without this long code, a malicious election administrator could substitute different encryptions that produce identical short selection codes in some or all contests (recall that the actual encryptions are *not* displayed on the ballot). These distinct encryptions could correspond to selections that do not match those printed on the ballot (for instance, switching two candidates) and allow votes to be thereby changed. Hashing all of the encryptions into the long ballot code makes it infeasible for an attacker to change any of the encryptions without causing the hash to no longer match the long ballot code (which *is* displayed on the ballot).

At the conclusion of an election, all of the selected encrypted votes are homomorphically combined to form encrypted tallies which are then verifiably decrypted to produce verified tallies—as in schemes with similar homomorphic tallying.

While the NIZK proofs above demonstrate that each ballot—and therefore each encrypted vote cast on each ballot—is well-formed, it does nothing to ensure that the short selection codes are matched against the correct candidates on each ballot. This is the function of the twin ballots which will be fully decrypted after the conclusion of voting.

5 Single-Ballot Variations

Whether it be due to cost or discomfort, some jurisdictions may prefer to not provide two blank ballots to each voter. The approach described above can be executed on a single-ballot design as follows.

Postal Delivery of Blank Ballots

Instead of a single short selection code beside each selectable option, two independent selection codes are printed (e.g., Q4-M1). A single ballot code computed as the hash of the two (implicit) ballot codes is printed at the bottom of this ballot. A voter may then indicate which of the two short code sets (left or right) are to be published as cast and which are to be fully decrypted. This choice may be made explicitly (by having the voter mark a choice directly on the ballot) or implicitly by another means (such as using the way that a ballot is folded[4] or the orientation in which it is placed in its return envelope[5] as a selector as in [5]).

The challenge here is usability for voters. While an explicit choice may be more natural for a voter who wishes to verify (e.g., "I chose to have the left codes revealed and the right codes used to record my vote."), it is difficult to present this choice to voters in a way that does not risk confusing voters who have no interest in verification. An implicit choice eliminates the risk of confusing uninterested voters, but it can complicate the process for both election administrators and voters who wish to verify their ballots. For instance, if ballot orientation is used, verifying voters would need to carefully note the orientations in which they insert their ballots into their envelopes, and election administrators would need to carefully note the orientations of received ballots and to take different actions based upon these orientations. While this can meet the definition of E2E-verifiability, it stretches credulity to suggest that this could be performed at scale by enough voters and jurisdictions to have a meaningful impact.

For these reasons, it may be preferable to use the simpler approach of providing each voter with two entirely distinct ballots and instructing that only one be marked and returned.

Electronic Delivery of Blank Ballots

If blank ballots are delivered to voters electronically, voters can "request" multiple ballots and return only one. In this case, unreturned ballots can be opened as though they were delivered by post. But it is no longer necessary to provide two ballots to each voter. Instead, the mere threat that a requested ballot may not be cast renders improper ballots detectable.

This process can be further improved if blank ballots are generated by voters themselves on their own devices. Uncast ballots can be challenged for integrity either by having the printing device open the encryptions directly or by voters returning blank ballots along with cast ballots for central decryption. When done this way, no device outside of the control of a voter will know the associations

---

[4] Tri-fold ballots have two natural distinct foldings—putting either the top third or the bottom third between the remaining two thirds.

[5] A typical rectangular ballot can naturally be inserted into an envelope in one of four orientations.

between ballot selections and short codes on any cast ballot. This gives voters far greater privacy guarantees than with centrally-printed ballots.

6 Usability

From the perspective of voters, there are many benefits to the basic approach of mailing two blank ballots.

- The explanation of one ballot being a spare is quite simple and natural. It seems less likely to cause confusion than many alternatives.
- Voters needn't be burdened with of the question of which set of encryptions to use.
- Simple disambiguation rules can be used by election officials to disambiguate cases when voters return both ballots—avoiding disenfranchisement of these voters.
- Interested voters who want to check the accuracy of their unreturned ballots can retain the entire ballots to facilitate these checks.
- A copy of the long ballot code can be printed onto a tear-off strip immediately below (or above) the copy that remains on the ballot.[6] This facilitates an easy check by voters prior to removing the strip.

Single ballot variants may be easier and more economical for election administrators, and they do not hinder voters who are not interested in verifying their ballots. But voters who want to verify the integrity of their ballots will need to somehow make (and record for their own use) decisions about which set of ballot codes to use and record some or all of the unused ballot codes and associated selections. This seems like quite a lot to ask—even from a diligent voter.

There would be great temptation—especially in the single ballot case—for a voter to retain a photograph of a ballot before returning it. But this should be discouraged because it could facilitate coercion (see the discussion of coercion and vote-selling in Sect. 8).

7 Hybrid Voting Systems

The encryption used in the above description of STROBE-Voting is compatible with that used in Helios, STAR-Vote, and ElectionGuard.

This is especially important because many jurisdictions that collect some votes in-person and others by mail do not wish to report tallies separately across modes. In such jurisdictions, the lack of an E2E-verifiable VbM method can inhibit the use of E2E-verifiability for in-person voting—even if only a small portion of votes are received by mail. STROBE-Voting can bridge this gap and thereby help promote the adoption of E2E-verifiable solutions.

Hybrid modes do impair statistical analysis since the models of ballot challenges are different. In Helios, STAR-Vote, and ElectionGuard, there is no limit

---

[6] The idea of a tear-off strip was suggested by an anonymous reviewer.

to the number of ballots that can be challenged or spoiled by a single voter—
although challenging of ballots is usually rare. With most instantiations of
STROBE-Voting, there is effectively one challenged ballot for every ballot cast.
A much larger proportion of VbM ballots than in-person ballots will be challenged, but a highly-skeptical individual voter has no means to raise the direct
confidence of an individual cast ballot beyond 50% unless the voter is offered
some means to request additional blank ballots.

While this does not seem to be a problem in practice, it does make it more
difficult to calculate the assurance level of an election. However, since there
would likely be a far greater portion of challenged ballots in the VbM votes, the
addition of STROBE-Voting to an in-person E2E-verifiable solution will almost
certainly not reduce the level of assurance in the integrity of the tally.

8   Attacks

Since this work is intended primarily to describe a concept that may serve as a
component of other systems, rigorous security proofs are not presented. However,
some potential attacks are addressed here.

Collision of Short Selection Codes

It might seem as though the short selection codes create a potential weakness.
However, longer codes would not provide any additional security. The security
is derived from the encryptions of the votes and the hash of these encryptions
that forms the full-length ballot code on each ballot. The short selection codes
serve only as simple deterministic identifiers to distinguish between the various encryptions. While it would not be difficult to create alternate ballots with
matching short selection codes that apply to different selections, there would be
no benefit in doing so. The association between the short selection codes and
the selections they represent is determined entirely by the long ballot code for
which it is infeasible to find collisions.

Small Perturbations

Since each voter receives two ballots (or two sets of codes on a single ballot), a
malicious election administrator could send a single voter one good ballot and
one corrupted ballot (or one corrupted code set) and hope that the voter casts
the corrupted ballot (or code set). In so doing, the malicious administrator would
be exposed to a 50% risk of its fraud being revealed, but there would be a 50%
chance of successfully corrupting a single ballot. The chance of corrupting n
ballots without being revealed would be 1 in 2^n, so this is not likely to be a very
fruitful attack.

A system can also be designed to allow particularly suspicious voters to
receive additional ballots—thereby enabling the voter's probability of detecting
fraud to be raised as far as desired (within practical limits).

Clash Attacks

Clash attacks involve an authority providing identical ballots to multiple voters who might be likely to cast identical votes. The authority might then record only one of the identical ballots. The intent would be to allow each voter to be able to verify the correct recording of a vote without revealing to the voter that this is a duplicate.

However, as with other E2E-verifiable designs following the "cast or spoil" approach of [4], clash attacks are not a concern. The ability to spoil a vote or ballot can reveal an attempt to create a clash in the same way that it can reveal an attempt to create an incorrect encryption—and with similar probabilities and risks to a malicious system. In the case of incorrect encryptions, the system will be revealed as malicious if a voter chooses to spoil an incorrectly encrypted vote. In the case of attempted clashes, the system will be revealed as malicious if one voter chooses to cast a particular ballot while another chooses to cast the twin. In this latter instance, the first voter would expect to find the associated ballot code on the list of cast ballots while the other would expect to find the same ballot code on the list of uncast/spoiled ballots. Putting the same ballot code on both lists would immediately implicate the voting system as malfeasant.

Note that the device that created an errant ballot may not be required to be involved in its spoiling—or even be aware of its spoiling. The election trustees who share the private key to decrypt election tallies can decrypt any spoiled ballots on their own. So failure to open a spoiled ballot would be a direct and public impeachment of the integrity of the election.

Attempting to Vote Two Ballots

Different jurisdictions manage their VbM ballots in vastly different ways. In some instances, blank ballots are considered a controlled resource and putting two ballots into the hands of voters might create a risk of double voting.

However, in many jurisdictions, the controls are placed at the time ballots are received. For example, in the author's home state of Washington in the U.S., voters can easily download and print as many blank ballots as they wish. Upon receipt of each completed ballot, election officials check a signature and eligibility (including that no prior vote from that voter has been received in that election) before accepting and counting the ballot.

Clearly a two-ballot approach is a better fit for a jurisdiction that does not place controls on blank ballots. A jurisdiction in which a vote on any legitimate ballot will be accepted and processed will presumably fair better with a single-ballot variation.

Susceptibility to Coercion and Vote-Selling

Like any unsupervised mode voting, vote-by-mail can subject voters to coercion and allow vote-selling more easily than supervised modes of voting.[7] No attempt

---

[7] Juels, Catalano, and Jakobsson [14] offers a possible approach to deter vote-selling and coercion in remote voting, but the usability creates practical challenges.

is made here to justify or advocate for VbM. However, it is reasonable to find ways to make VbM methods as strong as possible. Adding E2E-verifiability to VbM doesn't eliminate the coercion and vote-selling threats, but it nevertheless improves integrity by enabling verifiability of correct recording and counting of votes. This allows votes cast by mail using STROBE-Voting to be combined with votes cast by other modes to produce a single unified verifiable tally.

For better or worse, VbM is widely used and its prevalence is growing. VbM is stronger with STROBE-Voting than without. That said, STROBE-Voting can provide another vector for coercion and vote-selling beyond ordinary VbM. The combination of a genuine photograph of a ballot that has been cast together with the published short codes for that ballot offers a strong indication of the contents of a recorded vote. This can be mitigated by a variety of means—including the use of image editing and other tools—some of which may be provided by election administrators themselves. It should also be noted that this form of coercion is only possible before a vote is cast—a voter who, after following the instructions and casting a proper ballot, is asked to reveal the ballot contents will have no means to do so. This is why more direct means of verification are not offered to voters. However, it is important to maintain context and understand that with or without STROBE-Voting, remote voters can either choose to have or be coerced into having an observer during the voting process or to simply surrender a ballot entirely.

Privacy Implications of Centralized Ballot Printing

As with numerous other approaches to make paper delivery of blank ballots E2E-verifiable (e.g., [2,5,15]), centralized printing of blank ballots may enable a central entity to retain information that can later be used to compromise voter privacy. This concern can be mitigated with indirect approaches like code voting [6] at a significant cost to usability.

It is important to note that this threat can be eliminated entirely if ballots are delivered electronically and generated privately on voter devices as described at the end of Sect. 5.

9   Conclusions

STROBE-Voting is a technique that is simple both to understand and to implement. It enables E2E-verifiable election systems designed for in-person voting to be extended to serve mail-in and other remote voters.

While the acronym *STROBE* is only vaguely suggestive of the technique used in which some, but not all, of the ballots are "illuminated" by decryption, the methods have the potential to have an important impact on the use of E2E-verifiability and to promote new research to make E2E-verifiability even simpler to deploy and use.

Although the value of E2E-verifiability today is clear in an environment where numerous voters are questioning whether their votes have been correctly counted, there is ample room for new research and developments in areas such as dispute resolution, coercion-resistance for remote voting, and privacy enhancements for remote printing. STROBE-Voting adds another tool that can be used to enhance the applicability and value of E2E-verifiability.

Acknowledgements. The author would like to thank Jan Willemson and several anonymous reviewers for providing many helpful comments and suggestions that greatly improved this work.

References

1. Adida, B.: Helios: web-based open-audit voting. In: Proceedings of USENIX Security Conference, San Jose, CA, August 2008
2. Adida, B., Rivest, R.L.: Scratch & vote: self-contained paper-based cryptographic voting. In: Proceedings of WPES 2006 – ACM Workshop on Privacy in the Electronic Society, Alexandria, VA, October 2006
3. Bell, S., et al.: STAR-Vote: a secure, transparent, auditable, and reliable voting system. In: Proceedings of Electronic Voting Technology Workshop/Workshop on Trustworthy Elections, Washington, DC, August 2013
4. Benaloh, J.: Simple verifiable elections. In: Proceedings of Electronic Voting Technology Workshop, Vancouver, BC, August 2006
5. Benaloh, J., Ryan, P.Y.A., Teague, V.: Verifiable postal voting. In: Proceedings of 21st Cambridge International Workshop on Security Protocols, Cambridge, UK, March 2013
6. Chaum, D.: SureVote: technical overview. In: Proceedings of Workshop on Trustworthy Elections, Tomales Bay, CA, August 2001
7. Chaum, D., et al.: Scantegrity II: end-to-end verifiability for optical scan election systems using invisible ink confirmation codes. In: Proceedings of Electronic Voting Technology Workshop, San Jose, CA, July 2008
8. Chaum, D., Pedersen, T.P.: Wallet databases with observers. In: Brickell, E.F. (ed.) CRYPTO 1992. LNCS, vol. 740, pp. 89–105. Springer, Heidelberg (1993). https://doi.org/10.1007/3-540-48071-4_7
9. Chaum, D., Ryan, P.Y.A., Schneider, S.: A practical voter-verifiable election scheme. In: di Vimercati, S.C., Syverson, P., Gollmann, D. (eds.) ESORICS 2005. LNCS, vol. 3679, pp. 118–139. Springer, Heidelberg (2005). https://doi.org/10.1007/11555827_8
10. Cramer, R., Damgård, I., Schoenmakers, B.: Proofs of partial knowledge and simplified design of witness hiding protocols. In: Desmedt, Y.G. (ed.) CRYPTO 1994. LNCS, vol. 839, pp. 174–187. Springer, Heidelberg (1994). https://doi.org/10.1007/3-540-48658-5_19
11. Microsoft ElectionGuard Software Development Kit. https://github.com/microsoft/electionguard. (See also https://blogs.microsoft.com/on-the-issues/2019/09/24/electionguard-available-today-to-enable-secure-verifiable-voting/)
12. ElGamal, T.: A public key cryptosystem and a signature scheme based on discrete logarithms. IEEE Trans. Inf. Theory **31**, 469–472 (1985)
13. Fiat, A., Shamir, A.: How to prove yourself: practical solutions to identification and signature problems. In: Odlyzko, A.M. (ed.) CRYPTO 1986. LNCS, vol. 263, pp. 186–194. Springer, Heidelberg (1987). https://doi.org/10.1007/3-540-47721-7_12

14. Juels, A., Catalano, D., Jakobsson, M.: Coercion-resistant electronic elections. In: Proceedings of WPES 2005 – ACM Workshop on Privacy in the Electronic Society, Alexandria, VA, November 2005

15. Zagórski, F., Carback, R.T., Chaum, D., Clark, J., Essex, A., Vora, P.L.: Remotegrity: design and use of an end-to-end verifiable remote voting system. In: Jacobson, M., Locasto, M., Mohassel, P., Safavi-Naini, R. (eds.) ACNS 2013. LNCS, vol. 7954, pp. 441–457. Springer, Heidelberg (2013). https://doi.org/10.1007/978-3-642-38980-1_28

Assertion-Based Approaches to Auditing Complex Elections, with Application to Party-List Proportional Elections

Michelle Blom[1], Jurlind Budurushi[2], Ronald L. Rivest[3],
Philip B. Stark[4], Peter J. Stuckey[5], Vanessa Teague[6],
and Damjan Vukcevic[7,8(✉)]

[1] School of Computing and Information Systems, University of Melbourne,
Parkville, Australia
michelle.blom@unimelb.edu.au
[2] Cloudical Deutschland GmbH, Berlin, Germany
jurlind.budurushi@cloudical.io
[3] Computer Science and Artificial Intelligence Laboratory,
Massachusetts Institute of Technology, Cambridge, MA, USA
[4] Department of Statistics, University of California, Berkeley, CA, USA
[5] Department of Data Science and AI, Monash University, Clayton, Australia
[6] Thinking Cybersecurity Pty. Ltd., Melbourne, Australia
[7] School of Mathematics and Statistics, University of Melbourne, Parkville, Australia
[8] Melbourne Integrative Genomics, University of Melbourne, Parkville, Australia
damjan.vukcevic@unimelb.edu.au

Abstract. Risk-limiting audits (RLAs), an ingredient in evidence-based elections, are increasingly common. They are a rigorous statistical means of ensuring that electoral results are correct, usually without having to perform an expensive full recount—at the cost of some controlled probability of error. A recently developed approach for conducting RLAs, SHANGRLA, provides a flexible framework that can encompass a wide variety of social choice functions and audit strategies. Its flexibility comes from reducing sufficient conditions for outcomes to be correct to canonical 'assertions' that have a simple mathematical form.

Assertions have been developed for auditing various social choice functions including plurality, multi-winner plurality, super-majority, Hamiltonian methods, and instant runoff voting. However, there is no systematic approach to building assertions. Here, we show that assertions with *linear* dependence on transformations of the votes can easily be transformed to canonical form for SHANGRLA. We illustrate the approach by constructing assertions for party-list elections such as Hamiltonian free list elections and elections using the D'Hondt method, expanding the set of social choice functions to which SHANGRLA applies directly.

Keywords: Risk-limiting audits · Party-list proportional elections · Hamiltonian methods · D'Hondt method

© Springer Nature Switzerland AG 2021
R. Krimmer et al. (Eds.): E-Vote-ID 2021, LNCS 12900, pp. 47–62, 2021.
https://doi.org/10.1007/978-3-030-86942-7_4

1   Introduction

Risk-limiting audits (RLAs) test reported election outcomes statistically by manually inspecting random samples of paper ballots. An RLA terminates either by endorsing the reported outcome or by proceeding to a full manual count if the evidence is inconclusive. The outcome according to the full count corrects the reported outcome if they differ. The *risk limit* is an upper bound on the probability that a wrong election outcome will not be corrected—this is set in advance, typically between 1% and 10%.

SHANGRLA [4] is a general framework for conducting RLAs of a wide variety of social choice functions.[1] SHANGRLA involves reducing the correctness of a reported outcome to the truth of a set $\mathcal{A}$ of quantitative *assertions* about the set of validly cast ballots, which can then be tested using statistical methods. The assertions are either true or false depending on the votes on the ballots. If all the assertions are true, the reported outcome is correct.

This paper shows how to use the SHANGRLA RLA method to audit some complex social choice functions not addressed in the SHANGRLA paper. We give a recipe for translating sufficient conditions for a reported outcome to be correct into canonical form for SHANGRLA, when those conditions are the intersection of a set of linear inequalities involving transformations of the votes on each ballot. We focus on European-style party-list proportional representation elections, with the German state of Hesse as a case study.

1.1   Assertion-Based Auditing: Properties and Challenges

For some social choice functions, the reduction to assertions is obvious. For instance, in plurality (first-past-the-post) elections, common in the United States, Alice won the election if and only if Alice's tally was higher than that of each of the other $n - 1$ candidates (where n is the total number of candidates). That set of $n - 1$ assertions is clearly a set of linear inequalities among the vote totals for the n candidates.

In general, assertions involve not only the votes but also the reported results—the reported outcome and possibly the voting system's interpretation of individual ballots (CVRs) or tallies of groups of ballots.

SHANGRLA [4, Sec 2.5] shows how to make assorters for any 'scoring rule' (e.g. Borda, STAR-voting, and any weighted scheme). For more complex social choice functions, constructing sufficient sets of assertions may be much less obvious. Blom *et al.* [2] use a heuristic method, RAIRE, to derive assertions for Instant Runoff Voting (IRV) from the CVRs. RAIRE allows the RLA to test an IRV outcome—the claim that Alice won—without checking the entire IRV elimination. RAIRE's assertions are *sufficient*: if all of the assertions in $\mathcal{A}$ are true,

---

[1] Any social choice function that is a *scoring rule*—that assigns 'points' to candidates on each ballot, sums the points across ballots, and declares the winner(s) to be the candidate(s) with the most 'points'—can be audited using SHANGRLA, as can some social choice functions that are not scoring rules, such as super-majority and IRV.

then the announced election outcome is correct. However, the set of assertions might not be necessary—even if one of the assertions in $\mathcal{A}$ is false, Alice may still have won, but for reasons not checked by the audit.

A social choice function might be expensive to audit for two different reasons: it might require a very large sample for reasonable confidence, even when there are no errors (for instance, if it tends to produce small margins in practice); alternatively, it might be so complex that it is difficult to generate assertions that are sufficient to prove the reported election outcome is correct. Pilots and simulations suggest that IRV elections do not have small margins any more often than first-past-the-post elections. Hence IRV is feasible to audit in both senses.

Below, the sets of assertions we consider are *conjunctive*: the election outcome is correct if all the assertions in $\mathcal{A}$ are true. Although it is possible to imagine an audit method that tests more complex logical structures (for example, the announced outcome is correct if either all the assertions in $\mathcal{A}_1$ or all the assertions in $\mathcal{A}_2$ are true), this is not currently part of the SHANGRLA framework.

Summary: An audit designer must devise a set $\mathcal{A}$ of assertions.

- $\mathcal{A}$ generally depends on the social choice function and the reported electoral outcome, and may also depend on the CVRs, vote subtotals, or other data generated by the voting system.
- If every assertion in $\mathcal{A}$ is true, then the announced electoral result is correct.
- The announced electoral result may be correct even if not every assertion in $\mathcal{A}$ is true.

SHANGRLA relies on expressing assertions in terms of *assorters*.

1.2 Assorters

The statistical part of SHANGRLA is agnostic about the social choice function. It simply takes a collection of sets of numbers that are zero or greater (with a known upper bound), and decides whether to reject the hypothesis that the mean of each set is less than or equal to $1/2$—this is the *assorter null hypothesis*.

An *assorter* for some assertion $A \in \mathcal{A}$ assigns a nonnegative value to each ballot, depending on the selections the voter made on the ballot and possibly other information (e.g. reported vote totals or CVRs). The assertion is true iff the mean of the assorter (over all ballots) is greater than $1/2$. Generally, ballots that support the assertion score higher than $1/2$, ballots that cast doubt on it score less than $1/2$, and neutral ballots score exactly $1/2$. For example, in a simple first-past-the-post contest, A might assert that Alice's tally is higher than Bob's. The corresponding assorter would assign 1 to a ballot if it has a vote for Alice, 0 if it has a vote for Bob, and $1/2$ if it has a no valid vote or a vote for some other candidate.

The audit designer's first job is to generate a set $\mathcal{A}$ of assertions which, if all true, imply that the announced electoral outcome (the winner or winners) is correct. Then they need to express each $A \in \mathcal{A}$ using an assorter. Finally, they need to test the hypothesis that any assorter mean is less than or equal to 1/2. If all those hypotheses are rejected, the audit concludes that the reported outcome is correct. The chance this conclusion is erroneous is at most the risk limit.

Section 2 gives a more precise definition of an assorter and a general technique for transforming linear assertions into assorters.

1.3 Risk-Limiting Audits Using SHANGRLA: Pulling It All Together

An overview of the workflow for a sequential SHANGRLA RLA is:

1. Generate a set of assertions.
2. Express the assertions using assorters.
3. Test every assertion in $\mathcal{A}$, in parallel:
   (a) Retrieve a ballot or set of ballots selected at random.
   (b) Apply each assorter to every retrieved ballot.
   (c) For each assertion in $\mathcal{A}$, test its corresponding assorter null hypothesis (i.e. that the assorter mean is $\leqslant 1/2$) using a sequentially valid test.[2]
   (d) If the assorter null is rejected for $A \in \mathcal{A}$, remove A from $\mathcal{A}$.
   (e) If $\mathcal{A}$ is empty (i.e. all of the null hypotheses have been rejected), stop the audit and certify the electoral outcome.
   (f) Otherwise, continue to sample more ballots.
   (g) At any time, the auditor can decide to 'cut to the chase' and conduct a full hand count: anything that increases the chance of conducting a full hand count cannot increase the risk.

As with any RLA, the audit may not confirm the reported result (for example, that Alice's tally is the highest) even if all assertions are true (Alice's tally may actually be higher than Bob's, but the audit may not gather enough evidence to conclude so). This may happen because there are many tabulation errors or because one or more margins are small. When the audit proceeds to a full hand count, its result replaces the reported outcome if the two differ.

Conversely, the audit may mistakenly confirm the result even if the announced result is wrong. The probability of this kind of failure is not more than the *risk limit*. This is a parameter to SHANGRLA; setting it to a smaller value generally entails examining more ballots.

1.4 Party-List Proportional Representation Contests

Party-list proportional representation contests allocate seats in a parliament (or delegates to an assembly) in proportion to the entities' popularity within the electorate. The first step is (usually) rounding the party's fraction down to the nearest integer number of seats. Complexity arises from rounding, when the fractions determined by voters do not exactly match integer numbers of

---

[2] It can be more efficient to sample ballots in 'rounds' rather than singly; SHANGRLA can accommodate any valid test of the assorter nulls.

seats. *Largest Remainder Methods*, also called Hamiltonian methods, successively allocate leftover seats to the entities with the largest fractional parts until all seats are allocated. *Highest Averages Methods*, such as the D'Hondt method (also called Jefferson's method), weight this extra allocation by divisors involving a fraction of the seats already allocated to that party—they are hence more likely to allocate the leftover seats to small parties. The Sainte-Laguë method (also called Webster's method) is mathematically similar but its divisors penalise large parties even more.[3]

1.5 Related Work and Our Contribution

Blom *et al.* [1] showed how to construct a SHANGRLA RLA for preferential Hamiltonian elections with a viability threshold, applicable to many US primaries. Stark and Teague [5] showed how to construct an RLA for highest averages party-list proportional representation elections. Their method was not directly based on assertions and assorters, but it reduces the correctness of the reported seat allocation to a collection of two-entity plurality contests, for which it is straightforward to construct assorters, as we show below.

This paper shows how to extend SHANGRLA to additional social choice functions. We use party-list proportional representation elections as an example, showing how the assorter from [1] can be derived as a special case of the solution for more general Hamiltonian elections. We have simulated the audit on election data from the German state of Hesse; results are shown in Sect. 4. Auditing the allocation of integer portions of seats involves inspecting a reasonable number of ballots, but the correctness of the allocations based on the fractional remainders and the correctness of the particular candidates who receive seats within each party generally involve very small margins, which in turn require large audit sample sizes. We also show how to apply the construction to highest averages methods such as D'Hondt and Sainte-Laguë. Our contributions are:

- A guide to developing assertions and their corresponding SHANGRLA assorters, so that audits for contest types that are not already supplied can be derived, when correctness can be expressed as the intersection of a set of linear inequalities (Sect. 3).
- New SHANGRLA-based methods for auditing largest remainder methods that allow individual candidate selection (no audit method was previously known for this variant of largest remainder method) (Sect. 3.1).
- Simulations to estimate the average sample sizes of these new methods in the German state of Hesse (Sect. 4).
- SHANGRLA assorters for highest averages methods (RLAs for these methods were already known, but had not been expressed as assorters). (Sect. 5).

---

[3] Another source of complexity is the opportunity for voters to select, exclude, or prioritise individual candidates within the party.

2   Preliminaries

2.1   Nomenclature and Notation for Assertion-Based Election Audits

An election contest is decided by a set of 'ground truth' ballots $\mathcal{L}$ (of cardinality $|\mathcal{L}|$). Many social choice functions are used in political elections. Some yield a single winner; others multiple winners. Some only allow voters to express a single preference; others allow voters to select or rank multiple candidates or parties.

Here, we focus on elections that allow voters to select (but not rank) one or more 'entities,' which could be candidates or parties.[4]

Let S be the number of 'seats' (positions) to be filled in the contest, of which a_e were awarded to entity e. Each ballot might represent a single vote for an entity, or multiple votes for multiple entities. Important quantities for individual ballots $b \in \mathcal{L}$ include:

- m, the maximum permitted number of votes for any entity.
- $m_{\mathcal{L}}$, the maximum permitted number of votes in total (across all entities).
- b_e, the total number of (valid) votes for entity e on the ballot.
- $b_T := \sum_{e \in E} b_e$, the total number of (valid) votes on the ballot.

Any of these may be greater than one, depending on the social choice function. Validity requires $b_e \leqslant m$ and $b_T \leqslant m_{\mathcal{L}}$. If ballot b does not contain the contest in question or is deemed invalid, $b_e := 0$ for all entities E, and $b_T := 0$.

Important quantities for the set $\mathcal{L}$ of ballots include:

- $T_e = \sum_{b \in \mathcal{L}} b_e$, the *tally* of votes for entity e.
- $T_{\mathcal{L}} = \sum_{e \in E} T_e$, the total number of valid votes in the contest.
- $p_e = T_e / T_{\mathcal{L}}$, the *proportion* of votes for entity e.

2.2   Assertion-Based Auditing: Definitions

Here we formalize assertion-based auditing sketched in Sect. 1 and introduce the relevant mathematical notation. An *assorter* h is a function that assigns a non-negative number to each ballot depending on the votes reflected on the ballot and other election data (e.g. the reported outcome, the set of CVRs, or the CVR for that ballot). Each assertion in the audit is equivalent to 'the average value of the assorter for all the cast ballots is greater than $1/2$.' In turn, each assertion is checked by testing the complementary null hypothesis that the average is less than or equal to $1/2$. If all the complementary null hypotheses are false, the reported outcome of every contest under audit is correct.

Definition 1. *An* assertion *is a statement A about the set of paper ballots $\mathcal{L}$ of the contest. An* assorter *for assertion A is a function h_A that maps selections on a ballot b to $[0, M]$ for some known constant $M > 0$, such that assertion A holds for $\mathcal{L}$ iff $\bar{h}_A > 1/2$ where $\bar{h}_A$ is the average value of h_A over all $b \in \mathcal{L}$.*

---

[4] Below, in discussing assorters, we use the term 'entity' more abstractly. For instance, when voters may rank a subset of entities, the assorters may translate ranks into scoring functions in a nonlinear manner, as in [2]—we do not detail that case here.

A set $\mathcal{A}$ of assertions is *sufficient* if their conjunction implies that the reported electoral outcome is correct.

2.3   Example Assertions and Assorters

Example 1. First-past-the-post voting. Consider a simple first-past-the-post contest, where the winner w is the candidate with the most votes and each valid ballot records a vote for a single candidate. The result is correct if the assertions $p_w > p_\ell$ for each losing candidate ℓ all hold.

We can build an assorter h for the assertion $p_w > p_\ell$ as follows [4]:

$$h(b) := \begin{cases} 1 & b_w = 1 \text{ and } b_\ell = 0, \\ 0 & b_w = 0 \text{ and } b_\ell = 1, \\ \frac{1}{2} & \text{otherwise.} \end{cases}$$

Example 2. Majority contests. Consider a simple majority contest, where the winner is the candidate w achieving over 50% of the votes, assuming again each valid ballot holds a single vote (if there is no winner, a runoff election is held). The result can be verified by the assertion $p_w > 1/2$.

We can build an assorter h for the more general assertion $p_w > t$ as follows [4]:

$$h(b) := \begin{cases} \frac{1}{2t} & b_w = 1 \text{ and } b_\ell = 0, \forall \ell \neq w, \\ 0 & b_w = 0 \text{ and } b_\ell = 1 \text{ for exactly one } \ell \neq w, \\ \frac{1}{2} & \text{invalid ballot.} \end{cases}$$

3   Creating Assorters from Assertions

In this section we show how to transform generic linear assertions, i.e. inequalities of the form $\sum_{b\in\mathcal{L}} \sum_{e\in E} a_e b_e > c$, into canonical assertions using assorters as required by SHANGRLA. There are three steps:

1. Construct a set of linear assertions that imply the correctness of the outcome.[5]
2. Determine a 'proto-assorter' based on this assertion.
3. Construct an assorter from the proto-assorter via an affine transformation.

We work with social choice functions where each valid ballot can contribute a non-negative (zero or more) number of 'votes' or 'points' to various tallies (we refer to these as *votes* henceforth). For example, in plurality voting we have a tally for each candidate and each ballot contributes a vote of 1 to the tally of a single candidate and a vote of 0 to all other candidates' tallies. The tallies can represent candidates, groups of candidates, political parties, or possibly some

---

[5] Constructing such a set is outside the scope of this paper; we suspect there is no general method. Moreover, there may be social choice functions for which there is no such set.

more abstract groupings of candidates as might be necessary to describe an assertion (see below); we refer to them generically as *entities*.

Let the various tallies of interest be $T_1, T_2, \ldots, T_m$ for m different entities. These represent the total count of the votes across all valid ballots.

A *linear assertion* is a statement of the form

$$a_1 T_1 + a_2 T_2 + \cdots + a_m T_m > 0$$

for some constants $a_1, \ldots, a_m$.

Each assertion makes a claim about the ballots, to be tested by the audit. For most social choice functions, the assertions are about proportions rather than tallies. Typically these proportions are of the total number of valid votes, $T_{\mathcal{L}}$, in which case we can restate the assertion in terms of tallies by multiplying through by $T_{\mathcal{L}}$.

For example, a pairwise majority assertion is usually written as $p_A > p_B$, stating that candidate A got a larger proportion of the valid votes than candidate B. We can write this in linear form as follows. Let T_A and T_B be the tallies of votes in favour of candidates A and B respectively. Then:

$$p_A > p_B$$
$$\frac{T_A}{T_{\mathcal{L}}} > \frac{T_B}{T_{\mathcal{L}}}$$
$$T_A > T_B$$
$$T_A - T_B > 0.$$

Another example is a super/sub-majority assertion, $p_A > t$, for some threshold t. We can write this in linear form similar to above, as follows:

$$p_A > t$$
$$\frac{T_A}{T_{\mathcal{L}}} > t$$
$$T_A > t T_{\mathcal{L}}$$
$$T_A - t T_{\mathcal{L}} > 0.$$

For a given linear assertion, we define the following function on ballots, which we call a *proto-assorter*:

$$g(b) = a_1 b_1 + a_2 b_2 + \cdots + a_m b_m,$$

where b is a given ballot, and $b_1, b_2, \ldots, b_m$ are the votes contributed by that ballot to the tallies $T_1, T_2, \ldots, T_m$ respectively.[6]

Summing this function across all ballots, $\sum_b g(b)$, gives the left-hand side of the linear assertion. Thus, the linear assertion is true iff $\sum g(b) > 0$. The same property holds for the average across ballots, $\bar{g} = |\mathcal{L}|^{-1} \sum g(b)$; the linear assertion is true iff $\bar{g} > 0$.

---

[6] Note that $g(b) = 0$ for any invalid ballot b, based on previous definitions.

To obtain an assorter in canonical form, we apply an affine transformation to g such that it never takes negative values and also so that comparing its average value to $1/2$ determines the truth of the assertion. One such transformation is

$$h(b) = c \cdot g(b) + 1/2 \tag{1}$$

for some constant c.[7] There are many ways to choose c. We present two here. First, we determine a lower bound for the proto-assorter, a value a such that $g(b) \geqslant a$ for all b.[8] Note that $a < 0$ in all interesting cases: if not, the assertion would be trivially true ($\bar{g} > 0$) or trivially false ($\bar{g} \equiv 0$, with $a_j = 0$ for all j). If $a \geqslant -1/2$, simply setting $c = 1$ produces an assorter: we have $h \geqslant 0$, and $\bar{h} > 1/2$ iff $\bar{g} > 0$. Otherwise, we can choose $c = -1/(2a)$, giving

$$h(b) = \frac{g(b) - a}{-2a}. \tag{2}$$

(See [4, Sec. 2.5].) To see that $h(b)$ is an assorter, first note that $h(b) \geqslant 0$ since the numerator is always non-negative and the denominator is positive. Also, the sum and mean across all ballots are, respectively:

$$\sum_b h(b) = -\frac{1}{2a} \sum_b g(b) + \frac{|\mathcal{L}|}{2}$$

$$\bar{h} = -\frac{1}{2a}\bar{g} + \frac{1}{2}.$$

Therefore, $\bar{h} > 1/2$ iff $\bar{g} > 0$.

3.1   Example: Pairwise Difference Assorter

To illustrate the approach, we will now create an assorter for a fairly complex assertion for quite complicated ballots. We consider a contest where each ballot can have multiple votes for multiple entities; the votes are simple—not ranks or scores. Let $m_{\mathcal{L}}$ be the maximum number of votes a single ballot can contain for that contest. We can use the above general technique to derive an assorter for the assertion $p_A > p_B + d$. In Sect. 4 we will use this for auditing Hamiltonian free list contests, where A and B will be parties. This assertion checks that the proportion of votes A has is greater than that of B plus a constant, d. This constant may be negative.

We start with the assertion $p_A > p_B + d$. We can rewrite this in terms of tallies as we did in the previous examples, giving the following linear form:

---

[7] Note that $h(b) = 1/2$ if ballot b has no valid vote in the contest.

[8] If the votes b_j are bounded above by s and below by zero, then a bound (not necessarily the sharpest) on g is given by taking just the votes that contribute negative values to g, setting all of those votes to s, and setting the other votes to 0:

$$a = \sum_{j : a_j < 0} a_j s.$$

$$p_A > p_B + d$$
$$\frac{T_A}{T_\mathcal{L}} > \frac{T_B}{T_\mathcal{L}} + d$$
$$T_A > T_B + d\,T_\mathcal{L}$$
$$T_A - T_B - d\,T_\mathcal{L} > 0.$$

The corresponding proto-assorter is

$$g(b) = b_A - b_B - d \cdot b_T.$$

If the votes are bounded above by $m_\mathcal{L}$ then this has lower bound given by

$$g(b) \geqslant -m_\mathcal{L} - dm_\mathcal{L} = -m_\mathcal{L} \cdot (1 + d).$$

Therefore, an assorter is given by

$$h(b) = \frac{b_A - b_B - d \cdot b_T + m_\mathcal{L} \cdot (1 + d)}{2m_\mathcal{L} \cdot (1 + d)}.$$

When $m_\mathcal{L} = 1$ this reduces to the pairwise difference assorter for 'simple' Hamiltonian contests, where each ballot can only cast a single vote [1]. When $d = 0$ this reduces to the pairwise majority assorter in the more general context where we can have multiple votes per ballot.

4   Case Study: 2016 Hesse Local Elections

In the local elections in Hesse, Germany, each ballot allows the voter to cast S direct votes, where S is the number of seats in the region. Each party can have at most S candidates on the ballot. Voters can assign up to three votes to individual candidates; they can spread these votes amongst candidates from different parties as they like. Voters can cross out candidates, meaning none of their votes will flow to such candidates. Finally a voter can select a single party. The effect of this selection is that remaining votes not assigned to individual candidates are given to the party. At the low level these votes are then spread amongst the candidates of the party (that have not been crossed out) by assigning one vote to the next (uncrossed out) candidate in the selected party, starting from the top, and wrapping around to the top once we hit the bottom, until all the remaining votes are assigned. Budurushi [3] provides a detailed description of the vote casting and vote tallying rules.[9]

Example 3. Consider a contest in a region with 12 seats, and a ballot with 4 parties. The Greens have five candidates appearing in the order Arnold, Beatrix, Charles, Debra, and Emma. Consider a ballot that has 3 votes assigned directly to Beatrix, Charles crossed out, three votes assigned directly to Fox (a candidate for another party), and the Greens party selected.

---

[9] The description is based on the (German only) official information from Hesse, see https://wahlen.hessen.de/kommunen/kommunalwahlen-2021/wahlsystem, last accessed 24.07.2021.

Since 6 votes are directly assigned, the Greens receive the remaining 6 votes. We start by assigning one vote of the 6 to the top candidate, Arnold, then one to Beatrix, none to Charles, one to Debra, one to Emma, another to Arnold, and another to Beatrix. In total, the ballot assigns 2 votes to Arnold, 5 to Beatrix, 1 to Debra, 1 to Emma, and 3 to Fox.   □

The social choice function involves two stages. In the first stage, the entities we consider are the parties. This stage determines how many seats are awarded to each party. Each party is awarded the total votes assigned on a ballot to that party via individual candidates votes and the party selection remainder. There is a Hamiltonian election to determine the number of seats awarded to each party. Given S seats in the region, we award $s_e = \lfloor Sp_e \rfloor$ to each party $e \in E$. The remaining $k = S - \sum_{e \in E} s_e$ seats are awarded to the k parties with greatest remainders $r_e = Sp_e - s_e$. Let a_e be the total number of seats awarded to party e (which is either s_e or $s_e + 1$).

In the second stage, seats are awarded to individual candidates. For each party e awarded a_e seats, those a_e candidates in the party receiving the most votes are awarded a seat.

Performing a risk-limiting audit on a Hesse local election involves a number of assertions. The first stage is a Hamiltonian election. The assertions required to verify the result are described by Blom et al. [1]. For each pair of parties $m \neq n$ we need to test the assertion

$$p_m > p_n + \frac{a_m - a_n - 1}{S}, \quad n, m \in E, n \neq m. \tag{3}$$

While Blom et al. [1] define an assorter for this assertion, it is made under the assumption that each ballot contains a vote for at most one entity. The assorter defined in Sect. 3.1—with $A = m$, $B = n$ and $d = (a_m - a_n - 1)/S$—is more general and allows for multiple votes per ballot.

These (All-Seats) assertions may require large samples to verify. We can verify a simpler assertion—that each party e deserved to obtain at least s_e seats—using the assertion $p_e > s_e/S$. We check this with an 'All-But-Remainder' audit.

The second stage of the election is a multi-winner first-past-the-post contest within each party: party e's a_e seats are allocated to the a_e individual candidates with highest tallies. An audit would require comparing each winner's tally to each loser's. The margins are often very small—the example data includes margins of only one vote—so these allocations are likely to require a full recount, and we have not included them in our simulations.

For experiments we consider a collection of 21 local district-based elections held in Hesse, Germany, on March 6, 2016. An 'All-But-Remainder' audit checks that each party e deserved the seats awarded to it in the first phase of distribution (s_e), excluding those assigned to parties on the basis of their 'remainder'. An 'All-Seats' audit checks a_e, i.e. all of the seats awarded to party e, including their last seat awarded on the basis of their remainder (if applicable).

Across the 21 district contests in our case study, the number of seats available varied from 51 to 87, the number of parties from 6 to 11, and the number of voters from 39,839 to 157,100. For each assertion, we estimate the number of ballot checks required to audit it, assuming no errors are present between each paper ballot and its electronic record. Table 1 shows the number of ballot checks required to audit the most difficult assertion in each of these contests as the contest's ASN (average sample number) for the two levels of auditing (All-But-Remainder and All-Seats). An ASN of ∞ indicates that a full manual recount would be required. We record the ASN for risk limits, of 5% and 10%. The Kaplan–Kolmogorov risk function (with $g = 0.1$) was used to compute ASNs, given the margin for an assertion, following the process outlined in Sect. 4.1.

Table 1 shows that an All-Seats audit can be challenging in terms of the sample size required, but that an All-But-Remainder audit is usually quite practical. The estimated sample size required in an audit depends on the margin of each assertion being checked. Where these margins are small—for example, where two parties receive a similar remainder—the average sample size is likely to be large. This is an inherent property of the social choice function, not a failure of our method. For example, the All-Seats audit for Limburg-Weilburg has an infinite ASN. The vote data shows why: the lowest remainder to earn an extra seat is the CDU Party's, with a remainder of 24,267 votes; the highest remainder *not* to earn an extra seat is the FW Party's, with 24,205 votes. An audit would need to check that the FW did not, in fact, gain a higher remainder than the CDU. However, a single ballot can contain up to 71 votes, so this comparison (and hence the electoral outcome) could be altered by a single misrecorded ballot. An electoral outcome that can be altered by the votes on one ballot requires a full manual count in any election system, regardless of the auditing method.

Even the All-Seats audit is quite practical when the margins represent a relatively large fraction of ballots. This is consistent with prior work [1] on US primaries, showing that an All-Seats audit is quite practical in that context.

4.1   Estimating an Initial Sample Size Using a Risk Function

We use the margin of the assorter for each assertion to estimate the number of ballot checks required to confirm that an assertion holds in an audit. As defined in [4], the margin for assertion A is 2 times its assorter mean, $\bar{h}_A$, minus 1.

Let V the total number of valid ballots and I be the total number of invalid ballots cast in the contest. Note that the sum $V + I$ may differ from the total number of votes, $T_{\mathcal{L}}$, since there may be multiple votes expressed on each ballot.

For an All-But-Remainder assertion indicating that party e received more than proportion t of the total vote, $T_{\mathcal{L}}$, the assorter mean is

$$\bar{h} = \frac{1}{V+I} \left(\frac{1}{2t}T_e - \frac{1}{2}T_{\mathcal{L}} + \frac{1}{2}(V+I) \right),$$

where T_e is the total number of votes for all candidates in party e. We compute t for a given assertion as follows:

$$q = \frac{T_{\mathcal{L}}}{S}, \quad \delta = \left\lfloor \frac{T_e}{q} \right\rfloor, \quad t = \frac{q\delta}{T_{\mathcal{L}}}.$$

For an All-Seats comparative difference assertion between two parties, A and B, we need to test a pairwise difference assertion where the difference is given by

$$d = \frac{(a_A - a_B - 1)}{S}.$$

The assorter mean for testing this assertion is given by

$$\bar{h} = \frac{1}{V+I} \left(\frac{T_A - T_B - T_{\mathcal{L}}d + VS \cdot (1+d)}{2S \cdot (1+d)} + \frac{I}{2} \right).$$

Once we have computed the assorter mean for an assertion, we use functionality from the SHANGRLA software implementation,[10] using the Kaplan–Kolmogorov risk function with $g = 0.1$, and an error rate of 0.

Table 1. Estimates of audit sample sizes for each local district election held in Hesse on March 6th, 2016. We record the number of assertions to be checked in an All-But-Remainder and All-Seats audit, alongside the estimated number of ballot checks required to complete these audits for risk limits of 5% and 10%, assuming no discrepancies are found between paper ballots and their electronic records. S is the number of seats, $|\mathcal{L}|$ is the total number of ballots cast, $|E|$ is the total number of parties, and V is the total number of valid ballots. $|\mathcal{L}|$ and V are recorded to the nearest thousand.

District	S	$|\mathcal{L}|$	$|E|$	V	All-But-Remainder.			All-Seats		
						RL 5%	RL 10%		RL 5%	RL 10%
					$|\mathcal{A}|$	ASN	ASN	$|\mathcal{A}|$	ASN	ASN
Marburg-Biedenkopf	81	92k	8	88k	8	128	99	56	2,004	1,544
Fulder	81	95k	8	91k	8	27	20	56	34,769	28,142
Wetterau	81	122k	11	115k	11	26	20	110	12,570	9,790
Groß Gerau	71	85k	11	80k	11	291	224	110	7,844	6,101
Limburg-Weilburg	71	67k	7	64k	7	879	677	42	∞	∞
Kassel	81	100k	7	95k	7	1,180	909	42	4,580	3,540
Darmstadt-Dieburg	71	113k	8	107k	8	39	30	56	86,480	76,879
Bergstrasse	71	101k	9	96k	9	19	14	72	5,329	4,123
Werra-Meißner	61	45k	6	42k	6	8	6	30	3,252	2,522
Hersfeld-Rotenburg	61	52k	7	50k	7	29	23	42	5,173	4,026
Offenbach	87	119k	9	113k	9	35	27	72	25,691	20,323
Rheingau Taunus	81	78k	7	74k	7	27	21	42	4,382	3,392
Lahn-Dill	81	88k	8	83k	8	50	38	56	2,752	2,124
Waldeck-Frankenberg	71	65k	8	62k	8	234	180	56	1,508	1,162
Main-Taunus	81	95k	8	91k	8	66	51	56	23,669	18,808
Schwalm-Eder	71	82k	8	78k	8	24	18	56	35,724	29,301
Odenwald	51	40k	7	38k	7	74	57	42	933	719
Main-Kinzig	87	157k	10	148k	10	15	12	90	4,105	3,165
Landkreis Gießen	81	103k	8	98k	8	41	24	56	8,324	6,464
Hochtaunus	71	94k	8	90k	8	83	64	56	36,978	30,069
Vogelsberg	61	50k	7	47k	7	10	8	42	9,668	7,624

---

[10] `TestNonnegMean.initial_sample_size()` from https://github.com/pbstark/SHAN GRLA/blob/main/Code/assertion_audit_utils.py, last accessed 24.07.2021.

5   Example: Assorters for D'Hondt and Related Methods

Risk-limiting audits for D'Hondt and other highest averages methods were developed by Stark and Teague [5]. In this section we show how to express those audits in the form of assertions, and develop the appropriate assorters.

5.1   Background on Highest Averages Methods

Highest averages methods are used by many parliamentary democracies in Europe, as well as elections for the European Parliament (which uses D'Hondt).[11]

Highest averages methods are similar to Hamiltonian methods in that they allocate seats to parties in approximate proportion to the fraction of the overall vote they won. They differ in how they allocate the last few seats when the voting fractions do not match an integer number of seats.

A highest averages method is parameterized by a set of divisors $d(1), d(2), \ldots$ $d(S)$ where S is the number of seats. The seats are allocated by forming a table in which each party's votes are divided by each of the divisors, then choosing the S largest numbers in the whole table—the number of selected entries in a party's row is the number of seats that party wins. The divisors for D'Hondt are $d(i) = i$, $i = 1, 2, \ldots S$. Sainte-Laguë has divisors $d(i) = 2i - 1$, for $i = 1, 2, \ldots S$.

Let $f_{e,s} = T_e/d(s)$ for entity e and seat s. The *Winning Set* $\mathcal{W}$ is

$$\mathcal{W} = \{(e, s) : f_{e,s} \text{ is one of the } S \text{ largest}\}.$$

This can be visualised in a table by writing out, for each entity e, the sequence of numbers $T_e/d(1), T_e/d(2), T_e/d(3), \ldots$, and then selecting the S largest numbers in the table. Each party receives a number of seats equal to the number of selected values in its row.

Like Hamiltonian methods, highest averages methods can be used in a simple form in which voters choose only their favourite party, or in a variety of more complex forms in which voters can express approval or disapproval of individual candidates. We deal with the simple case first.

5.2   Simple D'Hondt: Party-Only Voting

In the simplest form of highest averages methods, seats are allocated to each entity (party) based on individual entity tallies. Let W_e be the number of seats won and L_e the number of the first seat lost by entity e. That is:

$$W_e = \max\{s : (e, s) \in \mathcal{W}\}; \perp \text{ if } e \text{ has no winners.}$$
$$L_e = \min\{s : (e, s) \notin \mathcal{W}\}; \perp \text{ if } e \text{ won all the seats.}$$

If e won some, but not all, seats, then $L_e = W_e + 1$.

---

[11] https://www.europarl.europa.eu/RegData/etudes/BRIE/2019/637966/EPRS_BRI (2019)637966_EN.pdf, last accessed 24.07.2021.

The inequalities that define the winners are, for all parties A with at least one winner, for all parties B (different from A) with at least one loser, as follows:

$$f_{A,W_A} > f_{B,L_B}. \tag{4}$$

Converting this into the notation of Sect. 3, expressing Eq. 4 as a linear assertion gives us, $\forall A$ s.t. $W_A \neq \perp, \forall B \neq A$ s.t. $L_B \neq \perp$,

$$T_A/d(W_A) - T_B/d(L_B) > 0.$$

From this, we define the proto-assorter for any ballot b as

$$g_{A,B}(b) := \begin{cases} 1/d(W_A) & \text{if } b \text{ is a vote for party } A, \\ -1/d(L_B) & \text{if } b \text{ is a vote for party } B, \\ 0 & \text{otherwise,} \end{cases}$$

or equivalently $\quad g_{A,B}(b) := b_A/d(W_A) - b_B/d(L_B)$

where b_A (resp. b_B) is 1 if there is a vote for party A (resp. B), 0 otherwise. The lower bound is clearly $a = -1/d(L_B)$. Substituting into Eq. 2 gives

$$h_{A,B}(b) = \begin{cases} 1/2\,[d(L_B)/d(W_A) + 1] & \text{if } b \text{ is a vote for party } A, \\ 0 & \text{if } b \text{ is a vote for party } B, \\ 1/2 & \text{otherwise.} \end{cases}$$

Note that order matters: in general, both $h_{A,B}$ and $h_{B,A}$ are necessary—the first checks that party A's lowest winner beat party B's highest loser; the second checks that party B's lowest winner beat party A's highest loser.

5.3   More Complex Methods: Multi-candidate Voting

Like some Hamiltonian elections, many highest averages elections also allow voters to select individual candidates. A party's tally is the total of its candidates' votes. Then, within each party, the won seats are allocated to the candidates with the highest individual tallies. The main entities are still parties, allocated seats according to Eq. 4, but the assorter must be generalised to allow one ballot to contain multiple votes for various candidates.

The proto-assorter for entities (parties) $A \neq B$ s.t. $W_A \neq \perp$, and $L_B \neq \perp$, is very similar to the single-party case, but votes for each party (b_A and b_B) count the total, over all that entity's candidates, and may be larger than one.

$$g_{A,B}(b) := b_A/d(W_A) - b_B/d(L_B).$$

The lower bound is $-m/d(L_B)$, again substituting in to Eq. 2 gives

$$h_{A,B}(b) = \frac{b_A d(L_B)/d(W_A) - b_B + m}{2m}.$$

Note this reduces to the single-vote assorter when $m = 1$ ($b_A, b_B \in \{0,1\}$).

6 Conclusion and Future Work

SHANGRLA reduces RLAs for many social choice functions to a canonical form involving 'assorters.' This paper shows how to translate general linear assertions into canonical assorter form for SHANGRLA, illustrated by developing the first RLA method for Hamiltonian free list elections and the first assertion-based approach for D'Hondt style elections.

We show that party-list proportional representation systems can be audited using simple assertions that are both necessary and sufficient for the reported outcome to be correct. In some settings, including in Hesse, elections are inherently expensive to audit because margins are frequently small, both between parties vying for the seats allocated by remainder, and between candidates in the same party.

There are social choice functions for which no set of linear assertions guarantees the reported winner really won, for instance, social choice functions in which the order of in which the votes are tabulated matters or that involve a random element. Some variants of Single Transferable Vote (STV) have one or the other of those properties.

Other variants of STV might be amenable to RLAs and to SHANGRLA in particular: the question is open. We conjecture that STV is inherently hard to audit. Although a sufficient set of conditions is easy to generate—simply check every step of the elimination and seat-allocation sequence—this is highly likely to have very small margins and hence to require impractical sample sizes. We conjecture that it is hard to find a set of conditions that imply an STV outcome is correct and that requires reasonable sample sizes to audit. Of course, this was also conjectured for IRV and turns out to be false.

References

1. Blom, M., Stark, P.B., Stuckey, P.J., Teague, V., Vukcevic, D.: Auditing Hamiltonian elections. In: M. Bernhard et al. (Eds.): FC 2021 Workshops, LNCS 12676, pp. 1–16 (2021). https://doi.org/10.1007/978-3-662-63958-0_21 (The original manuscript of this work is available at: arXiv:2102.08510)
2. Blom, M., Stuckey, P.J., Teague, V.: RAIRE: risk-limiting audits for IRV elections. arXiv:1903.08804 (2019)
3. Budurushi, J.: Usable security evaluation of EasyVote in the context of complex elections. Ph.D. thesis, Technische Universität Darmstadt, Darmstadt (2016). https://tuprints.ulb.tu-darmstadt.de/5418/
4. Stark, P.B.: Sets of half-average nulls generate risk-limiting audits: SHANGRLA. In: Bernhard, M., et al. (eds.) FC 2020. LNCS, vol. 12063, pp. 319–336. Springer, Cham (2020). https://doi.org/10.1007/978-3-030-54455-3_23
5. Stark, P.B., Teague, V., Essex, A.: Verifiable European elections: risk-limiting audits for D'Hondt and its relatives. USENIX J. Elect. Technol. Syst. (JETS) 3(1), 18–39 (2014)

Cyber Awareness Training for Election Staff Using Constructive Alignment

Thomas Chanussot[1,2] and Carsten Schürmann[1,2(✉)]

[1] IFES, Ho Chi Minh City, Vietnam
tchanussot@ifes.org
[2] Center for Information Security and Trust, IT University of Copenhagen,
Copenhagen, Denmark
carsten@itu.dk

Abstract. Cybersecurity awareness and cyber hygiene trainings are becoming standard practice for employees of election administrations. Election Management Bodies (EMBs) have specific needs: elections are cyclic with regards to the tasks and their associate risks, they are high value targets during a short time window, and they suffer from high turnover of staff making sustainable training difficult. With lots of training methodologies and training programs targeting election observers, officials, etc., there are limited quantifiable measures for the efficiency of this type of training. Evaluating the adequacy of the training objectives and methodologies to the specific needs of election administration is becoming a necessity. We propose to use constructive alignment for designing and evaluating cybersecurity awareness trainings.

1 Introduction

Elections worldwide have become the battlefield between national and foreign actors and cyber-criminals on one side, and election management bodies and political parties on the other. The objectives of threat actors vary from financially motivated extortion schemes to destructive attacks as proxies to delegitimize the electoral process. This trend has increased in frequency, with an intensification of cyber activities towards the date of the actual election. Most incidents are triggered by human behavior [9], foremost successful phishing attacks, with victims neglecting simple rules as the primary factor paving the way. It is now acknowledged that minimizing humans errors through cybersecurity awareness training is paramount for achieving any reasonable level of cybersecurity in election administration. What is not so clear, however, is how to design and evaluate training programs that are specifically tailored for election officials.

As cybersecurity awareness and cyber hygiene trainings are becoming more readily available, it has also become standard practice for employees of election management and temporary staff hired for election administration to partake in such trainings. To this end, many organizations rely on third-party providers for delivering cyber-hygiene training through online platforms to large customer

© Springer Nature Switzerland AG 2021
R. Krimmer et al. (Eds.): E-Vote-ID 2021, LNCS 12900, pp. 63–74, 2021.
https://doi.org/10.1007/978-3-030-86942-7_5

bases. Cybersecurity experts and consultancies do have the inside knowledge to keep training materials up to date with respect to the latest threats. Overall, it is acknowledged that cybersecurity training has to be offered on a regular basis to ensure that the employees' cybersecurity understanding and knowledge is always up to date. Elections are cyclic events with regards to tasks and their associated risks, they are high value targets for a limited amount of time, they typically suffer from high turnover of staff making sustainable training difficult, and they are critical to preserve public confidence in the quality of the democratic process.

To assess the quality of cybersecurity awareness and cyber hygiene training and to measure their effectiveness in addressing theses challenges, we develop in this paper a framework for evaluating existing and designing new courses based on the principle of constructive alignment [2]. Cyber hygiene refers to the ability of election administrators (1) to understand that their respective behaviors, online and also in relation with other persons has a direct effect on the security and credibility of the electoral process, (2) to learn to identify and react to common threats and therefore minimize their respective damage, and (3) to be prepared to respond to not-yet identified and future cyber threats.

Inspired by the Structure of Observed Learning Outcome (SOLO) taxonomy [3], we define four levels of understanding which encompass awareness, understanding of risks, comprehension of threats, and defense skills, empowering course participants to deal with future and yet unknown cyber threats. Our frameworks suggests that trainings should be assessed based on (1) the consistency of course prerequisites and how they accommodate participants with varying pre-existing knowledge, (2) the quality of the intended learning outcomes (ILOs) for each module and assess their consistency across several modules, (3) the intended retention policies, for each module, (4) the impact on the participants' cybersecurity behavior and understanding, and (5) expectation management.

When applying our framework, there are several insights to be gained how to design cybersecurity awareness training curricula. First, course participants usually work harder the more closely learning objectives are aligned with their assigned working tasks. Hence it is beneficial to distinguish between learning objectives that are general in nature and require additional mechanisms to capture the course participants' attention and those that are specific and targeted to a particular task. The latter can be aligned with particular threats anticipated by the EMB, and prepare the participant with the knowledge necessary to prevail in their professional role. Highly specialized curricula covering topics critical to running a credible election can be targeted to small selected audiences, the ILOs should be carefully aligned with the participants professional responsibilities. Curricula covering the basics of cyber hygiene training are usually designed for broader audiences with more diverse backgrounds and less consistent pre-existing knowledge and the ILOs need to be designed accordingly, especially if there are participants that have undergone similar trainings in preparation for earlier elections.

Second, online education can reach a much broader audience than facilitative-based teaching ever could. This is of particular interest for the electoral domain, where many election officials need to be educated prior to an election. It is possible to require election officials to have passed cybersecurity training before becoming an election official, for example, by presenting a certificate of the successful completion of his/her cyber-hygiene course. Online cybersecurity training can also be organized in alternative modules suitable for different backgrounds. A total beginner module on social engineering, for example, would spend effort to explain the motivation of an attacker to the course participant, whereas a module for the advanced participants could go more in detail about the different techniques used by a social engineer attacker. Another example would be a module highlighting privacy, data security, and integrity as well as protection against disclosure of confidential data for operators working on voter registration activities. Accidental disclosure [11] of voter lists [5] are not uncommon and have been reported numerous times [6].

In this paper, we propose an evaluation and design methodology for cybersecurity awareness training in Sect. 2 that is adapted to the specificities of electoral administrations. Using two existing training programs, as examples, we demonstrate how the methodology can be used to identify areas of improvement and to structure mature cybersecurity awareness trainings in Sect. 3. Finally, we assess results and conclude in Sect. 4.

2   Methodology

Cybersecurity awareness training has a bad reputation for being ineffective and boring. This, however, is not necessarily true, as demonstrated in prior work [7], which argues that if the training is tailored to the right audience with the right content, it is possible to measure the effectiveness of the training by relating pre-tests with post-tests. In this section, we push this point further and relate it to the theory of constructive alignment, which is a principle used for devising teaching and learning activities, and assessment tasks that directly address the intended learning outcomes (ILOs) in a way not typically achieved in traditional lectures, tutorial classes, and examinations [2]. Constructive alignment applies to in-person training as well as online training and the literature is extensive [4, 8,10]. It is a modern teaching philosophy based on cognitive psychology that is increasingly used at universities to guarantee a pleasant and effective learning experience for each and every student. The central idea of constructive alignment is that the course content is organized in such way that enables the teacher to make a deliberate alignment between the planned learning activity and the ILOs. We believe that this observation is central for designing effective cybersecurity awareness training programs, and it provides guidance for evaluating existing programs.

Compared to higher-education, cybersecurity training for election officials and poll-workers brings along additional challenges, such as the body of course participants is usually extremely diverse with different academic backgrounds, different skills, and different expectations. In practice, this heterogeneity presents quite a challenge and the solution requires a well-thought out and principled methodology that we structure according to five dimensions that we describe next.

2.1   Pre-existing Knowledge

To guarantee the effectiveness of cybersecurity training requires the organizers of the training to control the heterogeneity of the course participants. If the backgrounds of the participants are too diverse, some will be bored while others struggle to keep up. Skilled facilitators and trainers can accommodate the curriculum depth to the individual participant's needs by making it more immediate and more closely relatable. In self-paced online training programs, on the other hand, the participant can adjust the pace, for example by quickly skimming through content he is already familiar with, but will not be able to change the depth of the content. Through effectively understanding the pre-existing knowledge of each student allows the grouping of students with similar baselines. Suitable content can then be tailored for each group, for example, by identifying and presenting relevant modules of the training program. The group can then proceed at a comfortable pace. This also takes care of the challenge of course participants already having taken earlier editions of the same course for past elections. The design of the training should therefore be modular, which means that in can be reorganized into a personalized learning experience that engages effective participation.

Thus, a *first dimension* to assess quality of cyber-hygiene awareness training on is to evaluate if pre-existing knowledge is collected and used to adapt the training experiences to individual needs.

2.2   The Relevance and Specificity of the Learning Objectives

Intended learning objectives (ILOs) that accompany constructive alignment [3] serve two goals. First, every course participant is given the opportunity to identify with the learning objectives before training commences, which makes learning effective and allows expectations between facilitator and participant to be aligned. Second, learning objectives define the structure of entire training program, they specify in a way, how one module builds upon another. In fact, ILOs guarantee a satisfactory progression with respect to the participants' level of understanding from awareness to skills [1].

In Fig. 1, we propose a simple taxonomy that distinguishes four levels of understanding, (1) *awareness*, which means the course participants are able to learn to identify and describe individual topics that are central to cyber-hygiene, (2) *understanding of risks*, which refers to participants being able identify cyber-risks rendering cyber-hygiene necessary, (3) *comprehension of threats*, which means that course participants should learn to understand intent and objectives of an adversary, and lastly (4) *defense skills*, which allows course participants to recognize cyberattacks, take counter measures, and adopt personal behavior to minimize the risk of cyberattacks specific to electoral operations, even those not discussed explicitly in the course.

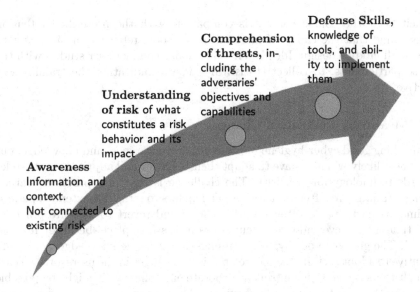

Awareness
Information and context.
Not connected to existing risk

Understanding of risk of what constitutes a risk behavior and its impact

Comprehension of threats, including the adversaries' objectives and capabilities

Defense Skills, knowledge of tools, and ability to implement them

Fig. 1. Taxonomy

Thus, a *second dimension* to evaluate cybersecurity awareness training is to evaluate if the learning objectives for the individual modules are clearly stated, consistent with respect to the level of understanding, and aligned with the needs of the participants with regards to their profession/role.

2.3 Retention Period

One of the challenges of cybersecurity awareness training is that topics can vary significantly in abstraction and relevance. Some threats and good practices seem intuitive, while others seem remote and unlikely. To cope with this enormous spread between the concrete and the abstract, each module should define an expected retention period that presupposes for how long the knowledge gained through the training should be actively applicable for the course participant.

Being explicit about the retention period has several advantages, including what topics and which materials can and should be covered in a module, and what mechanisms should be used to guarantee retention. When the expected retention period is shorter, emphasis should be given to materials that are immediately relevant to the participants learning experience. The very fact that interesting and relevant topics are covered is then usually enough to motivate the participants to perform well [7]. Longer expected retention periods will allow to engage with more general knowledge and good practices, which means that participants may require additional incentives, such as practical simulations, additional tests, etc. to ensure that the longer retention period can be guaranteed.

Thus, the *third dimension* to evaluate cybersecurity awareness training along is to verify that the expectations regarding retention have been set and made explicit, that the course content is compatible with the prescribed retention periods, and that the choice of mechanisms to boost retention are in line with the overall module design. Ideally, one should also conduct user studies with the course participants, to collect statistical evidence indicating the training was effective.

2.4   Measuring Behavioral Change

Establishing good cyber-hygiene requires not only awareness and knowledge, but users most likely will also have to adapt their behavior and adjust their attitudes towards technology and security. The challenge is that new practices learned during a training are often difficult for participants to retain for extended periods of time, as participants often tend to relapse and revert to insecure practices with time if they ever adopted secure ones in the first place, because "it's just easier". The goal of cyber-hygiene trainings is to provide knowledge, tools, and incentive to adopt sustainable secure practices. Changes in the users' attitude are difficult to measure. In a controlled corporate environment, it might be possible to use technology to measure behavioral change, by tracking the number of successful phishing attacks, for example. But in the larger context, one must rely on self-reported questionnaires to understand whether knowledge translated into improved behavior. These questionnaires, in which respondents select a response by themselves without interference, are inherently biased. Acknowledging this limitation, mechanisms to measure the adoption of a limited and pre-defined set of safe behavior is a *fourth dimension* through which the effectiveness of cyber-hygiene training should be evaluated.

2.5   Expectations Management

When election officials and poll workers are asked to participate in cybersecurity awareness training, there might be different expectations in play, which need to considered. Poll-workers and election official usually are assigned different tasks, and serve in different roles. This requires that the training program can cater to different needs, and be adaptive to different expectations. It is prudent, that the expectations of the participants are properly managed, which leads to the *fifth and final dimension* of our evaluation methodology, which is to what extent does the training program provide mechanisms to identify and integrate different expectations?

In summary, we propose an evaluation methodology for cyber hygiene training based on five dimensions, (1) the consistency of the course prerequisites and how they accommodate participants with varying pre-existing knowledge (2) the quality of the ILOs for each module and assessing their consistency across several modules, (3) the intended knowledge retention policies for each module, (4) the impact on the participants' cybersecurity behavior and understanding, and (5) expectation management. This methodology can also be used as a guide when developing new modules and courses, or when restructuring existing cyber-hygiene training into either several courses, or one course with several modules, so that returning participants will find a tailored and exciting curriculum to partake in.

3   Practical Application: Evaluating Cyber-Hygiene Trainings

To test our evaluation and design framework, we have applied our methodology to two training programs that have been provided to electoral administrations: IFES cybersecurity awareness training for EMBs (Regional Election Administration and Political Process Strengthening – REAPPS) and Cyber-hygiene for the Danish Election administration.

3.1   The IFES Cybersecurity Awareness Training

IFES' cybersecurity awareness training was developed in late 2018, it has been conducted with several hundreds of officials in Eastern Europe and Balkan States.

Pre-existing Knowledge. The course was developed for election staff with little to no exposure to cybersecurity. It does not test or categorize participants according to their pre-existing knowledge but aims to offer general awareness and an introduction to cybersecurity concepts as they apply to the electoral context. This means that no mechanism is provided to identify participants who have already taken this course in the past. As this training was specifically designed for participants with no prior exposure to cybersecurity concepts, this criteria does not directly apply, but would need to be integrated as the training reaches an audience with more mature cybersecurity awareness and skills.

The Relevance and Specificity of the ILOs. The content of the training can be classified in modules with different expected levels of understanding, as indicated in the table below. This classification of the topics highlights the priorities set forth during the training: identifying phishing and measures to protect accounts (passwords and multi-factor authentication in particular). These ILOs are aligned with global threats faced by EMBs.

Awareness	Understanding	Comprehension	Defense
Software patching; Antivirus tools; End-point protection; Backup strategies; BYOD; Public WiFi risks; USB security; Social media	Global Threats; Cyber-attacks	Election specific threats; Multi-factor authentication	Passwords management Detecting phishing red-flags

Retention Period. This training does not explicitly state an expected retention period. It has usually been conducted as an introductory course disconnected from the electoral cycle, or ahead of an election operation, for which the training is well suited as the defensive skills are aligned with types of attacks election staff must be ready to detect and respond to during the election period. The expected retention period can be derived from the mapping of the ILOs: *password management* and *phishing detection* are expected to be of immediate use to the participants, for these topics, the training goes in more depth and deliver practical and engaging learning exercises.

Measuring Behavioral Change. Pre-tests and post-tests measure the retention and understanding of the course material, improvement on the behaviors and practices of the participants is not measured over time. Reminders are sent to the participants on a regular basis and are used to reinforce key messages and good practices learned during the course.

Expectation Management. The course was designed to provide an introductory course to cyber hygiene and cybersecurity awareness. It is not specifically tailored to a particular group of participants and to specific classes of risks. It does align with participants expectations who had low previous exposure to cybersecurity concepts.

Overall Evaluation: IFES' cybersecurity awareness training has been developed with a dual purpose as clearly visible from the table of ILOs. It offers a generic, low level awareness of threats, risks and security good practices on the one hand, and more advanced ILOs with practical defense skills for threats that are considered global and highest risk. This clear distinction could provide a roadmap for future trainings, as several topics could be elevated from awareness to practical defense skills based on the risk environment, period of the electoral cycle, and specific needs of the EMB related to the adoption of new technologies for example.

3.2   Training Denmark's Digital Election Secretaries

Moving to Denmark, the cybersecurity training for digital election secretaries [7] was organized in a principled fashion follow a particular methodology for training design. By catering to a very narrow and homogeneous target group, the content of the training was defined by the role that the participants play during the election: the digital election secretaries were responsible for the voter registration technology deployed in polling stations. In the case of a cyberattack, it is the digital election secretary who decides to abandon the use of technology and move to the paper backup system. Attack trees were used to explore the threat space and then course modules were derived in response to the overall ILO that the participants should be able to recognize threats and to defend against them. The resulting course consists of three modules, (1) an introductory module to create a joint level of understanding among the participants, (2) an introduction to man-in-the middle attacks against election technologies, and (3) a module dedicated to spotting and mitigating social engineering attacks. All three modules were tailored to the particular role of the course participants.

Pre-existing Knowledge. This course was organized as a pilot study that does not make any assumptions about pre-existing knowledge of the course participants although all participants are public servants who work for the city of Copenhagen, and most like had already been exposed to cybersecurity awareness training. As this was the first time the course was offered, no attention was paid to the fact that some of the course participants might have taken this training in the past.

The Relevance and Specificity of the ILOs. No ILOs were explicitly mentioned in the course descriptions, but because the modules are directly derived from the role that the participants play during the election, they can be easily inferred. The training materials can be organized into the four classes of understanding. As this training is targeted to the practitioners, it aim to achieve a high level of understanding when addressing the ability of the digital election secretary to react efficiently in the case an attack is noticed.

Awareness	Understanding	Comprehension	Defense
BYOD; Ransomware; Disinformation	Election specific threats	Man-in-the-middle, USB security Key logger Computer virus Theft Social Engineering: Impersonation; Social Engineering: Authority; Urgency; Trust; Shoulder-surfing; Spear-phishing	Fall-back procedures Immediate response Escalation Proactive security Securing Evidence

Retention Period. Although the training does not explicitly state an expected retention period, it is clear that the course is designed to be taken a few days before election day activities commence and it is expected that the participants will remember the content until after the election. Since the course is offered online, it is easily possible to retake the course in preparation for another election.

Measuring Behavioral Change. This training requires the participants to take two tests, one before the training commences, and the other right after. These tests are organized to measure if new knowledge was acquired while taken the training of not. Improvement on the behaviors and practices of the participants is not measured over time.

Expectation Management. Since the course participants will play a similar role in the election, their expectations are closely aligned, and also their interest is heightened, because it is considered important to take such a training in preparation for assuming the role.

Overall Evaluation: The Danish course for training digital election secretaries has clear ILOs on a rather high level of understanding. The course will only work for its intended audience, and should not be mistaken for a general-purpose cybersecurity awareness training. The course could be improved by taking into account the pre-existing knowledge of the participants, possibly by integrating the course into a larger election official training program, where assumptions about pre-existing knowledge and prerequisites has been made explicit.

4   Conclusions

While cybersecurity awareness trainings are becoming standard practice for EMBs, there has been little study of how they answer the specific needs and unique threats during the election cycle. As election operations are increasingly digitalized (with a steep increase following the 2020 Covid pandemic), EMBs are adapting their stance with regards to cybersecurity.

Election administrations are unique in their threat model, with different risks inherent to different activities during different phases of the electoral cycle, and they are also unique in terms of providing verifiable results. As elections are becoming increasingly a battleground for cyber-attacks and disinformation campaigns, EMBs must rely on effective training methodologies with well-defined intended learning objectives (ILOs), and move rapidly to mature training and education programs that are consistently organized and well-defined along the dimensions that we have presented in this paper. We believe that evaluating cybersecurity awareness programs this way can not only ensure the adequation of the training content with the specific needs of election administration, it can also help trainers develop mature training programs in which content and objectives are quickly adjusted in terms of content and depth (from awareness to defensive skills). We believe that the evaluation strategy presented here applies to most elections and electoral systems, in developed as well as developing and post-conflict countries.

We conclude that *trainings need to incorporate the participants' profiles and their respective backgrounds* and identify and respond to their specific needs and risks. This will be a requirement for trainings targeting users with prior knowledge and exposure to cybersecurity issues.

Furthermore, *evolving learning objectives that range from awareness and information to higher levels of skills and know-how* will become key to maintain sustained users' engagement on cybersecurity issues. Cybersecurity evolves rapidly, new threats emerge, such as supply chain attacks, and new tools are being developed to mitigate these new risks. Cyber-hygiene is a long-term engagement and trainings should be conducted continuously upon entering new phases of the election cycle. Learning objectives should evolve and be refined to maintain ongoing engagement for users who have already received a training in the past.

In the case of heterogeneous groups of participants and roles, *questionnaire and tests prior to the training should influence the curriculum*. Collecting the necessary information regarding pre-existing knowledge of the participants could be done via a pre-training questionnaire using behavioral questions (what can participants do wrong on scenario-based questions). Knowledge based questions seem to remain the best method to measure success of the training.

Cyber-hygiene courses in general need to be conducted periodically to re-engage users and update them on the latest threats and techniques to mitigate cybersecurity risks. We believe that *the frequency of trainings should be aligned with the expected retention period and the electoral cycle*. Good practice in many industries put the periodicity of re-engaging users with cyber-hygiene practices around one year. However, election administration is cyclic, and subject to different types of threats. To increase the efficiency of the cyber-hygiene training and establish cybersecurity as a strategic objective of secure election preparation, planning of training periods should be based on the election cycle. Reminders in the forms of newsletter, posters, calendars are very important and should be ongoing, they support the training but do not provide new information.

Election officials are often under the pressure of an incoming electoral operation, without strong involvement of the management, cyber-hygiene training often receives little attention. A strong management support is a pre-requisite to any successful cyber-hygiene training. Therefore, *cyber-hygiene should be part of an overall security strategy*. Furthermore, a culture of trust is needed to ensure that election officials receive proper training and support rather than be blamed for cybersecurity incidents. Each EMB faces different threats, has a different risk acceptance level, and cybersecurity maturity, EMBs need to understand and formalize their needs and determine clear training course objectives.

Academic study and international good practice have also demonstrated that awareness and trainings can only go so far if they are not backed up by organizational policies. Cyber-hygiene cannot happen in a vacuum, election management administration need to *ensure that the training aligns with the cybersecurity objectives* and that recommendations are backed back appropriate administrative controls. They way to manage cyber risks due to the human factor is by high quality trainings and these are best designed and analyzed following the theory of constructive alignment.

References

1. Beyer, M., et al.: Awareness is only the first step. In: Hewlett Packard Enterprise, Technical report (2015)
2. Biggs, J.: Aligning teaching and assessing to course objectives. In: International Conference on Teaching and Learning in Higher Education: New trend and innovations, vol. 2 (2003)
3. Biggs, J.B., Collis, K.F.: Evaluating the quality of learning: the SOLO taxonomy (structure of the observed learning outcome). In: Educational Psychology Series (1982)

4. Brabrand, C.: Constructive Alignment for Teaching Model-Based Design for Concurrency. In: Jensen, K., van der Aalst, W.M.P.., Billington, J. (eds.) Transactions on Petri Nets and Other Models of Concurrency I. LNCS, vol. 5100, pp. 1–18. Springer, Heidelberg (2008). https://doi.org/10.1007/978-3-540-89287-8_1. ISBN 978-3-540-89287-8

5. EDRi. Massive political data leak in Malta (2020). https://edri.org/our-work/massive-political-data-leak-in-malta/. Accessed 6 May 2021

6. Volz, D., Finkle, J.: Database of 191 million U.S. voters exposed on Internet: researcher (2015). https://www.reuters.com/article/us-usa-voters-breach-idUSKBN0UB1E020151229. Accessed 6 May 2021

7. Schürmann, C., Jensen, L.H., Sigbjörnsdóttir, R.: Effective cybersecurity awareness training for election officials. In: Electronic Voting: E-Vote-ID 2020 12455, pp. 196–212 (2020)

8. Trigwell, K., Prosser, M.: Qualitative variation in constructive alignment in curriculum design. High. Educ. 67(2), 141–154 (2013). https://doi.org/10.1007/s10734-013-9701-1

9. Verizon. DBIR: Data Breach Investigations Report (2020). https://enterprise.verizon.com/resources/reports/2020-data-breach-investigations-report.pdf

10. Walsh, A.: An exploration of Biggs' constructive alignment in the context of work-based learning. Assess. Eval. High. Educ. 32(1), 79–87 (2007)

11. Wikipedia. Commission on elections data breach (2016). https://en.wikipedia.org/wiki/Commission_on_Elections_data_breach. Accessed 6 May 2021

Party Cues and Trust in Remote Internet Voting: Data from Estonia 2005–2019

Piret Ehin[✉][iD] and Mihkel Solvak[iD]

Johan Skytte Institute of Political Studies, University of Tartu,
Lossi 36, 51003 Tartu, Estonia
{piret.ehin,mihkel.solvak}@ut.ee

Abstract. Trust is crucial for the adoption and use of new technologies. This paper seeks to advance our knowledge of why people trust or distrust disruptive electoral technologies such as remote internet voting. It argues that because of the complexity of the systems in question, most potential users are unable to form independent opinions on the system's trustworthiness and are likely to rely on cues provided by trusted social actors such as their preferred political parties. The paper develops a set of hypotheses from this conjecture, and tests these with survey data on approximately 5200 Estonian voters in the context of 11 elections held between 2005 and 2019. The findings suggest that partisan attachments are an important determinant of trust in e-voting and that the partisan gap in trust cannot be reduced to differences in socio-demographic voter profiles. Our results, however, do not support the conjecture that less educated individuals are particularly likely to take cues from their preferred parties when assessing the trustworthiness of e-voting.

Keywords: e-voting · Internet voting · Trust

1 Introduction

In recent decades, trust has become an important focus in technology studies. As a precondition for the adoption and use of new technologies [26,35], trust can make or break specific innovations, with potentially far-reaching and cumulative macro-societal effects. In the context of the ongoing digital transformation affecting all spheres of life, it is vital to understand the nature, sources and effects of trust in the context of technological change.

The growing literature on the subject has clarified important conceptual questions and produced notable empirical findings. The conceptual work has focused on the role of uncertainty and vulnerability in trust situations, differences between various objects of trust, such as people, organizations or technologies, as well as the relevant properties of the trustor, trustee, and the broader

The work for this paper has received funding from European Union's Horizon 2020 research and innovation programme under grant agreement No. 857622.

R. Krimmer et al. (Eds.): E-Vote-ID 2021, LNCS 12900, pp. 75–90, 2021.
https://doi.org/10.1007/978-3-030-86942-7_6

institutional context. In terms of explaining trust in new technologies, the literature has tended to prioritize user perceptions of the functionality and reliability of specific technologies. In doing so, the literature on trust converges with technology acceptance models which emphasize perceived usefulness and perceived ease-of-use [10]. However, the literature has to date paid limited attention to how cognitively constrained individuals form opinions and beliefs about highly complex technological systems.

This paper focuses on the proposition that when forming beliefs about the trustworthiness of new technologies, potential users rely on cognitive shortcuts, taking cues from trusted social actors. Grounded in well-established theories of bounded rationality, this approach postulates that when forming judgments about new technologies, people behave as cognitive misers who rely on heuristics in order to reduce the time and effort associated with making up one's mind. Considering the complexity of new digital technologies as well as the rapid pace of technological replacement, the cue-taking approach has potential to lead to new insights about the determinants and dynamics of trust.

We use cue-taking theory to explain popular trust in remote internet voting (e-voting) in Estonia. E-voting is a disruptive technology that significantly alters the calculations and behavior of stakeholders in the electoral process, including voters, parties, candidates and electoral authorities [23]. Estonia introduced remote internet voting in 2005 and has used it since then in all local, national and European Parliament elections. Usage rates have grown rapidly, with e-votes constituting almost a half of all votes cast in national and European Parliament elections in 2019. While high and growing usage rates are suggestive of high levels of trust, our data shows that Estonian voters differ greatly in terms of the extent to which they trust e-voting. We derive a set of hypotheses about partisan attachments and voter trust in e-voting, and test these with survey data on approximately 5200 voters in the context of 11 elections held between 2005 and 2019.

This paper is organized in six sections. The next section examines the concept of trust in the context of technological innovation. The third section revisits the literature on cognitive shortcuts in opinion formation, and presents the argument that voters take cues from their preferred political parties in forming beliefs about e-voting. The fourth section introduces the research design, data and methods. The fifth section describes the positions of Estonia's main political parties on internet voting. The sixth section presents the results of the analysis, focusing on the level, correlates and predictors of trust in e-voting. We conclude with a brief discussion of the implications of our findings.

2   The Concept of Trust in the Context of Technological Innovation

Trust is generally understood as belief in the reliability, truth, or ability of someone or something. Trust has been defined in various ways in different disciplines, and the copious literature on the nature, causes and effects of trust has suffered from several problems including the lack of conceptual clarity and specificity. An Integrative Model of Organizational Trust that stands out for conceptual rigor and underlies a large body of subsequent scholarship defines trust as "willingness of a party to be vulnerable to the actions of another party based on the expectation that the other will perform a particular action important to the trustor, irrespective of the ability to monitor or control that other party" [28]. This model distinguishes between the characteristics of the trustor (propensity to trust) and the characteristics of the trustee (factors of perceived trustworthiness, including ability, benevolence and integrity). It argues that trust refers to the trustor's willingness to enter into a risk-taking relationship with the trustee, and makes an important distinction between trust as a belief and trusting behavior [28].

While most of the scholarship on trust is concerned with trust in people or organizations, a recent strand of research focuses on trust in technology. Several studies have proposed relevant definitions and measures, arguing that we need a better understanding of what makes technology itself trustworthy, "irrespective of the people and human structures that surround the technology" [29, p. 2] This approach has strong affinities with technology acceptance models which emphasize the inherent characteristics of specific technologies, such as perceived usefulness and ease-of-use [10] as well as performance expectancy and effort expectancy [38].

Focusing on technology as the object of trust calls for specifying how trust in technology differs from trust in people, and what the implications of these differences are. To trust a person is to trust "a volitional and moral agent" while to trust technology means to trust "human-created artifact with a limited range of capabilities" that lacks free will and moral agency [29, p. 5]. However, these differences do not challenge the basic definition of trust as a belief that the trustee has the attributes necessary to perform as expected in a situation. Both types of trust are compatible with definitions that emphasize vulnerability and willingness to assume risks as being central to trust. Both types of trust are affected by contextual conditions such as situational normality and structural assurance which refer to the belief that risks will not materialize because the situation is "normal, favorable, or well-ordered" and because "promises, contracts, regulations and guarantees are in place" [29,30]. Furthermore, it is important to understand that the diverse objects of trust may form complex systems in which technologies, people, organizations, and contextual conditions such as institutional and legal settings are intertwined and interdependent. Whether people distinguish among the different components of the system, whether they trust some components more than others, and how trust in specific components affects trust in the system as a whole remain questions for empirical inquiry.

The above clarifications enable us to spell out what we mean by trust in remote internet voting. The trustor is the potential user – i.e. a person eligible to vote. The object of trust is a system consisting of people, organizations, institutions, laws, rules, norms and specific technologies. The system is highly complex, consisting of multiple interconnected components each of which can constitute a separate object of trust. For instance, a user could have different levels of trust in each of the specific technologies used (e.g. ID cards, authentication, e-voting software, vote encryption systems, protocols and algorithms, servers, etc.), as well as in people and organizations involved in the design, production, testing, operation, control, promotion and evaluation of these technologies (including developers, tech companies, governments, lawyers, electoral authorities, etc.). Importantly, a lack of trust in one specific component of the system may undermine trust in the system as a whole. Remote internet voting entails a plethora of potential vulnerabilities and risks, including the risk that the vote is not cast as intended, that the vote cast does not remain secret, and that by downloading e-voting applications, users infect their devices with viruses and malware. Beyond personal risks, e-voting can be associated with a range of macro-level risks (e.g. failure to conduct free and fair elections, a crisis or breakdown of democracy). Trust in remote internet voting thus means willingness to rely on the diverse components of such a voting system based on the expectation that the system performs its declared functions (secure and fast location-independent voting in free and fair elections) irrespective of the voters' ability to monitor or control the system.

While the growing literature on trust in technology has done much to clarify the concept and illuminate the sources and effects of trust, it has not yet paid sufficient attention to the question of how people form beliefs about highly complex (systems of) objects. Arguing that the literature on trust in technology would benefit from insights from the broader literature on opinion and belief formation on complex issues, the next section revisits the literature on cognitive heuristics and contemplates the role of political parties in shaping public beliefs about the trustworthiness of e-voting.

3 Trust or Not to Trust Technology? Taking Cues from Political Parties

For decades, scholarship on opinion formation and decision-making has emphasized the cognitive limitations of human judgment, arguing that individuals tend to rely on cognitive heuristics in order to reduce informational and computational costs [6,17,32,34]. A heuristic is a mental shortcut that leads to fast, frugal and mostly accurate decisions in many situations characterized by uncertainty [18]. However, reliance on cognitive heuristics is also associated with errors and reduced accuracy, cognitive bias, stereotyping and prejudice [34].

Cue-taking is one type of heuristic that individuals use in order to reduce cognitive effort involved in problem-solving, opinion formation and decision-making. Because of the cognitive and temporal costs of rational reasoning, individuals look to other trusted social actors, such as political elites, for signals suggesting what to think or how to behave [27,41]. The likelihood that individuals rely on elite cues when forming opinions and making decisions increases when information is scarce or difficult to obtain, when issues are complex, uncertainty is high, when time is constrained, and when the ability to process information is low.

In the context of competitive democracies, a theory of opinion formation based on elite cues must take into account partisanship. There is a large and diverse literature focusing on party cues and the effects of party attachments on individual opinions and decision-making [3,7–9,22]. It is argued that citizens follow the lead of the party they sympathize with the most in forming policy opinions, and are particularly likely to do so when the issues in question are complex. There is significant evidence that individuals rely on party cues when making up their minds on issues such as European integration [2,19,20,31], the state of the national economy [5], climate change [12], foreign policy [4] or nuclear energy [25]. While much of the literature on partisanship effects has focused on the United States, party attachments have been shown to affect policy opinions in a variety of contexts, including multi-party systems and new democracies [7].

Despite the prominence of the party cues theory in political research, it seems that this approach has not been applied to explaining opinion formation on new digital technologies. Widely used models of technology acceptance and use, such as UTAUT [38] include social influence as one of the explanatory factors. Social influence is defined as "the degree to which an individual perceives that important others believe he or she should use the new system" [38, p. 451]. However, the category of social influence in these models is concerned with subjective norms, culture, image and reputation, not with cue-taking as a form of cognitive shortcut.

There are three interrelated reasons why opinion formation on e-voting is highly likely to involve cue-taking from political parties. First, because remote internet voting is quick and convenient, saving voters time and money, many voters will want to use it. Before doing so, however, they need to determine whether the system can be trusted. In other words, there are strong incentives to form an opinion on e-voting in the first place. Second, the issue is highly complex: few voters have the time and ability to form independent opinions on the trustworthiness of the technological, legal and institutional aspects of remote internet voting. Thus, voters are highly likely to look for and rely on informational and computational shortcuts in forming opinions. Third, political parties can be expected to be important cue-givers because they have much at stake in the introduction of new technologies that transform the electoral process. Technological innovations that alter both the cost-benefit calculations involved in the act of voting, as well as perceptions, norms and understandings related to elections, have the potential to differentially impact electoral support for specific parties. Thus, parties are likely to form positions, corresponding to their perception of how e-voting affects their electoral prospects and those of their contenders. They may frame new technologies in particular ways, seeking to legitimize or de-legitimize their use. In sum, the combination of these three factors makes it highly likely that parties engage in cue-giving and voters in cue-taking regarding e-voting.

We derive the following hypotheses from the above discussion:

H1: *Citizens who vote for parties that endorse remote internet voting are more likely to trust remote internet voting than citizens who vote for parties that criticize this voting mode.*

H2: The partisan gap in trust in remote internet voting cannot be reduced to differences in the socio-demographic profiles of party voters.

H3: The effect of party cues on an individual's trust in remote internet voting is conditioned by the individual's level of cognitive sophistication.

4   Research Design, Data and Methods

The hypotheses specified above are tested using individual-level survey data as well as party-level data from Estonia from 2005 to 2019. During these fifteen years, eleven nation-wide elections with an e-voting option have been held, including four local, four national and three European Parliament elections. Estonia remains the only country in the world that offers all of its voters the opportunity to cast a vote online. E-voting has been available in all nation-wide elections since 2005, and the share of e-votes has grown steadily, reaching almost 50 per cent of all votes cast in 2019. In Estonia, e-voting is highly institutionalized and has become part of the regular framework for conducting elections. In the context of a study focusing on trust in e-voting, this means that the object of trust is an existing, widely used system that all voters have the option of using. This differentiates the Estonian case from all other currently existing electoral contexts in the world. For more information on the organization and uptake of internet voting in Estonia see [1,33,36].

In this context, Estonian political parties have had more reason and more time to form positions on e-voting than their counterparts around the world. Party positions have evolved together with the Estonian e-voting system, and have both reflected and influenced societal and expert debates on the matter. As there have been no initiatives to systematically collect data on Estonian parties' positions on internet voting, such as a survey or manifesto study, this study infers party positions from a range of available sources, including votes in the parliament, party manifestos and campaign materials, statements by party leaders and officials, as well as media and social media coverage of party activities. This analysis focuses on the positions of six largest parties, three of which have, at various times, expressed skepticism towards e-voting.

To examine voter trust in e-voting, we use individual-level survey data from the Estonian electronic voter study 2005–2019, which is comprised of 11 post-election cross-sectional surveys covering all elections in which the option of remote internet voting has been available. Each survey had a sample size of roughly 1000 respondents, and the samples are representative of eligible voters in terms of age, gender, ethnicity and region. We focus only on self-reported voters, resulting in a dataset of roughly 5200 respondents.

We use the following measure of trust in e-voting: "Do you trust the procedure of internet voting?". Answers to this question were recorded on a four-category Likert scale between 2005 and 2011 and on a 0–10 scale since 2013. In both cases, we split the responses mid-scale and turned the variable into a binary trust variable (0 - do not trust; 1 - trust) to be able to compare effects across the years. Respondents who chose category 5 on the 0–10 scale were randomly assigned to either side.

To investigate the hypotheses we employ the following approaches. After describing the level of trust in e-voting over the years, we turn to the question of whether trust in e-voting differs from trust in political institutions as well as trust in online transactions. To answer this question, we examine correlation matrices of various survey items. Second, we examine the dynamics of trust in e-voting over time according to party choice. Given that some Estonian parties have changed their stances on internet voting over time, an examination of whether and how voter attitudes have followed these changes provides particularly compelling evidence of cue-taking. Third, we run eleven separate logit models in the following setup:

$$ln\left\{\frac{Pr(trust_t = 1)}{1 - Pr(trust_t = 1)}\right\} = \beta_0 + \beta_1 demographics_t + \beta_2 partychoice_t + \beta_3 trust_t$$

(1)

The dependent variable is trust in e-voting in election t and the independent variables are standard socio-demographics (age, gender, income, education), weekly internet usage frequency, self-reported computer skills of the voter, party choice in the given election, average trust in other state institutions and trust in internet transactions. We run a separate model for each election and include independent variables stepwise in order to assess whether and to what extent party cues override the effects of other factors. Given that we include trust in internet transactions, internet usage intensity as well as self-reported skills as controls, this approach should constitute a rigorous test of the party cues and non-reducibility hypotheses (H1 and H2). Finally, to test the sophistication hypothesis (H3) we examine the predictive margins of trust by party choice and education level.

Below, we will first elaborate on the positions of the Estonian political parties before turning to an analysis of voter attitudes.

5   The Positions of Estonian Political Parties on E-Voting

Despite a sustained political commitment to developing internet voting that spans two decades and ten coalition governments, there has been significant partisan conflict over e-voting in Estonia. Out of the six main parliamentary parties, three (Pro Patria, the Reform Party and Social Democrats) have endorsed and promoted e-voting. Pro Patria and the Reform Party, both on the center-right, were leading government parties in the early 2000s when expert and political discussions on e-voting were first launched, the decision to deploy internet voting was taken, and the necessary legislation prepared. The liberal, pro-market Reform Party has been the dominant government party during the observed period, leading coalition governments from April 2005 to November 2016. For most of this period, it was in coalition with Pro Patria and the Social Democrats. Throughout this period, the three parties' positions on internet voting – along with that of the government as a whole – have been highly positive, depicting e-voting as an important element of the Estonian e-state, a long-standing priority of Reform-led governments.

Three other major parties - the Center Party, the People's Union, and its successor, the Conservative People's Party – have adopted critical stances on internet voting at various points of time and with varying levels of intensity. For most of the observed period, the three parties were in opposition (with the exception of the Center serving as a junior partner in a Reform-led coalition government from April 2005 to April 2007, and the People's Union being included in government from April 2003 to April 2005). In November 2016, however, Center became the leading government party, ruling, initially, together with Pro Patria and the Social Democrats, and then, following March 2019 elections, with the Conservative People's Party and Pro Patria. Below, we summarize available evidence about negative cuing by the Center Party, the People's Union, and the Conservative People's Party.

The Center Party, a liberal centrist force with a recurring populist streak, was one of the two parties that voted against the introduction of internet voting in 2005. Between 2005 and 2013, it voiced occasional criticism of e-voting. For instance, following the 2011 national elections, MP Ando Leps claimed that the Estonian e-voting system was "completely untrustworthy," rendering the election legally invalid [37]. The Party stepped up criticism of e-voting after the October 2013 local elections. Party Chairman Edgar Savisaar published an article in the party newspaper *Kesknädal* in which he claimed that right-wing parties won elections by forging election results [39]. In spring 2013, an NGO connected to the Center Party ran a street campaign in Tallinn, featuring 68 posters with slogans such as "They may delete your vote", "Every e-vote is a potential threat to Estonia's independence" and "They can give your vote to whoever they want" (ibid.) In both 2011 and 2014, the Party helped fund visits of foreign experts who produced critical reports of the e-voting system. In 2014, the Center Party Board sent a letter to Estonian and EU top officials requesting immediate cancellation of e-voting due to "fundamental security problems" [40]. In April 2015, the Party's Council adopted a resolution which claimed that e-voting was a security risk, and argued that e-voting violates the requirement of uniformity and secrecy [24]. The resolution said that even if government parties had not abused e-voting to date, such abuse may occur in the future (ibid).

However, the Center Party appears to have discontinued its criticism of e-voting after it became the leading government party in November 2016. Still, in March 2017, the party proposed a bill which foresaw shortening the e-voting period from seven days to three [39]. However, Party Chairman and Prime Minister Jüri Ratas publicly confirmed that the government endorses internet voting. In September 2017, the government led by Ratas had to manage the most serious crisis in the history of Estonian e-government which occurred after foreign scientists found a vulnerability affecting hundreds of thousands of ID cards used in Estonia [21]. With the reputation of the Estonian e-government system at stake, the government led by Ratas worked hard to solve the crisis and control damage. Since the event, the Center Party has refrained from criticizing e-voting. In sum, the Center Party was critical of remote internet voting from 2005 until late 2016, while its position since November 2016 can be characterized as neutral or favorable.

The Estonian People's Union, a socially conservative rural party, was founded in 1999 and ceased to exist in 2012. It was one of the two parties that voted against the introduction of e-voting in 2005. Furthermore, its former Chairman Arnold Rüütel, then President of the Republic, twice refused to proclaim the law instituting internet voting, arguing that the provision that allows the voter to alter his or her e-vote violates the principle of uniformity of elections. He also asked the Supreme Court to declare the law invalid [13]. In 2006, Jaak Allik, Deputy Chair of the party group in the parliament, argued that e-voting is in principle not observable and electoral authorities are not able to ascertain whether the person who voted with a particular ID card is the legal holder of the card [11]. The party suffered major electoral losses in general elections held in spring 2007. This decline seems to coincide with the subsiding of negative rhetoric directed at e-voting.

The third major party that has criticized e-voting is the Estonian Conservative People's Party (EKRE). Founded in 2012, the populist far-right party first gained parliamentary representation in 2015 and entered the governing coalition in spring 2019. While the party seems to have kept a low profile on e-voting during the first four years of its existence, it has, over time, turned into a vocal critic of the system. In spring 2017, Henn Põlluaas, Deputy Chairman of the party group in the parliament, called for an international audit of the Estonian e-voting system. Half a year later, EKRE filed a complaint with the Electoral Committee, demanding that internet voting in upcoming local elections be cancelled due to security vulnerabilities affecting ID cards [14]. In March 2019, Deputy Chair of the party, Martin Helme, claimed that for him, the trustworthiness of e-elections was "non-existent" because the integrity of elections "cannot be monitored or verified" [16]. Over the course of 2017–2019, EKRE's news portal *Uued uudised* published 26 articles expressing various doubts about e-elections, pointing at shortcomings in procedures and emphasizing the need to evaluate and improve the security of the system. After EKRE joined the governing coalition in April 2019, it was assigned the portfolio of the Minister of Foreign Trade and Information Technology. Kert Kingo, who held the position for half a year in 2019, convened an e-voting working group to assess the verifiability, security and transparency of Estonia's electronic voting system – a move that many interpreted as being politically motivated [15]. In sum, between 2017 and 2019, EKRE's position on e-voting can be characterized as highly critical.

Differences in party positions appear to reflect the differential utilities that parties derive from e-voting. Voter uptake of e-voting varies by party choice as shown in Fig. 1. While the vote shares of the two largest parties (Reform and Center) have been fairly comparable, hovering between 23 and 29 per cent in national elections (Fig. 1a), the Reform Party gets about four times as many e-votes as its main political opponent (Fig. 1b). Also, Pro Patria and the Social Democrats are clearly more successful in attracting e-votes than the Center Party. Although previous studies have demonstrated that e-voting does not increase turnout or mobilize non-voters [33], it is clear that the importance of this voting channel varies greatly across parties.

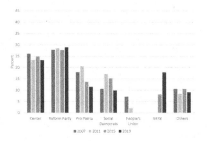
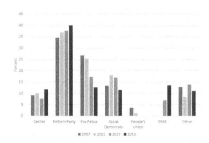

(a) Party vote shares in national elections 2007-2019

(b) Party e-vote shares in national elections 2007-2019

Fig. 1. Total vote shares and e-vote shares in national elections 2007–2019

6   Voter Trust and Its Correlates: Results Based on the Estonian Electronic Voter Study

Data from the Estonian electronic voter study suggests that e-voting has enjoyed high levels of trust in Estonia since its inception. According to the first survey conducted in 2005, a few months after the first e-enabled election, about 80 per cent of the voters said that they trusted the system. The level of trust has ebbed and flowed, reaching the lowest level of 54 per cent in 2013, but recovering after that and hovering around 69–70 per cent in the two elections held in 2019.

Before proceeding to analyze the predictors of trust in e-voting, it is important to establish whether and how this type of trust is related to trust in other institutions. Running bivariate correlations (coefficients not shown due to space limitations but available from authors upon request) between trust in internet voting and trust in the parliament, government, politicians, the state and internet transactions show that trust in e-voting is correlated with trusting other institutions but the correlations are systematically weaker compared to correlations between trust in different state institutions. This is a strong indication that trust in e-voting is substantively different from trust in other state institutions and that respondents are able to distinguish e-voting from other objects and evaluate its trustworthiness separately.

Also, it is important to establish whether and how much trust matters when it comes to the decision whether to use the system or not. Figure 2 shows the association between trust and usage of e-voting, extracted from a regression model where usage is the dependent variable and trust is an independent variable alongside conventional socio-demographic measures. The results confirm that trust is a persistent and potent predictor of usage.

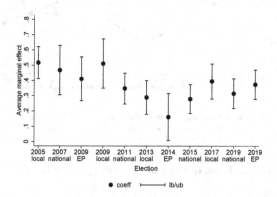

Fig. 2. The effect of trust on usage of e-voting (2005–2019)

Turning to the question of how party cues affect voter attitudes, Fig. 3 shows the level of trust in e-voting by party choice over time. Multiple things stand out. First, the figure shows that party supporters fall into two distinct groups, the low-trust (Center, EKRE voters) and the high-trust group (all others). Second, the share of trustors fluctuates over the observed period for two parties. Trust among Center Party supporters starts out high, then plummets and then grows again. These fluctuations reflect the temporal evolution of the Center Party position on e-voting: the Party was initially indifferent towards this voting mode, then started to heavily oppose it and finally switched to positive rhetoric after becoming the leading government party in late 2016. EKRE supporters have moved from a high-trust group to a low-trust group almost linearly as the party leadership's opposition to e-voting has grown more vocal.

Next, we ran a regression model in order to ascertain the effects of party choice on trust in e-voting, controlling for socio-demographic variables as well as computer literacy, internet usage and trust in political institutions as well as internet transactions. Table 1 presents a part of the regression model output (effects of control variables not shown). A number of findings stand out. First, in the early years of e-voting, party choice was not a significant predictor of trust. Statistically significant effects of party choice appear from 2011 onwards and persist when internet usage, PC skill level, trust in internet transactions as well as socio-demographics are controlled for. Second, we see how the explanatory power of these models, especially their ability to classify low-trust voters, improves over time and then diminishes again. These fluctuations correspond to shifts in the Center Party's stance on e-voting. Third, as the reference group are Center Party voters, we can conclude that the supporters of the Reform Party, Pro Patria and the Social Democrats are clearly more trusting of e-voting than Center Party

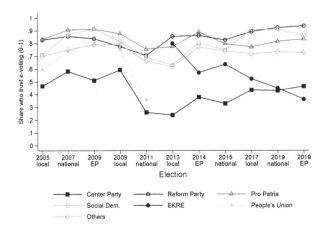

Fig. 3. Level of trust in e-voting by party choice

supporters. This finding is in line with the significantly larger share of internet votes accruing to these three parties compared to the Center Party.

Table 1. The effects of party choice on trust in e-voting (2005–2019)

	2005 Local	2007 National	2009 EP	2009 Local	2011 National	2013 Local	2014 EP	2015 National	2017 Local	2019 National	2019 EP
Reform Party	0.027	0.061	0.064	0.029	0.224	0.273***	0.238**	0.357***	0.149*	0.301***	0.311***
(ref: Center)	(0.058)	(0.052)	(0.050)	(0.064)	(0.127)	(0.071)	(0.081)	(0.081)	(0.063)	(0.062)	(0.073)
Pro Patria	0.041	0.109 *	0.119 **	0.077	0.259 *	0.198 **	0.307 ***	0.406 ***	0.075	0.162 **	0.229 **
	(0.058)	(0.050)	(0.047)	(0.063)	(0.127)	(0.070)	(0.084)	(0.081)	(0.079)	(0.075)	(0.085)
Social Democrats	−0.074	0.063	0.100*	0.014	0.226	0.110	0.237**	0.397***	0.227**	0.281***	0.241***
	(0.081)	(0.056)	(0.048)	(0.071)	(0.127)	(0.068)	(0.075)	(0.073)	(0.074)	(0.067)	(0.075)
People's Union	−0.101	0.001	–	–	0.234	na	na	na	na	na	na
	(0.086)	(0.081)	–	–	(0.184)	na	na	na	na	na	na
EKRE	na	na	na	na	na	0.161	0.080	0.324***	−0.102	−0.011	−0.176
	na	na	na	na	na	(0.217)	(0.129)	(0.089)	(0.088)	(0.073)	(0.098)
Other party	−0.011	0.052	0.027	0.079	0.232	0.217***	0.178*	0.325***	0.101	0.123	0.129
	(0.059)	(0.053)	(0.047)	(0.056)	(0.120)	(0.058)	(0.077)	(0.077)	(0.058)	(0.072)	(0.079)
Sensitivity	98.45	99.59	98.38	98.94	96.87	85.8	93.42	88.89	92.03	91.07	92.92
Specificity	16.67	2.00	27.66	10.64	34.21	78.33	68.89	63.83	53.73	60.26	52.14
Pseudo R^2	0.176	0.198	0.453	0.171	0.383	0.619	0.584	0.422	0.478	0.514	0.440
Observations	459	532	479	426	395	472	318	530	548	554	484

Average marginal effects with standard errors in parentheses.
* $p < 0.05$, ** $p < 0.01$, *** $p < 0.001$

Finally, we turn to the question of whether the effect of party cues on trust in e-voting is moderated by the voter's cognitive sophistication. Figure 4 shows the predictive margins of trust in e-voting according to the highest level of education attained. Overall, the results suggest that trust in e-voting does not depend on sophistication. However, regardless of which party we focus on, a pattern emerges where in the first years of e-voting lower education was associated with

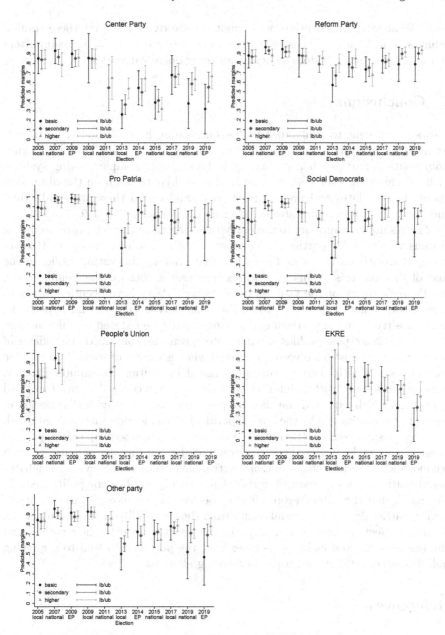

Fig. 4. The effect of education on trust in e-voting by party choice (predictive margins)

higher levels of predicted trust, while in the last four or five elections, the highly educated are more prone to trust e-voting than the less educated. It is not clear why such a reversal has occurred - because confidence intervals for the educational categories overlap, we cannot substantively interpret these results. What is clear, however, is that when trust in e-voting declines among supporters of a particular party, it does so across all educational categories.

7 Conclusions

This study sought to contribute to the burgeoning literature on trust in new technologies by systematically evaluating the proposition that voters take cues from political parties when evaluating technologically complex voting systems such as remote internet voting. It derived three hypotheses from the discussion about the correlates and predictors of trust, and tested these with individual and party-level data from Estonia, covering the period 2005–2019.

The results lend support to the party cues hypothesis, which postulated that citizens who vote for parties that endorse e-voting are more likely to trust e-voting than citizens who vote for parties that criticize this voting mode. In the case of Estonia, this means that voters who cast a vote for the Center Party, the People's Union or the Conservative People's Party have been less likely to trust e-voting than voters who voted for other parties. The second hypothesis, which posited that the partisan gap in trust cannot be reduced to differences in the socio-demographic profiles of party voters, was also confirmed. The effects of party choice on trust for e-voting persisted when a variety of socio-demographic controls, along with general trust in political institutions, computer literacy, internet usage and trust in internet transactions were controlled for. The third hypothesis which expected the effect of party cues on an individual's trust in e-voting to be conditioned by the level of political sophistication was not confirmed.

These results confirm the potential of societal actors to shape mass perceptions of new technologies, with consequences for the uptake and use of such technologies. The fact that political parties have 'skin in the game' in debates about voting modes increases the risk that e-voting will become politicized. To the extent that the voters' propensity to use e-voting technology varies by party choice, parties derive differential utility from the availability of this voting mode. Feedback effects among such utility, the cues parties send to their voters, and the resulting differences in usage rates have the potential to lead to a growing polarization of trust in and usage of e-voting along party lines.

References

1. Alvarez, R., Nagler, J.: Likely consequences of internet voting for political representation. Loyola Los Angeles Law Rev. **34**, 1115–1153 (2000)
2. Anderson, C.J.: When in doubt, use proxies: attitudes toward domestic politics and support for European integration. Comp. Pol. Stud. **31**(5), 569–601 (1998)
3. Bartels, L.: Beyond the running tally: partisan bias in political perceptions. Polit. Behav. **24**, 117–150 (2002)
4. Berinsky, A.J.: Assuming the costs of war: events, elites, and American public support for military conflict. J. Polit. **69**(4), 975–997 (2007)

5. Bisgaard, M., Slothuus, R.: Partisan elites as culprits? How party cues shape partisan perceptual gaps. Am. J. Polit. Sci. **62**, 456–469 (2018)
6. Bobadilla-Suarez, S., Love, B.: Fast or frugal, but not both: decision heuristics under time pressure. J. Exp. Psychol. Learn. Mem. Cogn. **44**(1), 24–33 (2018)
7. Brader, T., Tucker, J.A.: Following the party's lead: party cues, policy opinion, and the power of partisanship in three multiparty systems. Comp. Polit. **44**(4), 403–420 (2012)
8. Bullock, J.: Party cues. In: Suhay, E., Grofman, B., Trechsel, A.H. (eds.) The Oxford Handbook of Electoral Persuasion. Oxford University Press, Oxford (2019)
9. Campbell, A., Converse, P.E., Miller, W.E., Stokes, D.E.: The American Voter. Wiley, New York (1960)
10. Davis, F.D.: Perceived usefulness, perceived ease of use, and user acceptance of information technology. MIS Q. **13**(3), 319–340 (1989)
11. Delfi: Rahvaliit jätkab sõda e-hääletuse vastu (2006). https://www.delfi.ee/news/paevauudised/eesti/rahvaliit-jatkab-soda-e-haaletuse-vastu?id=13112352. Accessed 03 Nov 2019
12. Ehret, P., Van Boven, L., Sherman, D.K.: Partisan barriers to bipartisanship: Understanding climate policy polarization. Soc. Psychol. Pers. Sci. **9**(3), 308–318 (2018)
13. ERR: Rüütel sai e-valimistega lüüa (2005). https://www.err.ee/435363/ruutel-sai-e-valimistega-luua. Accessed 03 Nov 2019
14. ERR: EKRE vaidlustas e-valimiste korraldamise (2017). https://www.err.ee/617818/ekre-vaidlustas-e-valimiste-korraldamise. Accessed 03 Nov 2019
15. ERR: It minister convenes inaugural e-voting working group (2019). https://news.err.ee/958188/it-minister-convenes-inaugural-e-voting-working-group. Accessed 03 Nov 2019
16. ERR: Valimisteenistus EKRE-le: e-valimised on vaadeldavad ja kontrollitavad (2019). https://www.err.ee/921784/valimisteenistus-EKRE-le-e-valimised-on-vaadeldavad-ja-kontrollitavad. Accessed 03 Nov 2019
17. Gigerenzer, G.: Rationality for Mortals: How People Cope with Uncertainty. Oxford University Press, New York (2008)
18. Gigerenzer, G., Gaissmaier, W.: Heuristic decision making. Ann. Rev. Psychol. **62**, 451–482 (2011)
19. Hobolt, S.B.: Taking cues on Europe: voter competence and party endorsements in referendums on European integration. Eur. J. Polit. Res. **46**(February), 151–182 (2007)
20. Hooghe, L., Marks, G.: Calculation, community and cues: public opinion on European integration. Eur. Union Polit. **6**(4), 419–443 (2005)
21. Information System Authority: ROCA Vulnerability and eID: Lessons Learned (2019). https://www.ria.ee/sites/default/files/content-editors/kuberturve/roca-vulnerability-and-eid-lessons-learned.pdf. Accessed 03 Nov 2019
22. Jacoby, W.G.: The impact of party identification on issue attitudes. Am. J. Polit. Sci. **32**, 643–61 (1988)
23. Kersting, N., Baldersheim, H.: Electronic Voting and Democracy: A Comparative Analysis. Palgrave Macmillan, New York (2004)
24. Keskerakond: E-riigis on suurepärane kõik peale e-valimiste (2015). https://www.keskerakond.ee/et/530-keskerakonna-volikogu-avaldus-e-riigis-on-suurepaerane-koik-peale-e-valimiste. Accessed 03 Nov 2019
25. Latre, E., Thijssen, P., Perko, T.: The party politics of nuclear energy: party cues and public opinion regarding nuclear energy in Belgium. Energy Res. Soc. Sci. **47**, 192–201 (2019)

26. Lippert, S.K., Davis, M.: A conceptual model integrating trust into planned change activities to enhance technology adoption behavior. J. Inf. Sci. **32**(5), 434–448 (2006)
27. Lippmann, W.: Public Opinion. Harcourt, Brace and Co. (1922)
28. Mayer, R.C., Davis, J.H., Schoorman, F.D.: An integrative model of organizational trust. Acad. Manage. Rev. **20**(3), 709–734 (1995)
29. McKnight, D.H., Carter, M., Thatcher, J.B., Clay, P.F.: Trust in a specific technology: an investigation of its components and measures. ACM Trans. Manage. Inform. Syst. **2**(2), 1–25 (2011)
30. McKnight, D.H., Cummings, L.L., Chervany, N.L.: Initial trust formation in new organizational relationships. Acad. Manage. Rev. **23**(3), 473–490 (1998)
31. Pannico, R.: Parties are always right: the effects of party cues and policy information on attitudes towards EU issues. West Eur. Polit. **43**(4), 869–893 (2020). https://doi.org/10.1080/01402382.2019.1653658
32. Simon, H.A.: Rational choice and the structure of the environment. Psychol. Rev. **63**(2), 129–138 (1956)
33. Solvak, M., Vassil, K.: E-voting in Estonia: technological diffusion and other developments over ten years (2005–2015). University of Tartu (2016)
34. Tversky, A., Kahneman, D.: Judgment under uncertainty: heuristics and biases. Science **185**(4157), 1124–1131 (1974)
35. Vance, A., Elie-Dit-Cosaque, C., Straubl, D.W.: Examining trust in information technology artifacts: the effects of system quality and culture. J. Manag. Inf. Syst. **24**(4), 73–100 (2008)
36. Vassil, K., Solvak, M., Vinkel, P., Trechsel, A.H., Alvarez, R.M.: The diffusion of internet voting. Usage patterns of internet voting in Estonia between 2005 and 2015. Govern. Inform. Q. 33(3), 453–459 (2016). https://doi.org/10.1016/j.giq.2016.06.007
37. Veiserik, I.: Ando Leps: E-hääletus riigikogu valimistel õigustühine. Kesknädal (23 March) (2011)
38. Venkatesh, V., Morris, M.G., Davis, G.B., Davis, F.D.: User acceptance of information technology: toward a unified view. MIS Q. **27**(3), 425–478 (2003)
39. Vester, L., Olup, N.M.: Ülevaade: Keskerakonna võitlused e-valimiste vastu. Postimees (5 September) (2017)
40. Villmann, A.-L.: Keskerakond nõuab Euroopa Parlamendilt e-valimiste tühistamist (2014). https://www.err.ee/512935/keskerakond-nouab-euroopa-parlamendilt-e-valimiste-tuhistamist. Accessed 03 Nov 2019
41. Zaller, J.R.: The Nature and Origins of Mass Opinion. Cambridge University Press, Cambridge (1992)

To i-vote or Not to i-vote: Drivers and Barriers to the Implementation of Internet Voting

Nathan Licht[1] , David Duenas-Cid[2,3] , Iuliia Krivonosova[1] ,
and Robert Krimmer[2]

[1] Tallinn University of Technology, Ehitajate tee 5, 12616 Tallinn, Estonia
{nalich,iuliia.krivonosova}@taltech.ee
[2] University of Tartu, Ülikooli 18, 50090 Tartu, Estonia
robert.krimmer@ut.ee
[3] Kozminski University, 57/59 Jagiellonska, 03-301 Warsaw, Poland
dduenas@kozminski.edu.pl

Abstract. This paper investigates the drivers and barriers of internet voting and the implications of a global pandemic for the development of the respective technology. In contrast to the expected uptake in the early 2000s of internet voting, the technology is still rather seldomly used in election systems around the world. The paper at hand explores the different forces that drive or impede internet voting adoption from a political, social, legal, organizational, contextual, economic and technological perspective. In an exploratory approach, 18 expert interviews and extensive complementary desk research were conducted.

The findings identified 15 general drivers and 15 general barriers for the process of internet voting adoption. The evidence suggests that for a large part, the political features, trust and perception are the most pivotal factors to internet voting development.

Keywords: Internet voting · Drivers and barriers · Framework of internet voting · Technology adoption · e-Democracy

1   Introduction

From Richard Buckminster Fuller [1] in the mid 20th century over Bill Gates [2], who predicted in his book The Road Ahead that "voters will be able to cast their ballots from home or their wallet PCs" to Apple's CEO, Tim Cook that "dream[s] of [voting on phones]" [3], the idea of deploying remote electronic voting has been envisioned by technology leaders since the first half of the last decade. A vision that was increasingly voiced at the beginning of the early 2000s as the interest in the internet and information and communication technologies (ICT) grew bigger.

Bill Gates' quote translated into present understandings probably refers to what is nowadays called internet voting (i-voting), which is a form of remote voting that is conducted in unsupervised environments such as one's home. If one compares his quote with the quote by Tim Cook, it does not sound very different, despite being said around

R. Krimmer et al. (Eds.): E-Vote-ID 2021, LNCS 12900, pp. 91–105, 2021.
https://doi.org/10.1007/978-3-030-86942-7_7

26 years earlier. In fact, the technology has been around for over two decades and has not diffused as it was expected that it would be. During the early 2000s, a great interest in novel technology existed, and much investment occurred alongside the general developments of ICTs to enhance democratic processes. Experts and politicians back then were convinced that in the course of the following 20 years, every democratic election would be conducted via electronic voting and even using the internet [4]. Although today that is still not the reality that we live in, the quote by Tim Cook seems to reflect a still present vision for contemporary leaders to be able to conduct elections online.

Therefore, the question can be raised why i-voting has not adopted as it had been expected and what are factors that drive internet voting. Moreover, due to the current global COVID-19 pandemic, several elections that were meant to take place were postponed, and discussions about whether to implement novel, sustainable and long-term voting solutions in response to the current events have appeared [5]. Remarkably, the interest in i-voting technology has heightened due to the global developments in response to the COVID-19 pandemic [6] which makes our research more timely and relevant. The understanding of i-voting's diffusion, its driving as well as impeding forces seem to be common questions that have been raised in academia and yet lack a holistic overview and common first understanding, which this paper aims to provide.

This paper solely focusses on i-voting, which is a specific form of electronic voting (e-voting), but for a better understanding of research intersections between these two topics, the following section depicts previous work related to both issues.

Previous works on e-voting have investigated diffusions of e-voting in Europe and drivers and barriers around e-voting [7] on adoption factors of e-voting by young people [8] the evolution of e-voting [9], the global e-voting status [10] and to provide an e-voting framework [11]. On i-voting, previous studies examined the global status quo [12, 13], studied the origins of remote online voting [4], aimed at providing a historical overview on i-voting usage [14, 15] and facilitating conditions for i-voting implementation on the examples of Estonia and Switzerland [16]. Furthermore, i-voting adoption was explicitly investigated for the Estonian case [17], and respective adoption phases were identified for the Estonian case [18]. Last, another work looked at the adoption stages and on what levels internet voting will occur [19]. This respective paper identified two levels and five adoption stages of internet voting diffusion on which this paper is building on to investigate the respective drivers and barriers that impact the technology acceptance on these levels.

In conclusion, previous research either looked at part drivers and barriers or facilitating conditions in specific contexts. However, no comprehensive study has been conducted so far that investigates general drivers and barriers that are observable along the various adoption and trialed contexts. In line with that identified research gap, this paper poses the following research question: *What is driving internet voting and what barriers exist to further adoption?* In order to answer this question, the work at hand conducted in an exploratory way some 18 expert interviews and extensive complementary desk research. The applied methodology used for this paper, is explained subsequently.

2 Methodology

In order to study what hinders or benefits the implementation of internet voting, we want to identify its drivers and barriers. To do so, we conducted a qualitative empirical study with a nonexperimental design including expert interviews, as promoted by Brown & Hale [20]. This research was conducted using an inductive epistemological approach to acquire knowledge. The inductive process, as opposed to the deductive method, is a "bottom-up [technique in which] evidence is collected first, [from the observation of the world] and knowledge and theories built from this" [21]. In order to guide the data analysis, a conceptual model was created *ad hoc*[1], integrating propositions included in five innovation diffusion theories. This model (see Fig. 1) explains how different dimensions are embedded into one context that shapes the process of diffusion of internet voting, in an evolutionary process that is impacted by perceptions, adopter categories and discourses. Furthermore, it establishes the differentiation of internet voting adoption on two levels: political and individual. The model presents five dimensions, various stakeholders and factors that impact the technology acceptance process within societies.

In order to make this paper better readable, we will briefly introduce some necessary stakeholders. First, the *relevant social groups* [23] which have a need or specific interest in the new innovation which creates a demand within society for the respective technology. Second, *change agents* or *opinion leaders* [24] shape public debate around an innovation due to their privileged position in society. Third, *individual drivers* are the citizens themselves who would be accepting technology based on the expected utility against the expected effort [25]. The following empirical research will explore the drivers and barriers and their allocation on the respective level of adoption.

The data collection of this research was conducted via semi-structured expert interviews and complemented by desk research, allowing cross checking experts opinions with other sources. The study followed the framework provided by Krimmer's mirabilis [9] that aids to identify the respective stakeholders involved in the implementation process of e-voting technology. In the context of this research, it was limited to three stakeholders: i) Media/observer, ii) election management and iii) inventors or vendors of voting technology. More precisely, it was focused on practitioners/EMBs/policymakers, scholars and election observers, as well as vendors or inventors of i-voting technology. A total of 18 interviews were conducted, transcribed, confirmed and analyzed in NVivo, via a deductive codification approach proposed by Mayring [26]. Data triangulation is granted through confirming cross-checking answers against either statement of other interviewees or findings from the literature [27][2].

This research has natural limitations with regard to its research design. Primarily, the finding of appropriate experts can limit the findings of the study to the extent that either not the most applicable experts might have been identified or that specific experts did not confirm to participate in the research [28]. In particular, it was more challenging to

---

[1] For a better understanding, see: 22. Licht, N.: Insights into Internet Voting: Adoption Stages, Drivers & Barriers, and the Possible Impact of COVID-19. Ragnar Nurkse Department of Innovation and Governance. Tallinn University of Technology (2021).

[2] The empirical findings will be cited as in-text citations with the interview number in brackets, in the following format: e.g., single citation (1), multiple citations (1;2; 3…).

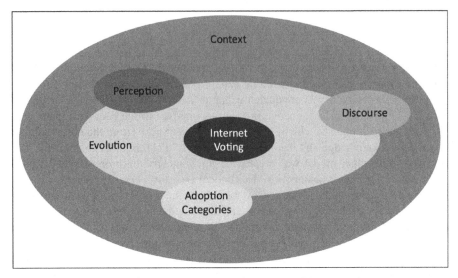

Fig. 1. Framework of Internet Voting

achieve an even distribution among gender and geographics. Also, during the interview process, issues may arise, mainly due to the lack of testing the human language, which may cause ambiguity and hence distort the originally intended meaning of words by the expert. Furthermore, qualitative research as such, as to their lack of generalizability as it would be the case in quantitative research [29].

3   Analysis and Discussion of Drivers and Barriers

Given the dual nature of the process of adoption of technology we divide the information obtained from the expert interviews as well as the desk research in two main framing contexts, on the one hand, the context referring to the Political and Socioeconomic situation and, on the other hand, the Technological one.

3.1   Political and Socio-economic Context Dimension

In line with the theory, the context is very influential in the establishment of election systems [30]. The findings further resemble the supporting framework and can be divided into social, economic, cultural/historical, political, organizational, legal and procedural elements.

Civil Society
The different processes of construction of a society favor or disfavor the discussion, critique, and proposition of i-voting technology. A more diverse society consisting of academia, civil society organizations (CSO) and experts, enable a more varied discourse about i-voting and can be either driving or impeding diffusion. These groups are drivers if they, for example, promote the inclusion of excluded voter groups through i-voting or

might be barriers if they voice security or transparency concerns. Furthermore, regions with a high number of IT-related content creation and the communication thereof, due to strong CSOs and expert groups, are somewhat reticent to adopting new voting technologies as they have stronger groups driving the discourse around the risks (5;8;10;13&14). However, the presence of solid lobby groups within society, fighting for the rights of visually impaired persons and expatriate voters, have been, on the other hand, identified as strong drivers for internet voting adoption on the political level (7;9;10;11&15).

Vendors

Also, the lack of expert communities and hence a lack of expertise within society tends to make these contexts more susceptible to be targeted by vendors. High-level lobbyism by vendors is very effective when no counterparties contribute to expertise to the debate (2;8). Technology in elections is considered because of the commercial implications and strong lobbying efforts by vendors that persuade governments to adopt new technologies in their elections (1;2). One of the interviewees (1) specifically mentioned the push of the commercial drive and its implications for voting technology adoption. Moreover, contexts with less regulated procurement methods, and the lack of civil opposition that is run by non-governmental actors, who are knowledgeable in that field, tend to faster purchase new voting technologies (NVTs) and in less sustainable way (1;2). Academia and expert groups have been identified as vital stakeholders in the adoption discussion due to their ability to aid in overcoming suspicions or doubts through investigating challenges, proposing solutions and creating prototypes (5;14).

Economic Situation

Internet voting systems (IVS) and the respective infrastructure that is necessary to promote i-voting can be very costly in short-term consideration, not only in terms of purchasing but also maintenance of an IVS (4;6;16). From a long-term perspective, the associated costs per vote via IVS are remarkably lower than conventional votes and some cases have considered internet voting for the reason of cost reduction (1;4;11) [31, 32]. However, most cases that have introduced i-voting still provide traditional paper voting, i.e., postal voting, as an alternative option to prevent vote coercion, which in fact adds additional costs (2;6).

Culture and History

Our findings suggest the existence of differences in the interpretation of vote secrecy and universal suffrage depending on the cultural context, which influences the perception of IVS (6). In more detail we observed that a relatively relaxed understanding of secrecy and a strong approach towards universal access might lead to enhanced i-voting efforts. On the contrary, where a particular emphasis on secrecy is present, further i-voting diffusion might be rejected if not enough proof is given via universal verifiability of how a vote is cast, counted and kept secret. Last, an increased emphasis on universal suffrage, and therefore, a strong focus on the inclusion of diaspora voters or visually impaired people might lead to higher IVS uptake (6;15).

Elections are, in some contexts, seen as a community-based exercise in which the electorate follows their duty to go and vote. That exercise might be perceived as an act of physically convening and voicing one's opinion and would culturally not accept to replace that with technology (5). This case does not describe the opposition of technology per se but the predominant proposition of tradition (3;6). Regarding historical influences, our interviews conclude that post-crisis situations or the newly gained independence of regions impact the creation of new voting systems (1). Often, the act of removing old election systems is an act of trust-building and demonstration of recent ruling in which NVTs are perceived as neutral third party that politicians and administrations have no influence over (1;3;5).

Political Context

In nearly all interviews, the political will was identified as both a powerful driver as well as a strong barrier. First, governments use i-voting technology as political agenda to demonstrate modernity and progress in their political activity (17). Some contexts have attributed electoral affairs to a ministry and restructuring the state alongside the electoral system is used for political campaigning purposes (2;18). In essence, political actors aim to appear progressive and modern and wish to use tools like IVS to prove also tech-savviness (18). Significant technological developments can be traced back to politically motivated events and decisions. If technology is perceived to be beneficial for the incumbent party, it is promoted; if not, the same party may become the greatest opponent to NVT development (1;2;3;5;10;15). This observation, also known as the "middleman paradox", refers to the phenomenon that incumbents resist the move towards e-democracy because they perceive that the altered election system might lead to a decrease of their own political power and control [33]. In line with further evidence, change of government was named to be another influential factor. Two scenarios were identified which have been concrete barriers to IVS diffusions: 1) the election of a new governing party, also ascribable to the middleman paradox (6;14); and 2) a civil conflict in which the transformation of the election system is put on halt (2). Regarding the first scenario: If certain political actors identify that their electorate is opposing the idea of i-voting and that their competitor might benefit from online voting more than they expect to do, evidence shows that this actor tends to discontinue i-voting for purely political reasons [34] (6;11;14). Furthermore, the findings show that i-voting is a highly sensitive subject with attached political risks, associated costs and resources needed; therefore, unless a concrete need requires it, governments tend to refrain from touching that subject (4;6;11;14;15).

The second dimension refers to accessibility and universal suffrage, which have been identified to be among the strongest general drivers for i-voting adoption. Accessibility refers to the idea that "people with disabilities should be able to use all public spaces and services in the same way as other people" [35]. Online voting can enfranchise disabled people as they can more easily register and authenticate themselves and cast their vote from their home (3;7;9;10;15). The provision of universal suffrage identified by the OSCE [36] entails, further, the idea to integrate the entire electorate into the elections. Universal suffrage can be interpreted in different ways, and countries, as well as semi-autonomous regions, have been considering for a significant part to introduce i-voting because of their aspiration to include overseas or territorially challenged voters into their elections more efficiently. Nearly all conducted interviews mentioned the aspect of voting provision for the diaspora, overseas diplomats, consular staff, general populations in extreme territorial conditions or overseas soldiers. Essentially, the intrinsic motivation is political and only promoted if the incumbent expects to gain from including these groups of voters, as sometimes the diaspora consists of political opponents and hence its exclusion from electoral matters is deliberate (5;6;8;9;10;18). Another impact of diaspora voters concerns their foreign impact through campaign donations and exercising of their often-strong socioeconomic status and power on domestic political debate (2).

Organizational Context
Another element to mention is, that as populations increase and administrative capacities need to be restructured to enable higher procedural efficiency, new technologies allow better election management and further ease electoral processes, especially regarding cumbersome remote voting processes such as postal voting (4;5;8;15;16). And yet, from the study, it is clear that voter coercion and vote-buying in remote and uncontrolled election environments still remain to endanger the integrity of elections, and for that, specific contexts that initially have seen technology as a practical solution refrain from particularly adopting i-voting (4). Also, the context's set-up, procedural traditions and hurdles as well as the degree of digital governance and the understanding of digital services play a substantial role in driving i-voting adoption due to the spill-over effect that tends to occur in digital ecosystems (2;7;9;14;17).

Legal Context
The obtained results present evidence that legal frameworks need to be established for an effective i-voting introduction (14;16). Passing appropriate legislation, however, tends to be rather difficult because the law is rigid in nature, and ICT is relatively flexible and needs to be evaluated regularly. Law, once passed, will remain as a reference text for future considerations and cannot simply be changed on demand (14). Specific contexts experience the already written law to be a barrier, and lawmakers would need to pursue passing actively or amending the law, which allows for IVS considerations.

Furthermore, empirical data shows that law is subject to interpretation and that certain regions may therefore understand the legal text differently and hence court interpretations can be essential in the development of IVS (6;7;8). Cases were identified in which important court decisions prevented further NVT adoption and influenced third parties not to adopt (6;8), or judgements existed that paved the way for i-voting to be adopted (15). In the interviews, it was further identified that there is a lack of a general legal and technical framework/design that describes and defines the appropriated provisions of i-voting systems. This lack becomes a barrier because the standard according to which a potentially suitable system would be compared against does not exist, and hence the debate is less structured (9;10;11). The other scenario was described that a legal framework exists, but it is impossible to comply with the requirements, and it makes it merely impossible to proceed with i-voting development (9).

3.2 Technological Context Dimension

The following issue concerning technology and security features mainly concern the adoption process on the pollical level but is influenced by the narratives and discourses on the individual level. Although, during the interviews, it was mentioned that various technology designs exist, we generically refer to 'the technology' as such in order to enable a more holistic discussion. Besides the existing technological capabilities to host and conduct elections using i-voting, a threshold for many countries in terms of technology and security is the concrete definition of what technology should be used for the elections in form of a concrete framework (10;14). Furthermore, certain contexts lack respective experts that know how the systems work and that are able to provide the right guidance for it to be successfully implemented (11;13). Hence, a legal framework could also become a barrier, not just a facilitator for sustainable implementation. Legal frameworks can be worded in various ways, promoting or demoting the usage of remote online voting components (9).

Furthermore, technology is considered so complex that most citizens tend not to understand how the vote is being cast, counted, kept secret and how they can verify that their vote was counted as intended (3;16). Therefore, it is technically possible but often not viable to exchange a functioning system that is operating with paper (e.g. postal voting) with a new system that needs to provide transparency, secrecy and integrity proof to all stakeholders. Hence, the complex nature, in cases, is seen to be a barrier (1). It is, moreover, important to differentiate hereby between full-scale adoption and partial adoption. In contexts of partial adoption, technical failures and security breaches seem less concerning than if they were to occur in full-scale adoption contexts. Therefore, imposing the task of expanding with i-voting diffusion is a more complex endeavor than offering it for a share of the eligible electorate (2;15).

One of the biggest challenges from the technology side is to provide either individual or universal verifiability (1). The technical abilities exist to provide these features in a reliable way, but need to be acknowledged by the decision-making party in order to be fully useful (10). Although the demand for such verifiability feature to be present in the election system has increased, barely any state legislator has acknowledged and integrated such features into their requirements which can be both a barrier as well as a driver (14). On the one hand, it facilitates eased implementation efforts as they need to meet fewer requirements. On the other hand, the system is also more vulnerable to criticism of transparency and integrity.

Furthermore, internet voting does require not only the technology but also the infrastructure that would facilitate the execution of the election. Such infrastructure would be broadband networks with high penetration rates, especially in remote areas. If no internet access exists in remote areas, there is no utility gain from adopting IVS for the purpose of including remote areas better into elections (5;16;18). The mentioned issue is subject to the geographical context and is related to the digital divide, which is a term used to describe the gap between contexts that benefit from digital technology and those who do not [37]. The empirical findings suggest that the digital divide, which had been more so visible in the early 2000s, was a barrier to many non-Western contexts (4;16) [38–40].

Hence, these findings suggest that while none sufficient ICT infrastructure seemed to have been a barrier for IVS in non-Western contexts, the increase in broadband penetration with the beginning of the second decade drove IVS development to see the first advent of IVS cases in non-Western contexts [38]. Still, the digital divide remains to exist and further is a barrier to IVS development in certain regions (16;18) [41]. The following section analyzes and discusses the perception and discourse dimension.

3.3 Perception and Discourse Dimension

One of the major findings from the interviews in terms of perception is regarding the issue of trust. Although trust is hard to measure and still subject to ongoing academic investigations, certain parameters could have been identified. The public perception is mostly referring to the drivers and barriers that impact the diffusion that occurs on the individual level after the political decision has been made to introduce IVS in society.

The findings support the assumption that election systems are as much trustworthy as the people who erected and proposed them. Hence, if people mistrust the government and or EMBs who implement IVS, they tend to mistrust the technology (5). Furthermore, regardless of the previous trust given to one election system, it is not granted that this trust is simply transferable to any novel election system. On the contrary, it seems that strong trust in EMBs in primarily Western democracies might be one of the bigger barriers to i-voting adoption as the primary assumption is to question whether new technology is necessary and simultaneously to endanger a well working system (1;10;14). This may be further supported by the concept of path dependency, which states that individuals would decide to trust and use a system based on previous experiences, decisions and preferences that they made [42, 43]. That phenomenon exists along with all fields of social spheres and might certainly affect the choice of usage of election systems.

Internet voting technology requires a great amount of trust from the electorate since its technological setup is relatively complex, and very few experts do understand the system entirely (1). Whether one may trust in one particular aspect or not is rather incoherent with objective measurements. Regardless of objectively measured and relatable evidence that would suggest that appropriate i-voting technology exists, many cases experience one of the biggest barriers to be the lack of trust (1;3;5;11;14). Additionally, objectivity and trust tend to be fragmented by public discourse and the strong presence of social media that influences public opinion on electoral matters [44]. Moreover, specific expert groups and CSOs have made it their duty to detect and inform about vulnerabilities in i-voting systems particularly, since the 2016's US presidential election, increased interest in cybersecurity around elections (6;7;9;18). Although public discourse has been identified to be a barrier in many instances, there are also cases in which pressure by CSOs and media on politicians have paved the way for the introduction of IVS (15).

Although certain risks had been already present in the early 2000s and cyber hacking and lobbyism against the introduction of i-voting existed since the first hour (10), it was, however, on a much smaller scale. In comparison to nowadays, there was less awareness of the entirety of cyber-risks and also less internet usage penetration in general (6) which can nowadays be seen as a barrier to further diffusion. The perception of technology its potentials and risks has shifted. Common cyber threats and dangers have been put more in focus around the discussion for i-voting introduction than it was the case in the early 2000s. That is mostly due to the fact that the technology was relatively novel and less experimented with than it is nowadays. Hence, more threat and risk awareness exist as common knowledge in the electorate, and hence success stories back then might not be as successful today (6;7).

Since i-voting technology is to a degree somewhat intangible for the large share of people, i-voting demonstrations are used to build trust in the system (1;10;14). Including rhetoric and competence demonstration seem to be useful in convincing the electorate about the system, as suggested by the findings. These demonstrations can be of bureaucratic nature, in which the focus is rather on the institutions and has been proven to be successful in contexts in which a history of malfunctioning of institutions exists. In a context in which previously technical failures in election systems had occurred, trust-building via technology demonstrations have proven to be successful (14). Perception, then, may be impacted by security breaches and technical failures. The identified cases in which that occurred show different results for the degree of usage (6;7;14). Hereby, a necessary differentiation has to be made between the roles that academia or CSOs play and the media. These stewards of discourse certainly have identified to be impacting the diffusion process and certainly media on the individual diffusion level. However, more data is needed to look into the issue impact of trust in election systems as a result of technical failures.

From the empirical findings, we identified the drivers for the political decision level, to be universal access and accessibility for disabled voters, the pursuit of a contactless democracy, they wish to appear modern, the vendor's push, the process improvements, the perception of technology to be a neutral third party, the perception of increased administrative integrity, cost reductions, strong lobby groups, expected increase in voter turnouts and the presence of high socioeconomic power and well-established technical infrastructure. On the individual adoption level, we presented evidence that drivers exist such as convenience voting, spill-over effects within a digital society and the socioeconomic status of voters. Following barriers were identified for the political level adoption process: the middleman paradox, political crisis, change of government, security concerns, theoretical technical vulnerabilities, strong opposition from CSOs and academia, lack of a framework, lack of technological infrastructure, lack of verifiability, procedural barriers and the change of legal requirements. Barriers to adoption on the individual level have been identified as path dependency, cultural traditions, mistrust in technology and mistrust in EMBs and governments (Tables 1 and 2).

Table 1. Overview of the Drivers of Internet Voting

Drivers
Political level
Universal access (Expatriate & overseas staff voting, voting in territorially challenging locations)
Accessibility
The political will to appear modern and innovative
Contactless democracy
Vendor's commercial drive
Increase turnout/prevent further decline
Strong lobby groups

(continued)

Table 1. (*continued*)

Drivers
Perception of technology as neutral third party
Cost reductions
Process improvements
Integrity improvements in administrative operations
Socioeconomic status and high technological infrastructure (geographics)
Individual level
Convenience voting
Spill-over effect within already digitised societies and their ecosystem
Socioeconomic status of the voter

Table 2. Overview on the Barriers of Internet Voting

Barriers
Political level
Middleman Paradox
Political crisis
Change of government (related to middleman paradox)
Security concerns
Theoretical technical vulnerabilities
Strong opposition from academia & CSOs
Lack of a framework
Lack of technological infrastructure/Digital divide
Lack of verifiability
Procedural barriers
Change of legal requirements
Individual level
Path dependency
Cultural traditions
Mistrust in technology
Mistrust in government and EMBs

4   Conclusion

In order to answer the question on what drivers and barriers exist that prevent further internet voting diffusion, subsequently, the discussion occurs first on the political level and then on the individual level.

The driving or lobbying stakeholders on the political decision level, are the diaspora, territorially challenged voters or disabled voters which resemble the described relevant social groups. Further the groups lobbying for these relevant social groups on the political level and hence driving stakeholders as for example lobby groups, academia, CSOs or vendors have a resemblance to the change agents and opinion leaders identified in the conceptual model. Further findings suggest that the political will is a major driver for i-voting adoption on the political level as to prevent decreasing voter turnouts or the urgency to provide an appropriate election system for the context of an evolving contactless democracy or to appear modern through the introduction of NVTs. Last, the degree of the socioeconomic status, influences whether the political level even considers the move towards NVTs to be feasible or not.

On the individual adoption level, although, the aspect of convenience voting is still under further academic investigation, the empirical findings suggest that the proposed theory of relative utility in regard to effort can be confirmed for the individual level. Furthermore, the findings have also identified that, although an early interest might exist for i-voting, individuals tend to not maintain that interest if they experience no further usage of the infrastructure than for merely voting online from time to time. In the case of Estonia, this steady interest was achieved through the wider usage avenues of the e-ID for bank transactions for example [45]. In contrast, the Austrian case failed to mobilize enough supporters for its online voting systems because it had no further utility to its voters than to vote [4]. Ergo, a wider-context deployment of ICT technology and the practicality of a digital ecosystem might create a spill-over effect and hence drive i-voting technology for the technology acceptance on the individual level.

From the finding, a central part that impedes further global i-voting adoption has been the middleman paradox. This is a central barrier for many regions as the first adoption decision is made on the political level and later transferred to the individual level. However, the fear of losing one's own power that could only be bypassed if an urgent need for the election reform would appear, impedes further i-voting in many contexts around the world. Further contextual barriers were identified to be security concerns, lack of verifiability and theoretical vulnerabilities. Moreover, mistrust and in combination with public discourse are opposing forces to the development of NVTs as CSOs, academia and expert groups in many cases actively oppose the idea of i-voting implementation due to security and verifiability concerns. Their ability to provide expertise, facilitate communication, to have access to prototypes and further resources such as data and expert knowledge makes them to effective change agents and opinion leaders that frequently lobby against IVS diffusion.

A particular barriers to adoption on the individual level has identified to be path dependency [43, 46]. It being a purely social issue, cultural norms and values amplify the problem of path dependency and confirm the cultural explanation for why technology is adopted. The social construction of society and perception of technology are decisive in explaining adoption and would be confirmed by the issue of path-dependency. Mistrust in technology is strongly depending on perception and consists of the fear that the technology might not be secure, which mostly is related to the fact that the technology is too complex for the average person to understand fully. Furthermore, the mistrust might also exist towards the decision-makers generally, and therefore the technology might not be accepted.

In conclusion, the research question can be answered through the depicted evidence showing that in total, 15 drivers, 12 on the political and three on the individual level and 15 barriers, with 11 on the political and four on the individual level, have been identified. Strong driving and impeding forces alike were found on the political level to be the absence or presence of political will, necessity and the so-called middleman paradox. Even if the list of drivers and barriers is balanced, the reality shows that the implication of them is not following the same pattern, since the reduced number of adopters of i-voting brings to the conclusion that barriers play a more important role in the process of adoption than drivers. Further detailed case studies in selected countries could shed new light on how these drivers and barriers interact in particular administrative and political contexts and bring to the final decision of implementing or not i-voting. Additional research would be necessary in the field of trust in elections and specifically in election technology as well as the respective roles attributed to building or harming trust through the two discourse drivers that are academia or CSOs and on the other side the media. From the interviews it became apparent that these groups another study is merited but in which their roles especially in the individual diffusion process is further investigated. Possible questions to consider could be how can trust be measured and how can trust-building of new voting technologies be formed and what roles do media and academia play in that process? Last, in order to understand how various contexts, deal with electoral crises and why certain regions stopped their internet voting, while others remain to deploy IVS in their elections, a follow-up study on Estonia's foreign cyber interference, France's discontinuation in 2017 and Norway's case of their technical vulnerabilities may be appropriate. In this proposed study, it would be sensible to look at the positioning of academia and CSOs and the reasons why that may be the case and under what circumstances that might change and impact the adoption and diffusion of internet voting. In summary, internet voting has been around for more than two decades and identified to be a logical tool for democracy and yet lacks large-scale adoption. In this paper we analyzed and presented general drivers and barriers that impact the adoption and diffusion process and illustrated further research areas that merit further investigation. Internet voting, being a process in a political process is also highly impacted by political factors itself and therefore significant qualitative differences between the respective drivers and barriers for the respective contexts might exist.

Acknowledgements. This work received support from mGov4EU and eceps grants - 857622 and 959072 and, in the case of Dr. David Duenas-Cid, also from Polish National Research Center grant (Miniatura 3 - 2019/03/X/HS6/01688 "Zaufanie do technologii w e-administracji: Powtórna analiza nieudanego wdrożenia elektronicznych maszyn do głosowania w Holandii (2006–07)".

References

1. Buckminster Fuller, R.: No More Secondhand God and Other Writings. Southern Illinois University Press, Carbondale and Edwardsville (1963)
2. Gates, B., Myhrvold, N., Rinearson, P., Domonkos, D.: The road ahead (1995)
3. Cook, T.: Apple's C.E.O. Is making very different choices from Mark Zuckerberg. In: Swisher, K. (ed.) New York Times (2021)
4. Krimmer, R.: Internet Voting in Austria: History, Development, and Building Blocks for the Future. WU Vienna University of Economics and Business (2017)
5. IDEA. https://www.idea.int/news-media/multimedia-reports/global-overview-covid-19-imp act-elections
6. Krimmer, R., Duenas-Cid, D., Krivonosova, I.: Debate: safeguarding democracy during pandemics. Social distancing, postal, or internet voting—the good, the bad or the ugly? Public Money Manag. **41**, 8–10 (2021)
7. Kersting, N., Baldersheim, H.: Electronic Voting and Democracy: A Comparative Analysis. Springer, Heidelberg (2004). https://doi.org/10.1057/9780230523531
8. Schaupp, L.C., Carter, L.: E-voting: from apathy to adoption. J. Enterp. Inf. Manag. (2005)
9. Krimmer, R.: The evolution of e-voting: why voting technology is used and how it affects democracy. Tallinn University of Technology Doctoral Theses Series I: Social Sciences, no. 19 (2012)
10. Vegas, C., Barrat, J.: Overview of current state of E-voting worldwide. In: Real-World Electronic Voting: Design, Analysis and Deployment, p. 51 (2016)
11. Risnanto, S., Abd Rahim, Y.B., Herman, N.S., Abdurrohman: E-voting readiness mapping for general election implementation. J. Theor. Appl. Inf. Technol. **98**, 3280–3290 (2020)
12. Gibson, J.P., Krimmer, R., Teague, V., Pomares, J.: A review of e-voting: the past, present and future. Ann. Telecommun. **71**, 279–286 (2016). https://doi.org/10.1007/s12243-016-0525-8
13. Krimmer, R., Triessnig, S., Volkamer, M.: The development of remote e-voting around the world: A review of roads and directions. In: Alkassar, A., Volkamer, M. (eds.) E-Voting and Identity. LNCS, vol. 4896, pp. 1–15. Springer, Heidelberg (2007). https://doi.org/10.1007/978-3-540-77493-8_1
14. ACE - The Electoral Knowledge Network. http://aceproject.org/ace-en/focus/e-voting/countr ies/mobile_browsing/onePag
15. Khutkyy, D.: Policy paper Internet Voting: Challenges and Solutions. European Digital Development Alliance (2020)
16. Górny, M.: I-voting–opportunities and threats. Conditions for the effective implementation of Internet voting on the example of Switzerland and Estonia. Przegląd Politologiczny, pp. 133–146 (2021)
17. Vassil, K., Solvak, M., Vinkel, P., Trechsel, A.H., Alvarez, R.M.: The diffusion of internet voting. Usage patterns of internet voting in Estonia between 2005 and 2015. Gov. Inf. Q. **33**, 453–459 (2016)
18. Vinkel, P., Krimmer, R.: The how and why to internet voting an attempt to explain E-Stonia. In: Krimmer, R., et al. (eds.) E-Vote-ID 2016. LNCS, vol. 10141, pp. 178–191. Springer, Cham (2017). https://doi.org/10.1007/978-3-319-52240-1_11
19. Anonymous: Anonymous. In: International Joint Conference on Electronic Voting. Springer (Year)
20. Brown, M., Hale, K.: Applied Research Methods in Public and Nonprofit Organizations. Wiley, Hoboken (2014)
21. Ormston, R., Spencer, L., Barnard, M., Snape, D.: The foundations of qualitative research. In: Qualitative Research Practice: A Guide for Social Science Students and Researchers, no. 2, pp. 52–55 (2014)

22. Licht, N.: Insights into Internet Voting: Adoption Stages, Drivers & Barriers, and the Possible Impact of COVID-19. Ragnar Nurkse Department of Innovation and Governance. Tallinn University of Technology (2021)
23. Pinch, T.J., Bijker, W.E.: The social construction of facts and artefacts: or how the sociology of science and the sociology of technology might benefit each other. Soc. Stud. Sci. **14**, 399–441 (1984)
24. Rogers, E.: Diffusion of Innovation, 5th edn. Free Press, New York (2003)
25. Venkatesh, V., Morris, M.G., Davis, G.B., Davis, F.D.: User acceptance of information technology: toward a unified view. MIS Q. **27**, 425–478 (2003)
26. Mayring, P.: Qualitative content analysis: theoretical foundation, basic procedures and software solution (2014)
27. Flick, U.: Triangulation - Eine Einführung VS Verlag (2008)
28. Flick, U.: An Introduction to Qualitative Research. SAGE, Hamburg (2014)
29. Ochieng, P.: An analysis of the strengths and limitation of qualitative and quantitative research paradigms. Probl. Educ. 21st Century **13**, 13 (2009)
30. Derichs, C., Heberer, T.: Wahlsysteme und Wahltypen: politische Systeme und regionale Kontexte im Vergleich. Springer, Heidelberg (2007)
31. Krimmer, R., Duenas-Cid, D., Krivonosova, I.: New methodology for calculating cost-efficiency of different ways of voting: is internet voting cheaper? Public Money Manag. **41**, 17–26 (2021)
32. Krimmer, R., Duenas-Cid, D., Krivonosova, I., Vinkel, P., Koitmae, A.: How much does an e-Vote cost? Cost comparison per vote in multichannel elections in Estonia. In: Krimmer, R., et al. (eds.) Electronic Voting. LNCS, vol. 11143, pp. 117–131. Springer, Cham (2018). https://doi.org/10.1007/978-3-030-00419-4_8
33. Mahrer, H., Krimmer, R.: Towards the enhancement of e-democracy: identifying the notion of the 'middleman paradox.' Inf. Syst. J. **15**, 27–42 (2005)
34. Postimees. Tallinn. http://s3-eu-west-1.amazonaws.com/pdf.station.ee/epl/epl/2020/11/17/p2.pdf?AWSAccessKeyId=AKIAJMCAZLEYS3TMYI7Q&Expires=1619606705&Signature=5yLZkaC0Jyt2IOGQ6E2NrzA7oS8%3D
35. OSCE/ODIHR: A Booklet about: Watching Elections and Helping People with Disabilities take part in Elections. OSCE/ODIHR, Warsaw (2017)
36. OSCE: Document of the Copenhagen Meeting of the Conference on the Human Dimension of CSCE. In: OSCE (ed.) OSCE, Copenhagen (1990)
37. Hilbert, M.: The end justifies the definition: the manifold outlooks on the digital divide and their practical usefulness for policy-making. Telecommun. Policy **35**, 715–736 (2011)
38. Ronquillo, C., Currie, L.: The digital divide: Trends in global mobile and broadband Internet access from 2000–2010. In: Nursing Informatics: Proceedings of the International Congress on Nursing Informatics, vol. 2012, p. 346 (2012)
39. UNCTAD: The Digital Divide Report: ICT Diffusion Index 2005. United Nations (2005)
40. Norris, P.: Digital Divide: Civic Engagement, Information Poverty, and the Internet World-wide. Cambridge University Press, Cambridge (2001)
41. https://cipesa.org/2021/03/south-africas-parliament-rejects-plan-to-introduce-e-voting/
42. Investopedia. https://www.investopedia.com/terms/p/path-dependency.asp
43. David, P.A.: Clio and the economics of QWERTY. Am. Econ. Rev. **75**, 332–337 (1985)
44. Krimmer, R., Rabitsch, A., Kuzel, R.O., Achler, M., Licht, N.: Elections & Internet, Social Media and Artificial Intelligence (AI): A Guide for Electoral Practitioners. UNESCO (2021, forthcoming)
45. Martens, T.: Electronic identity management in Estonia between market and state governance. Identity Inf. Soc. **3**, 213–233 (2010)
46. Gross, R., Hanna, R.: Path dependency in provision of domestic heating. Nat. Energy **4**, 358–364 (2019)

Who Was that Masked Voter? The Tally Won't Tell!

Peter Y. A. Ryan[1]($\boxtimes$)(iD), Peter B. Roenne[1]($\boxtimes$)(iD), Dimiter Ostrev[1]($\boxtimes$)(iD),
Fatima-Ezzahra El Orche[1,3]($\boxtimes$), Najmeh Soroush[1]($\boxtimes$)(iD),
and Philip B. Stark[2]($\boxtimes$)(iD)

[1] Interdisciplinary Centre for Security, Reliability, and Trust, SnT,
University of Luxembourg, Luxembourg City, Luxembourg
{peter.ryan,peter.roenne,dimiter.ostrev,fatimaezzahra.elorche,
najmeh.soroush}@uni.lu
[2] Department of Statistics, University of California, Berkeley, CA, USA
stark@stat.berkeley.edu
[3] ENS, CNRS, PSL Research University, Paris, France
fatimaezzahra.elorche@ens.fr

Abstract. We consider elections that publish anonymised voted ballots or anonymised cast-vote records for transparency or verification purposes, investigating the implications for privacy, coercion, and vote selling and exploring how partially masking the ballots can alleviate these issues.

Risk Limiting Tallies (RLT), which reveal only a random sample of ballots, were previously proposed to mitigate some coercion threats. Masking some ballots provides coerced voters with plausible deniability, while risk-limiting techniques ensure that the required confidence level in the election result is achieved. Risk-Limiting Verification (RLV) extended this approach to masking a random subset of receipts or trackers.

Here we show how these ideas can be generalised and made more flexible and effective by masking at a finer level of granularity: at the level of the components of ballots. In particular, we consider elections involving complex ballots, where RLT may be vulnerable to pattern-based vote buying. We propose various measures of verifiability and coercion-resistance and investigate how several sampling/masking strategies perform against these measures. Using methods from coding theory, we analyse signature attacks, bounding the number of voters who can be coerced. We also define new quantitative measures for the level of coercion-resistance without plausible deniability and the level of vote-buying-resistance without "free lunch" vote sellers.

These results and the different strategies for masking ballots are of general interest for elections that publish ballots for auditing, verification, or transparency purposes.

1 Introduction

Some voting systems, including many end-to-end verifiable systems and some conventional elections, publish the (plaintext) ballots. If these ballots are suitably

© Springer Nature Switzerland AG 2021
R. Krimmer et al. (Eds.): E-Vote-ID 2021, LNCS 12900, pp. 106–123, 2021.
https://doi.org/10.1007/978-3-030-86942-7_8

anonymised, by for example verifiable mixes published on a bulletin board, then this is typically quite safe. But in some contexts, revealing such information may be problematic: certain corner cases, such as unanimous votes or absence of any votes for a candidate and coercion threats, such as signature attacks.

In [4] the idea of Risk-Limiting Tallies (RLT) and Risk-Limiting Verification (RLV) was proposed to mitigate such threats. The idea is to shroud a proportion of the (anonymised) votes so voters can plausibly claim to have complied with the coercer, even though no votes appear for the candidate demanded by the coercer or no ballot with the pattern demanded by the coercer shows up in the tally. The proportion left shrouded can be adjusted using risk-limiting techniques to ensure that the confidence in the announced outcome achieves the required threshold, e.g., 99%. The idea extends to the verification aspects: shrouding some proportion of receipts or trackers. This proves particularly effective in for example the Selene scheme to counter the "sting in the tail": the coercer claiming that the voter's fake tracker is his own.

In this paper we note that, despite the pleasing features of the constructions of [4] there are still some drawbacks, in particular if the ballots are rather complex. While RLT may disincentivize *coercion*, there may still be an incentive for *vote buying*: the voter might still cast the required pattern vote in the hope that it will be revealed. Further, it has been suggested that RLT is arguably undemocratic in that some voters' ballots do not contribute to the final tally. The second objection can be countered by arguing that every vote has an equal probability of being included in the count and that the outcome will be, with whatever confidence level required, a correct reflection of all votes cast. Nonetheless, it is an aspect that some people find troubling. A pleasing side effect of our construction is that all ballots are treated on an equal footing.

These observations suggest exploring different ways to apply RLT and RLV when ballots are complex: rather than shrouding entire ballots at random, we shroud, at random, some preferences on each ballot. In effect we are filtering the tally horizontally rather than vertically. This hits both of the issues above: the chance any given pattern remains identifiable after the filtering is reduced, and every ballot contributes to the outcome, albeit not necessarily to every contest. In the *full tally* construction below, every ballot contributes fully to the announced outcome, but we shroud the link between the tracker and some components of the ballots. For tracker-based schemes, the voters can verify some but not all of their selections. This paper seeks to quantify these effects and explore trade-offs among them.

Our techniques allow us to state and prove bounds on the number of voters an adversary is able to attack using pattern-based or "signature" attacks. Note that assigning the same, or similar, complex ballot pattern to many voters is counterproductive for the adversary: if even a few voters comply, the rest can point to the signature ballots that already appear and claim compliance. Thus, an adversary who wants to influence many voters with a signature attack must be able to produce many distinguishable ballot patterns. This observation motivates us to prove lower and upper bounds on the number of distinguishable patterns an adversary can construct. We prove these bounds using a connection to a well-studied problem in the theory of error-correcting codes.

This ballot-masking method and its privacy implications are interesting not only in for RLT and RLV but for all schemes where all or some ballots are published for auditing, verification, or transparency. As an example, Colorado is currently redacting cast-vote records (CVRs) by removing entire CVRs, e.g., for rare ballot styles; partial masking has been considered as an alternative. We note, however, that masking parts of the ballot might make it hard to detect ill-formed, e.g., over-votes etc.

We also note that this idea has similarities to the SOBA constructions for Risk-Limiting-Audits (RLAs), [1], which also publishes each audited ballot "disassembled" into different contests, whereas the auditors will see the intact ballot. The VAULT approach [2] also uses homomorphic encryption of the cast-vote records to achieve the SOBA goals more easily. (VAULT was used for the first time in a risk-limiting audit in Inyo County, California, in 2020.) The purpose and the underlying cryptographic constructions are quite different, but our analysis applies to these cases as well.

For some tally algorithms, we can separate ballots into their atomic parts and reveal these independently after anonymising them, which effectively counters signature attacks. However, that reduces public transparency and may reduce public confidence in the election result. For Selene, where voters verify their votes via trackers, this separation provides a method to verify without revealing individual ballots: we simply assign a distinct tracker to each element of the ballot. Voters can then verify some or all components of their ballot using those trackers. A coerced voter could use the Selene tracker-faking mechanism to assemble a ballot that matches the coercer's instructions. Technically this is straightforward but from a usability standpoint seems problematic. Moreover, even if the voter were prepared to go the effort of concocting such a fake ballot, the necessary ingredients might not be available, so coercion threats will remain, and the probability that one of atomic trackers is the same as the coercer's increases. Thus it makes sense to look for alternatives.

Below, we present the main ideas and analyse differences in privacy, coercion-resistance, and receipt-freeness for the different methods. Section 2 introduces the idea of partially masking ballots. Section 3 describes how it can be used in masked RLT and RLV. Section 4 defines a distinguishing distance between randomly masked ballots, establishes a connection to the Hamming distance, characterizes the class of masking strategies for which this connection holds, and proves bounds on the number of voters that can be approached with a pattern-based attack. It provides another application of the distinguishing distance: to quantify the effect of masking on individual verifiability. Section 5 considers quantitative game-based notions of privacy, coercion-resistance, and receipt-freeness. Section 6 concludes.

2   Masking Complex Ballots

Many elections use simple plurality voting: the voter selects at most one candidate from a set, in the simplest case, a referendum, a choice between "yes" and "no." The next level of complexity is single-winner plurality, aka "first past the post." More complex social choice functions and correspondingly more complex ballots are common. Perhaps the next level in complexity are *approval voting* in which the voter can cast votes for several candidates for a single office, and multi-winner plurality, in which a voter can vote for up to k candidates for k offices. In some cases voters may have a quota of votes and is allowed to cast more than one vote for a given candidate, up to some limit. Some methods allow voters to give a preference ranking to the candidates.

Common to all of these social choice functions, if the ballots are published, is that they are vulnerable to signature attacks (also known as "Italian" attacks), i.e. a coercer chooses a particular, unlikely, pattern, instructs the victim to mark a ballot with that pattern and checks whether a ballot with that pattern appears in the tally.

Let us assume that the ballots are of the form $(v_1, v_2, \ldots, v_k)$ with k the number of candidates and v_i taking values from a specified set $\mathcal{V}$. $\mathcal{V}$ might for example just be $\{0, 1\}$ or a set of integers plus a blank: $\{1, \ldots, s\} \bigcup \{\text{blank}\}$ etc.

In many types of elections, these ballot-level selections, or subsets thereof, will reappear as part of the tally procedure (e.g. in electronic mixnet tallies), as part of an audit trail or for transparency (electronic scans of paper ballots), in Risk-Limiting Audits using samples of votes, or verification procedures (e.g. in tracker-based schemes such as Selene). In order to preserve privacy, the mapping between the published votes and the voter is normally anonymised.

As mentioned above, revealing these ballots may endanger the receipt-freeness of the election. With *Masked Tallies*, introduced here, only parts of each ballot are revealed:

$$(\text{mask}_{i1}(v_1^{(i)}), \text{mask}_{i2}(v_2^{(i)}), \ldots, \text{mask}_{ik}(v_k^{(i)})) \quad \text{for } i = 1, \ldots, n.$$

The functions mask_{ij} are either the identity, displaying the component of the vote, or a constant, e.g. $*$ $(\notin \mathcal{V})$, masking the component. n is the number of ballots cast.

Risk-Limiting Tallies [4], involved unmasking only as many randomly selected ballots as are needed to determine the election result with a chosen risk limit. The remaining ballots were kept completely masked. Here we suggest a generalization, allowing partial masking of the ballots, and we will discuss the impact on risk limits, privacy, coercion-resistance, and resistance to vote-buying.

3   Partially Masked RLTs and RLVs

We reprise risk-limiting tallies and verification, RLT and RLV [4], before extending these to general masks. First we recapitulate the idea of tracker-based verification in terms of Selene.

Outline of Selene. Selene [8] enables verification by posting the votes in the clear on the BB along with private tracking numbers. Voters are only notified of their tracker some time after the vote/tracker pairs have been publicly posted, giving a coerced voter the opportunity to choose an alternative tracker to placate the coercer. The voter is able to fake the tracker and related cryptographic data using a secret trapdoor key. The notification of the trackers is carefully designed to provide assurance to the voter that it is their correctly assigned tracker, i.e. unique to them, while being deniable to any third party.

Assuming that votes are encrypted component-wise, at the end of the mixing we will have encrypted votes and trackers on the bulletin board:

$$(\{tr_i\}_{PK}, (\{v_1^{(i)}\}_{PK}, \{v_2^{(i)}\}_{PK}, \dots \dots \{v_k^{(i)}\}_{PK}))$$

where $\{\cdot\}_{PK}$ denotes encryption under the public key PK. These ballots can now be verifiably decrypted to reveal the vote/tracker pairs that can be checked by the voters, and anyone can compute the tally directly on the plaintext votes.

Risk-Limiting Tallies and Verification with Partially Masked Ballots. In the original approach to RLT (where ballots are without trackers) and RLV (with trackers for individual verification), see [4], the idea was to only decrypt a random subset of the ballots. The number decrypted being controlled by a risk-limit that bounds the probability that the announced election result will be wrong.

In the new masked RLV and RLT approach, we instead reveal randomly selected components of the ballots (and the trackers for RLV). If there is more than one contest on the ballot, the contests can be treated independently. How much we reveal will again be governed by a specified risk limit, as in [4]. A natural choice is to first decrypt m of the k entries in each ballot at random, and to increase m if necessary to meet the risk limit. This is simplest and will be used in the analysis below. In practice, it may make sense to dynamically change the rate of openings per candidate, e.g. if a candidate is popular we might be able to decrease the rate of unmasking of votes for that candidate, maintaining the risk limit while improving coercion-resistance.

Using this masked approach for RLV with tracker verification, the masking means that only parts of the ballot can be verified, but unlike to the original RLV every voter can verify *something*. We will quantify how much.

Full Tally with Partial Verification (FTPV). A social choice function is *separable* if, for the purposes of tallying, the components of each vote can be considered separately. Plurality, approval, and Borda count are separable; instant-runoff voting and single transferrable vote are not. For separable social choice functions, it is possible to compute the full tally, i.e. achieve 100% confidence in the outcome while partially masking selections. For each ballot, we randomly select some components. All selected components for all ballots are gathered in another part of the BB and subjected to a full, componentwise shuffling before decryption. Their positions in the original ballots are replaced by $*$. Thus, the way that these selected components appeared in the original ballots is lost.

The FTPV approach above might still hit corner cases, for instance if no vote was cast for a particular candidate. This suggests using a hybrid approach in which we use the approach above but reveal a random subset of the components separated out from the ballots. Thus we reveal enough of each ballot linked to the tracker to make verification meaningful while mitigating coercion threats, while a larger portion of the ballots is revealed without a link to the trackers to attain the required risk limit for the tally.

4 Distinguishing Distance and Applications to Signature Attacks and Individual Verifiability

In this section, we define a metric on the set of complex ballots that characterizes how well pairs of strings can be distinguished under random masking. We then observe that in some cases this metric is a monotone transformation of the Hamming distance used in coding theory. We also precisely characterize the cases when this occurs. Next, we use the connection to coding theory to answer the following question: how many simultaneous signature attacks can a coercer and/or vote-buyer launch? Finally, we give another application of the distinguishing distance: we use it to quantify the effect of a masking strategy on individual verifiability.

Throughout this section, we consider complex ballots with k components taken from the set $\mathcal{V}$; thus, the set of possible ballots is $\mathcal{V}^k$. We ignore here any constraints on what constitute valid ballots. For $x \in \mathcal{V}^k$ and $S \subset \{1, \dots, k\}$, we denote by x_S the substring of x on the positions in S.

4.1 Definition and Basic Properties of Distinguishing Distance

How distinguishable are pairs of elements of $\mathcal{V}^k$ under masking? For every probability distribution p_S over subsets of $\{1, \dots, k\}$, for every $x \in \mathcal{V}^k$ there is an induced probability distribution q_{S,x_S} of the pair (S, x_S), given by $q_{S,x_S}(s, \alpha) = p_S(s)\delta_{x_s,\alpha}$. If we keep p_S fixed and consider a pair $x, y \in \mathcal{V}^k$, we can define the distance between x and y as the statistical distance of q_{S,x_S}, q_{S,y_S}; thus, we take

$$d_{p_S}(x, y) = \frac{1}{2}\|q_{S,x_S} - q_{S,y_S}\|_1 = \sup_D |\Pr(D(S, x_S) = 1) - \Pr(D(S, y_S) = 1)|, \quad (1)$$

where the supremum is over distinguishers D. We can obtain the following formula for d_{p_S}:

Proposition 1. *For all distributions p_S, for all $x, y \in \mathcal{V}^k$,*

$$d_{p_S}(x, y) = \sum_{s:x_s \neq y_s} p_S(s) = \sum_s p_S(s)\mathbb{I}(s \cap t \neq \emptyset)$$

where t is the set of positions on which x, y differ and the operator $\mathbb{I}$ transforms the true/false value of a statement to $1, 0$ respectively.

Proof.

$$d_{p_S}(x,y) = \frac{1}{2}\|q_{S,x_S} - q_{S,y_S}\|_1 = \sum_{(s,\alpha):q_{S,x_S}(s,\alpha)>q_{S,y_S}(s,\alpha)} (q_{S,x_S}(s,\alpha) - q_{S,y_S}(s,\alpha))$$

$$= \sum_{(s,\alpha):q_{S,x_S}(s,\alpha)>q_{S,y_S}(s,\alpha)} (p_S(s)\delta_{x_s,\alpha} - p_S(s)\delta_{y_s,\alpha})$$

$$= \sum_{s:x_s \neq y_s} p_S(s) = \sum_s p_S(s)\mathbb{I}(s \cap t \neq \emptyset).$$

$\square$

Under the mild assumption that each position is revealed with strictly positive probability, d_{p_S} is a metric on $\mathcal{V}^k$.

Proposition 2. *For all p_S, d_{P_S} is symmetric, satisfies the triangle inequality and satisfies $\forall x, d_{P_S}(x,x) = 0$. If in addition $\forall i, \Pr(i \in S) > 0$, then $d_{p_S}(x,y) = 0 \implies x = y$.*

Proof. The first three claims follow directly from (1). For the last claim, take any i, any $v \in \mathcal{V}$, any x, y with $d_{p_S}(x,y) = 0$. Consider the distinguisher D given by "On input s, α, if i is among the revealed positions and the corresponding entry is v output 1, else output zero." Then,

$$\Pr(i \in S)\delta_{x_i,v} = \Pr(D(S,x_S) = 1) = \Pr(D(S,y_S) = 1) = \Pr(i \in S)\delta_{y_i,v}.$$

Therefore, $\forall i \forall v, x_i = v \iff y_i = v$, so $x = y$. $\square$

Now, we look at another question: how to find an optimal distinguisher between a pair of strings. For each $x \in \mathcal{V}^k$, define distinguisher D_x by "On input (s, α), if $x_s = \alpha$, output 1, else output 0." This is optimal regardless of the particular p_S, and regardless of the particular second element y.

Proposition 3. *For all distributions p_S, for all $x, y \in \mathcal{V}^k$,*

$$d_{p_S}(x,y) = \Pr(D_x(S,x_S) = 1) - \Pr(D_x(S,y_S) = 1).$$

Proof.

$$\Pr(D_x(S,x_S) = 1) - \Pr(D_x(S,y_S) = 1)$$

$$= \sum_s p_S(s)(\Pr(D_x(s,x_s) = 1) - \Pr(D_x(s,y_s) = 1))$$

$$= \sum_s p_S(s)(1 - \delta_{x_s,y_s}) = \sum_{s:x_s \neq y_s} p_S(s) = d_{p_S}(x,y).$$

$\square$

4.2   Distinguishing Distance and Hamming Distance

From Proposition 1, we see that for any p_S, $d_{p_S}(x,y)$ does not depend on all details of the strings x, y, but only on the set of positions where x, y differ. It turns out that there is a class of distributions p_S such that d_{p_S} does not even depend on all details of the set of positions where x, y differ, but only on the Hamming distance between x and y, $d_H(x, y) = |\{i : x_i \neq y_i\}|$. This class of probability distributions is precisely those that assign equal weight to subsets of equal size.

Theorem 1. *For all p_S, the following are equivalent:*

1. *There exists a probability vector $(r(0), \ldots r(k))$ such that $\forall s, p_S(s) = \frac{r(|s|)}{\binom{k}{|s|}}$*

2. *There exists a function f_{p_S} such that for all $x, y \in V^k$, $d_{p_S}(x, y) = f_{p_S}(d_H(x, y))$.*

We prove the forward direction of Theorem 1 by computing an explicit formula for the function f_{p_S}.

Theorem 2. *Suppose $\exists (r(0), \ldots r(k)) \forall s, p_S(s) = \frac{r(|s|)}{\binom{k}{|s|}}$ Then,*

$$d_{p_S}(x, y) = \sum_{i=1}^{d_H(x,y)} \sum_{j=0}^{k-d_H(x,y)} \frac{\binom{d_H(x,y)}{i} \binom{k-d_H(x,y)}{j} r(i+j)}{\binom{k}{i+j}}.$$

Proof (Theorem 2). Take any x, y and let t be the subset of positions where x, y differ. Then,

$$d_{p_S}(x, y) = \sum_{s: x_s \neq y_s} p_S(s) = \sum_{s: s \cap t \neq \emptyset} p_S(s) = \sum_{i=1}^{|t|} \sum_{j=0}^{k-|t|} \frac{\binom{|t|}{i} \binom{k-|t|}{j} r(i+j)}{\binom{k}{i+j}}.$$

$\square$

To prove the reverse direction of Theorem 1, we think of the $2^k - 1$ dimensional vector space over $\mathbb{C}$ with entries indexed by non-empty subsets of $\{1, \ldots k\}$, we think of the subspace

$$W = \{w \in \mathbb{C}^{2^k - 1} : |s| = |t| \implies w(s) = w(t)\}$$

and we also think of the $(2^k - 1) \times (2^k - 1)$ matrix M with entries $M(s, t) = \mathbb{I}(s \cap t \neq \emptyset)$ indexed by non-empty subsets of $\{1, \ldots, k\}$.

From Theorem 2, we see that $w \in W \implies Mw \in W$, that is, M leaves the subspace W invariant. Next, we observe that M is self-adjoint, and that M is also invertible:

Theorem 3. *For all $k \in \mathbb{N}$, the matrix M_k with entries $M_k(s, t) = \mathbb{I}(s \cap t \neq \emptyset)$ indexed by non-empty subsets of $\{1, \ldots k\}$ is invertible.*

a fact that we will prove at the end of this subsection. From this, we see that M^{-1} also leaves subspace W invariant.

Now, assume $\exists f_{p_S}, \forall x, y : d_{p_S}(x, y) = f_{p_S}(d_H(x, y))$. Form the vector $w \in W$ with entries $w(t) = f_{p_S}(|t|)$. The relation $d_{p_S}(x, y) = f_{p_S}(d_H(x, y))$ and Proposition 1 imply $\forall t, w(t) = \sum_{s \neq \emptyset} M(t, s) p_S(s)$. Then, $(p_S(s))_{s \neq \emptyset} = M^{-1} w \in$

W, so p_S assigns equal weight to subsets of equal size. This completes the proof of Theorem 1, assuming Theorem 3 holds.

It remains to prove Theorem 3. The proof is by induction on k. When $k = 1$, $M_1 = (1)$ is invertible. Assume now M_k is invertible and consider M_{k+1}. We order subsets according to the following: a subset corresponds to a string of 0s and 1s, and this encodes an integer between 1 and $2^{k+1} - 1$. With this ordering of the subsets, the matrix M_{k+1} has the following block form:

$$\begin{pmatrix} M_k^{(2^k-1)\times(2^k-1)} & 0^{(2^k-1)\times 1} & M_k^{(2^k-1)\times(2^k-1)} \\ 0^{1\times(2^k-1)} & 1^{1\times 1} & 1^{1\times(2^k-1)} \\ M_k^{(2^k-1)\times(2^k-1)} & 1^{(2^k-1)\times 1} & 1^{(2^k-1)\times(2^k-1)} \end{pmatrix}$$

where the sizes of the blocks are indicated in the superscript, and a 0 or 1 indicates that all entries of that block are 0 or 1.

Now we consider the following elementary row operations: subtract the middle row from all the bottom rows, then subtract the top block of rows from the bottom block of rows. We arrive at the matrix

$$\begin{pmatrix} M_k^{(2^k-1)\times(2^k-1)} & 0^{(2^k-1)\times 1} & M_k^{(2^k-1)\times(2^k-1)} \\ 0^{1\times(2^k-1)} & 1^{1\times 1} & 1^{1\times(2^k-1)} \\ 0^{(2^k-1)\times(2^k-1)} & 0^{(2^k-1)\times 1} & (-M_k)^{(2^k-1)\times(2^k-1)} \end{pmatrix}$$

and this is invertible by the inductive hypothesis. Hence, M_{k+1} is also invertible.

4.3   Bounds on the Number of Simultaneous Signature Attacks

We consider a coercer and/or vote buyer who wants to launch signature attacks on multiple voters simultaneously. Thus, the adversary chooses r signatures $x_1, \ldots, x_r \in \mathcal{V}^k$ and approaches many voters requiring each to submit one of the signature ballots.

What is the largest number r_{max} of different signatures that a coercer can use subject to the natural constraint that the strings $x_1, \ldots, x_r$ are pairwise distinguishable under random masking? We use the connection to coding theory from Subsect. 4.2 to answer this question.

First, we prove some properties of the function f_{p_S} from Theorem 1.

Lemma 1. *For every p_S that satisfies $\exists (r(0), \ldots, r(k)) \forall s, p_S(s) = \frac{r(|s|)}{\binom{k}{|s|}}$, the function f_{p_S} is non-decreasing, $f_{p_S}(0) = 0$, and $f_{p_S}(k) = 1 - p_S(\emptyset)$.*

Proof. Take any $i < j \in \{0, \ldots, k\}$. Take $x, y \in \mathcal{V}^k$ that differ in the first i positions and $x', y' \in \mathcal{V}^k$ that differ in the first j positions. Using Proposition 1 we get $f_{p_S}(i) = f_{p_S}(d_H(x,y)) = d_{p_S}(x,y) = \sum_s p_S(s)\mathbb{I}(s \cap \{1, \ldots, i\} \neq \emptyset)$ $\leq \sum_s p_S(s)\mathbb{I}(s \cap \{1, \ldots, j\} \neq \emptyset) = d_{p_S}(x',y') = f_{p_S}(d_H(x',y')) = f_{p_S}(j)$.

For the other two claims, take $z, w \in \mathcal{V}^k$ that differ in all positions. Then,

$$f_{p_S}(0) = f_{p_S}(d_H(z, z)) = d_{p_S}(z, z) = 0$$
$$f_{p_S}(k) = f_{p_S}(d_H(z, w)) = d_{p_S}(z, w) = \sum_s p_S(s)\mathbb{I}(s \cap \{1, \ldots, k\} \neq \emptyset) = 1 - p_S(\emptyset).$$

□

The properties of f_{p_S} established in Lemma 1 allow us to define a partial inverse of f_{p_S}. Take $g_{p_S} : [0, 1 - p_S(\emptyset)] \rightarrow \{0, 1, \ldots k\}$ given by

$$g_{p_S}(q) = \min\{d \in \{0, 1, \ldots, k\} : f_{p_S}(d) \geq q\}$$

so that we have

$$f_{p_S}(d) \geq q \iff d \geq g_{p_S}(q). \tag{2}$$

Now, we are ready to state and prove our bounds on the number of simultaneous signature attacks under a pairwise distinguishability constraint.

Theorem 4. *For every finite set $\mathcal{V}$, for every $k \in \mathbb{N}$, for every probability distribution p_S on subsets of $\{1, \ldots, k\}$ satisfying $\exists (r(0), \ldots, r(k)) \forall s, p_S(s) = \frac{r(|s|)}{\binom{k}{|s|}}$, for every $q \in [0, 1 - p_S(\emptyset)]$, let $r_{max}(\mathcal{V}, k, p_S, q)$ denote the size of the largest collection $\{x_1, \ldots x_r\}$ with the property $\forall i \neq j, d_{p_S}(x_i, x_j) \geq q$. Then*

$$\frac{|\mathcal{V}|^k}{\sum_{j=0}^{g_{p_S}(q)-1} \binom{k}{j}(|\mathcal{V}| - 1)^j} \leq r_{max}(\mathcal{V}, k, p_S, q) \leq \frac{|\mathcal{V}|^k}{\sum_{j=0}^{\lfloor (g_{p_S}(q)-1)/2 \rfloor} \binom{k}{j}(|\mathcal{V}| - 1)^j}.$$

Proof. We use the same argument that is used in coding theory to establish the Gilbert-Varshamov lower bound and the Hamming upper bound on the maximum number of codewords subject to a pairwise Hamming distance constraint.

First, we observe that a collection $\{x_1, \ldots x_r\}$ satisfies $\forall i \neq j, d_{p_S}(x_i, x_j) \geq q$ if and only if it satisfies $\forall i \neq j, d_H(x_i, x_j) \geq g_{p_S}(q)$. This follows from the relation $d_{p_S}(x_i, x_j) = f_{p_S}(d_H(x_i, x_j))$ and the property (2) of the partial inverse g_{p_S}.

Now, take a collection $\{x_1, \ldots x_{r_{max}(\mathcal{V}, k, p_S, q)}\}$ with the maximum number of elements subject to the constraint $\forall i \neq j, d_H(x_i, x_j) \geq g_{p_S}(q)$. To prove the upper bound, note that the Hamming balls of radius $\lfloor (g_{p_S}(q) - 1)/2 \rfloor$ around $x_1, \ldots, x_{r_{max}}$ must be disjoint, that each such ball contains $\sum_{j=0}^{\lfloor (g_{p_S}(q)-1)/2 \rfloor} \binom{k}{j}(|\mathcal{V}| - 1)^j$ elements, and that the total number of elements in all these balls must not exceed the size of the whole set $\mathcal{V}^k$.

To prove the lower bound, note that the Hamming balls of radius $g_{p_S}(q) - 1$ around $x_1, \ldots, x_{r_{max}}$ must completely cover $\mathcal{V}^k$, or else another element could be found that has Hamming distance $\geq g_{p_S}(q)$ to all of $x_1, \ldots, x_{r_{max}}$ and this would contradict the choice of $\{x_1, \ldots x_{r_{max}(\mathcal{V},k,p_S,q)}\}$ as having the maximum number of elements. Now, we have r_{max} Hamming balls with $\sum_{j=0}^{g_{p_S}(q)-1} \binom{k}{j}(|\mathcal{V}|-1)^j$ elements each and their total number of elements must exceed $|\mathcal{V}|^k$, giving the lower bound on r_{max}. $\square$

These upper and lower bounds are exemplified in Fig. 1 for an election with $k = 5$ candidates and $|\mathcal{V}| = 2$ (like the student election example in next section). We have $g_{p_S}(q) = k - m + 1$ when g is applied to a uniform distribution over m-element subsets (m openings) evaluated at $q = 1$ (perfect distinguishability).

4.4   Quantifying the Effect of Masking on Individual Verifiability

We would like to quantify the effect of a particular masking strategy, specified by the probability distribution p_S, on individual verifiability. We propose the following quantity:

$$IV(p_S) = \inf_{x \neq y \in \mathcal{V}^k} d_{p_S}(x, y).$$

This quantity takes values between 0 and 1, where $IV(p_S) = 1$ means that the masking strategy p_S leaves the individual verifiability of the underlying voting protocol invariant, while $IV(p_S) = 0$ means that the masking strategy p_S destroys any individual verifiability that was present in the underlying voting protocol.

The motivation for choosing the quantity $IV(p_S)$ is the following: a voter who has voted x obtains a pair (s, α) where $s \subset \{1, \ldots, k\}$ and $\alpha \in \mathcal{V}^{|s|}$ and must decide whether this revealed vote was obtained from his submitted vote x or from some $y \neq x$. Taking the infimum over $x \neq y$ corresponds to considering the worst case over voter choices x and modifications of the voter choice y.

One attractive feature of this setup is that an individual voter does not need to know the distribution p_S or the modification y in order to apply the optimal verification strategy; indeed the optimal strategy for a voter who has chosen x is to apply the distinguisher D_x considered in Proposition 3.

For distributions p_S that satisfy $\exists (r(0), \ldots, r(k)) \forall s, p_S(s) = \frac{r(|s|)}{\binom{k}{|s|}}$, Theorem 2 gives a simple formula for $IV(p_S)$:

$$IV(p_S) = \sum_{j=0}^{k-1} \frac{\binom{k-1}{j} r(j+1)}{\binom{k}{j+1}} = \sum_{l=1}^{k} \frac{l}{k} r(l),$$

where we have used the fact that the transformation from Hamming to distinguishing distance is non-decreasing (Lemma 1), and so the smallest distinguishing distance is between x, y such that $d_H(x, y) = 1$.

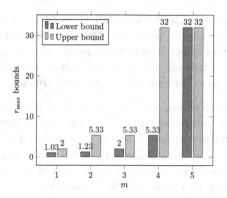

$m \setminus p$	p_{col}	$(1 - p_{col})^n$
1	0.16	$1.46 \cdot 10^{-79}$
2	0.018	$8.3 \cdot 10^{-9}$
3	0.0005	0.60
4	$9.7 \cdot 10^{-6}$	0.99
5	$1.6 \cdot 10^{-7}$	0.9998

Fig. 1. Example for $|\mathcal{V}| = 2$ and $k = 5$. Here r_{max} is the number of different signatures that a coercer can distinguish pairwise.

Fig. 2. The probability, p_{col} that a single (resp. no) honest voter casts a ballot which after masking equals the mask of $v_0^O = (0, 1, 1, 1, 1)$ for the student election. Here n is the number of voters, and m is the number of unmasked components.

5   Quantitative Privacy-Type Properties

We now want to measure and compare privacy-properties for different masked tally methods. When computing concrete values we will consider approval voting with k candidates only 0 or 1 is allowed for each candidate, without any overall constraint, $(v_1, \ldots, v_k) \in \{0, 1\}^k$. For the n honest voters we assume for simplicity that the probability to vote $v_i = 1$ is p_i and these probabilities are independent. As a special concrete case we consider a student election with $n = 1001$ voters (one voter is under observation), $k = 5$ candidates with probabilities $(0.6, 0.4, 0.01, 0.01, 0.01)$, i.e. two popular candidates and three unpopular.

5.1   Privacy

In order to compare the different approaches we first consider the quantitative δ-privacy definition from [5]. The main other quantitative privacy definition is [3], but it is less suited considering signature attacks. The parties are an observer O, who can use public data, n_h honest voters and an additional voter under observation V_{obs}, whose vote the observer tries to guess.

Definition 1 (δ-privacy). *Let P be a voting protocol and V_{obs} be the voter under observation. We say that P achieves δ-privacy if*

$$\Pr[(\pi_O || \pi_{V_{obs}}(v_0^O) || \pi_v)^{(l)} \to 1] - \Pr[(\pi_O || \pi_{V_{obs}}(v_1^O) || \pi_v)^{(l)} \to 1]$$

is δ-bounded as a function of the security parameter ℓ for all vote choices v_0^O and v_1^O of the observed voter. Here π_O, $\pi_{V_{obs}}$ and π_v are respectively the programs run by the observer O, the voter under observation V_{obs} and all the honest voters.

The value δ will depend on the chosen vote distribution, and we see that it is especially relevant to penalize signature attacks: if we assume that there is a vote choice $v^* = (v_1^*, \ldots, v_k^*)$ which rarely gets selected and has a probability close to zero, then an unmasked tally which reveals all cast plaintext ballots, even in anonymised form, will have $\delta = 1$—the adversary simply checks if v^* appears.

Full Ballot Disclosure. When we reveal all ballots, we can consider the case where the observer tries to distinguish a voter casting the most unpopular vote vs the most popular vote, as in a signature attack. That is, in the definition we let $v_0^O = (v_1, \ldots, v_k)$ with $v_i = 1$ if $p_i \leq 1/2$ and $v_i = 0$ if $p_i > 1/2$, and we have $v_1^O = (1 - v_1, \ldots, 1 - v_k)$. Denote the corresponding probability p_{min}. Now a good strategy is simply to check if at least one $(v_1, \ldots, v_k)$ appears in the disclosed ballots, and the algorithm then outputs "1". This means $\Pr[(\pi_O || \pi_{V_{obs}}(v_0^O) || \pi_v)^{(l)} \to 1] = 1$ but $(\pi_O || \pi_{V_{obs}}(v_1^O) || \pi_v)$ will also output "1" if another voter chooses v_0^O. This happens with probability $1 - (1 - p_{min})^{n_h}$. We conclude that $\delta \geq (1 - p_{min})^{n_h}$. For the case of the student election we have that $v_0^O = (0, 1, 1, 1, 1)$ with $p_{min} = 0.4^2 \cdot 0.01^3 = 1.6 \cdot 10^{-7}$. Thus for $n_h = 1000$ we have $\delta \geq (1 - p_{min})^{n_h} \approx 0.99984$, i.e. close to 1.

Result Only. We now consider the case where we only reveal the overall result $r = (r_1, \ldots, r_k)$. In this case we can follow an analysis close to [5,7] for calculating δ. For every possible result r we calculate the probability that the result happened if the observed voter cast v_0^O or v_1^O. The algorithm will then output one if the former probability is larger. We get $\delta = \sum_{r \in M^*_{v_0^O, v_1^O}} (A_r^{v_0^O} - A_r^{v_1^O})$ where $M^*_{v_0^O, v_1^O} = \{r \in \mathbb{R} : A_r^{v_1^O} \leq A_r^{v_0^O}\}$, $\mathbb{R}$ is the set of all possible results of the election and A_r^v denotes the probability that the choices of the honest voters yield the result r given that V_{obs}'s choice is v. These probabilities can explicitly be calculated since each candidate count from the honest voters, X_i, is binomially distributed, $X_i \sim BD(n_h, p_i)$. We thus have $A_r^v = \mathbb{P}(X_1 = r_1 - v_1) \cdots \mathbb{P}(X_k = r_k - v_k) = \prod_{i=1}^k \binom{n-1}{r_i - v_i} p_i^{r_i - v_i} (1 - p_i)^{n - r_i + v_i - 1}$.

RLT. In the original RLT method we keep a certain fraction, f_{blind}, of the ballots hidden, that is $(1 - f_{blind})n$ ballots are published. If we consider the optimal algorithm from the full ballot disclosure and the corresponding δ_{full} we see that $\delta = (1 - f_{blind})\delta_{full}$ since the probability that observed voter's ballot is hidden is $(1 - f_{blind})$.

Masked RLT. We now consider the case of masked RLTs where the we release all ballots but with only m out of k components unmasked. A good strategy to lower bound δ is to count the number N_b of colliding ballots v which satisfy $\text{mask}_v v = \text{mask}_v v_b^O$ for $b = 0, 1$. We choose v_0^O as the most unlikely ballot, as above and take v_1^O as the opposite ballot to discriminate optimally between the two counts. The main distinguishing power comes from N_0, and we let the distinguishing algorithm output "1" if the probability of the honest voters casting $N_0 - 1$ colliding votes is higher than getting N_0 collisions. The probability for each honest voter to have a collision is $p_{col} = 1/\binom{k}{m} \cdot \sum_{1 \leq i_1 < i_2 < \ldots < i_m \leq k} p_{i_1} \cdots p_{i_m}$

and $N_0 \sim BD(n_h, p)$, where p_i is the probability of a match in the ith candidate. In Fig. 2 we have displayed the probabilities for the student election example. The algorithm above will then simply give the probability at the mode of the binomial distribution with p_{col}. For $m = 3$ we find $\delta \geq 0.6$ for the student election.

5.2 Coercion-Resistance

In [6] the authors present a definition of quantitative coercion-resistance following similar ideas as in Definition 1. We will here use their strategy version and not go into all details. We let S denote the election system with specified number candidates, honest (n_h) and dishonest voters (mostly neglected here) and a ballot distribution, and attacker, C_S, and voter, V_S, interactive Turing machine models. We let γ denote a property defining the goal of the coerced voter, e.g. to vote for a specified candidate.

Definition 2. S *achieves* δ^{cr}-*coercion-resistance if for all dictated coerced strategies* $\pi_{V_{co}} \in V_S$ *there exists a counter-strategy* $\tilde{\pi}_{V_{co}} \in V_S$ *s.t. for all coercer programs* $\pi_c \in C_S$:

- $\Pr[(\pi_c || \tilde{\pi}_{V_{co}} || \pi_v)^{(l)} \mapsto \gamma]$ *is overwhelming,*
- $\Pr[(\pi_c || \pi_{V_{co}} || \pi_v)^{(l)} \mapsto 1] - \Pr[(\pi_c || \tilde{\pi}_{V_{co}} || \pi_v)^{(l)} \mapsto 1]$ *is* δ^{cr}-*bounded,*

with bounded and overwhelming defined in the security parameter. The first part says that the voter is able to achieve her goal (e.g. vote for a specific candidate) and the second part says that the coercer's distinguishing power is bounded by δ^{cr}. This level of coercion-resistance depends on several parameters especially the probability distribution on the candidates.

Whereas this definition gives a level of coercion-resistance, it does not tell the full story. To see this let us consider two different election systems. System A outputs voter names and corresponding votes with probability $1/2$, completely breaking privacy, and otherwise it only outputs the election result. Neglecting the information from the election result we get $\delta^A = 1/2$. In system B the voter secretly gets a signed receipt of her vote with probability $1/2$ and otherwise the protocol works ideally. In this case a coerced voter can always cast her own choice and claim that no receipt was received. A voter following the coercer's instruction will with probability $1/2$ give the corresponding receipt, i.e. we again have $\delta^B = 1/2$. However, the two systems are very different from the point of view of the voter: in system A the coerced voter gets caught cheating with probability $1/2$, whereas in system B, the voter always has plausible deniability.

Since plausible deniability is an essential factor for the usability of coercion-resistance mechanisms, we need a new definition to be able to measure this aspect.

5.3 No Deniability

The level of plausibility of a voter claiming to have followed the coercer, while actually following the counter strategy, relates to the probability of false positives when the coercer tries to determine if the voter disregarded the instructions. In the following we assume without loss of generality that the coercer outputs 1 when blaming the voter. We now want to define the maximal probability of getting caught without any deniability, i.e. we consider the case where $\Pr[(\pi_c||\pi_{V_{co}}||\pi_v)^{(l)} \mapsto 1] = 0$ or negligible, i.e. the coercer only uses strategies where he never blames an honest voter.

Definition 3. *S achieves $\delta^{cr,no-d}$-coercion-resistance if for all dictated coerced strategies $\pi_{V_{co}} \in V_S$ there exists a counter-strategy $\tilde{\pi}_{V_{co}} \in V_S$ s.t. for all coercer programs $\pi_c \in C_S$:*

- $\Pr[(\pi_c||\tilde{\pi}_{V_{co}}||\pi_v)^{(l)} \mapsto \gamma]$ *is overwhelming.*
- $\Pr[(\pi_c||\tilde{\pi}_{V_{co}}||\pi_v)^{(l)} \mapsto 1]$ *is $\delta^{cr,no-d}$-bounded and $\Pr[(\pi_c||\pi_{V_{co}}||\pi_v)^{(l)} \mapsto 1]$ is negligible.*

Note that the coercer's optimal strategy to obtain this $\delta^{cr,no-d}$ and the voter's strategy might be different from the ones in Definition 2 but $\delta^{cr,no-d} \leq \delta^{cr}$.

The no deniability probability clearly separates the RLT approaches. The original RLT always has plausible deniability if we choose to keep some ratio of ballots shrouded and the voter can claim her ballot was not revealed. This is e.g. important for RLV giving deniability against an attack where the coercer provides a ciphertext to cast and asks for its decrypted vote.

In the case of masked ballots, there can be a chance of getting caught undeniably. This will depend strongly on the number of revealed ballot components m, the vote distribution and the voter's goal. For the student election analysed above, the worst case when the goal of the voter is to cast $(1,0,0,0,0)$. The coercer's optimal strategy is then to demand a vote for $(0,1,1,1,1)$. The coercer will blame the voter if there is no matching masked ballot, i.e. if no honest voters produce a collision which happens with probability $(1 - p_{col})^{n_h+1}$ computed Fig. 2. The probability of no deniability is then $p = 8 \cdot 10^{-9}$ for $m = 2$ but jumps abruptly to $p = 0.6$ for $m = 3$.

An interesting case is when the voter has a relaxed goal allowing to cast a signature part or not, and when the vote distribution has some ballots strictly zero probability. Let us consider a three candidate 0/1 election with 1-vote probabilities $(1/2, 1/2, 0)$. The voter's goal is to cast a 1 for the first candidate. The coercer's optimal strategy is to demand a signature ballot $(0,0,1)$. The voter has two counter-strategies: 1) cast a vote $(1,0,0)$ without the 0 probability signature part or 2) casting a vote $(1,0,1)$ with the signature part. For 1) the there is no deniability if no other voter casts a matching ballot and the coerced voter's ballot does not match either. For $m = 1$ this happens with $p = (2/3)^{n_h+1}$ and for $m = 2$ with $p = (11/12)^{n_h}$, both are small if we have many voters. For 2) there will always be a matching vote if the first part of the coerced voter's ballot is masked. However, if the last part is revealed the coercer can deduce this ballot comes from the coerced voter since this candidate had probability 0, and if the 1 vote in the first part is revealed as well then the voter is caught with no deniability. Thus is no deniability with probability $(1/3) \cdot (2/3)^{n_h}$ for $m = 1$ and $1/3 + (1/3) \cdot (11/12)^{n_h}$ for $m = 2$. Thus for $m = 1$ strategy 2) is always better, but for $m = 2$ strategy 1) is better when we have more than 13 voters. In some cases the voter strategy thus depends on m, which might not be know beforehand.

Finally, it is also natural to define the level of plausability we can provide. The average plausability that a voter has e.g. in Definition 2 is a useful quantity for the voter, but it would be more useful to guarantee that the voter always has a certain level for coercion-resistance. We leave a precise definition for future work.

5.4   Receipt-Freeness

Following [6], Definition 2 also covers receipt-freeness. However, we again argue that modelling some variants is useful. The following definition is based on a swap of $\pi_{V_{co}}$ and $\pi_{\tilde{V}_{co}}$ in Definition 3, and models vote buyers who do not want to pay a "free lunch" to vote sellers who follow their own goal. The voter goal γ can here be to cast a specified vote or set of votes.

Definition 4 (Weak Vote Buying Resistance). *For a given small p_{fl}, S achieves δ^{wvb}-coercion-resistance if for all dictated coerced strategies $\pi_{V_{co}} \in V_S$ there exists a counter-strategy $\tilde{\pi}_{V_{co}} \in V_S$ s.t. for all coercer programs $\pi_c \in C_S$:*

- $\Pr[(\pi_c || \tilde{\pi}_{V_{co}} || \pi_v)^{(l)} \mapsto \gamma]$ *is overwhelming.*
- $\Pr[(\pi_c || \pi_{V_{co}} || \pi_v)^{(l)} \mapsto 1] - \Pr[(\pi_c || \tilde{\pi}_{V_{co}} || \pi_v)^{(l)} \mapsto 1]$ *is δ^{wvb}-bounded and* $\Pr[(\pi_c || \tilde{\pi}_{V_{co}} || \pi_v)^{(l)} \mapsto 1]$ *is p_{fl}-bounded.*

We here interpret outputting "1" as paying the vote seller and this definition bounds how often an instruction-following vote seller gets paid by a vote-buyer (by $\delta^{wvb} + p_{fl}$), but under the condition that a voter who casts another vote is only paid with a (very) small probability p_{fl}. This is a weakened vote-buyer model but interesting since a vote buyer should avoid vote sellers going for a "free lunch". If the probability of an honest vote seller getting paid is low, it would help curb vote selling (even though the vote buyer could increase the price and create a "vote selling lottery"). In this definition, it also makes sense to drop the quantification over the coercer's strategies to see the resistance to vote buying for different vote choices.

RLT. In the original RLT a signature ballot will get revealed with probability $1 - f_{blind}$. If the vote buyer sees this he can pay the vote seller and will only pay the voter seller wrongly with a small probability p_{fl} equal to the probability that one of the honest voters cast the signature ballot, i.e. $\delta^{vb} \simeq 1 - f_{blind}$ which can be rather high and protects badly against vote buying.

Masked RLT. For the masked ballots we can however choose m such that several ballots will have the same masking as the signature ballot and makes it hard for the vote buyer to assess if the signature ballot was cast. For the student election we see from Fig. 2 that the number of matches with the optimal signature ballot $(0, 1, 1, 1, 1)$ is binomially distributed with an expectation value of 18.4 colliding ballots and a standard deviation of around 4.

For a more precise example, we can consider the three-candidate election with probabilities $(1/2, 1/2, 0)$ as above and assume that the goal of the voter is to cast 0 for candidate 1 and $p_\mathrm{fl} = 0$. For $m = 1$ we will have $\delta^{vb} = 0$, but for $m = 2$ the vote-buyer can demand a vote for candidate 1 and 3 and pay out if he sees $(1, *, 1)$. Any counter-strategy with 0 for candidate 1 gives $\delta^{vb} = 1/3$.

We note that the new quantitative definitions for no deniability coercion-resistance (Definition 3), the weak vote buying resistance (Definition 4) and the original δ^{cr}-coercion-resistance (Definition 2) are considering different aspects of coercion-resistance and stating the three different δ-values gives a more nuanced description of the security of a given voting protocol. Also note that the δ values are calculated using potentially different strategies for the coercer and voter, and finding unified strategies optimising the parameters is an interesting line of future work. Finally, there are natural, more fine-grained, definitions extending these which should be also considered in the future.

6   Conclusion

We have shown that the idea of risk-limiting tallies and risk-limiting verification can be applied effectively to complex ballots. By partially masking each ballot rather than simply masking a subset of the ballots as in the original RLT and RLV we gain far greater flexibility in terms of masking strategies. This will be explored further in order to optimise the trade-offs between the various measures defined here in future work.

The approach is more robust against any claims of being undemocratic: all ballots are counted, and indeed in the full tally/partial verification option, all are counted fully. The only compromise then is some reduction in the level of verifiability, but this can be adjusted and is probably acceptable. If we compare this with ThreeBallot, there the chance of detecting a manipulated ballot is $1/3$, assuming that the attacker does not learn which ballot was retained by the voter. In our case we can achieve a good level of coercion mitigation with say a shrouding of about $1/2$ of each ballot. Finally, we did a preliminary analysis of the quantitative privacy for the different tally methods, and the coercion-resistance, in particular, the probability a coerced voter gets undeniably caught. The new masked tallies however, are more appropriate for receipt-freeness, in particular with upper bounds on the number of vote sellers, whereas the old RLT provides good plausible deniability to coerced voters. This suggests combining both methods when possible, but future work is needed to define the precise level of vote-buying resistance.

Acknowledgements. This research was funded in part by the Luxembourg National Research Fund (FNR) grant references STV C18/IS/12685695, Q-CoDe CORE17/IS/11689058 and PRIDE15/10621687/ SPsquared.

References

1. Benaloh, J., Jones, D., Lazarus, E.L., Lindeman, M., Stark, P.B.: SOBA: Secrecy-preserving observable ballot-level audit. In: 2011 Electronic Voting Technology Workshop/Workshop on Trustworthy Elections (EVT/WOTE 11). USENIX Association, San Francisco, CA (2011). https://www.usenix.org/conference/evtwote-11/soba-secrecy-preserving-observable-ballot-level-audit
2. Benaloh, J., Stark, P.B., Teague, V.J.: VAULT: Verifiable audits using limited transparency. In: Krimmer, R., Volkamer, M., Cortier, V., Beckert, B., Küsters, R., Serdült, U., Duenas-Cid, D. (eds.) Proceedings of E-Vote ID 2019. LNCS, vol. 11759. Springer, Chem (2019)
3. Bernhard, D., Cortier, V., Pereira, O., Warinschi, B.: Measuring vote privacy, revisited. In: Proceedings of the 2012 ACM Conference on Computer and Communications Security, pp. 941–952 (2012)
4. Jamroga, W., Roenne, P.B., Ryan, P.Y.A., Stark, P.B.: Risk-limiting tallies. In: Krimmer, R., et al. (eds.) E-Vote-ID 2019. LNCS, vol. 11759, pp. 183–199. Springer, Cham (2019). https://doi.org/10.1007/978-3-030-30625-0_12
5. Küsters, R., Truderung, T., Vogt, A.: Verifiability, privacy, and coercion-resistance: new insights from a case study. In: 2011 IEEE Symposium on Security and Privacy, pp. 538–553. IEEE (2011)
6. Küsters, R., Truderung, T., Vogt, A.: A game-based definition of coercion resistance and its applications. J. Comput. Secur. **20**(6), 709–764 (2012). https://doi.org/10.3233/JCS-2012-0444
7. Liedtke, J., Küsters, R., Müller, J., Rausch, D., Vogt, A.: Ordinos: a verifiable tally-hiding electronic voting protocol. In: IEEE 5th European Symposium on Security and Privacy (EuroS&P 2020) (2020)
8. Ryan, P.Y.A., Rønne, P.B., Iovino, V.: Selene: voting with transparent verifiability and coercion-mitigation. In: Clark, J., Meiklejohn, S., Ryan, P.Y.A., Wallach, D., Brenner, M., Rohloff, K. (eds.) FC 2016. LNCS, vol. 9604, pp. 176–192. Springer, Heidelberg (2016). https://doi.org/10.1007/978-3-662-53357-4_12

RiLACS: Risk Limiting Audits
via Confidence Sequences

Ian Waudby-Smith[1]([⊠]) ⓘ, Philip B. Stark[2] ⓘ, and Aaditya Ramdas[1] ⓘ

[1] Carnegie Mellon University, Pittsburgh, PA, USA
{ianws,aramdas}@cmu.edu
[2] University of California, Berkeley, Berkeley, CA, USA
stark@stat.berkeley.edu

Abstract. Accurately determining the outcome of an election is a complex task with many potential sources of error, ranging from software glitches in voting machines to procedural lapses to outright fraud. Risk-limiting audits (RLA) are statistically principled "incremental" hand counts that provide statistical assurance that reported outcomes accurately reflect the validly cast votes. We present a suite of tools for conducting RLAs using confidence sequences—sequences of confidence sets which uniformly capture an electoral parameter of interest from the start of an audit to the point of an exhaustive recount with high probability. Adopting the SHANGRLA [13] framework, we design nonnegative martingales which yield computationally and statistically efficient confidence sequences and RLAs for a wide variety of election types.

Keywords: Martingales · Sequential hypothesis tests · SHANGRLA

1 Introduction

The reported outcome of an election may not match the validly cast votes for a variety of reasons, including software configuration errors, bugs, human error, and deliberate malfeasance. Trustworthy elections start with a trustworthy paper record of the validly cast votes. Given access to a trustworthy paper trail of votes, a risk-limiting audit (RLA) can provide a rigorous probabilistic guarantee:

1. If an initially announced assertion $\mathcal{A}$ about an election is *false*, this will be corrected by the audit with high probability;
2. If the aforementioned assertion $\mathcal{A}$ is *true*, then $\mathcal{A}$ will be confirmed (with probability one).

Here, an electoral assertion $\mathcal{A}$ is simply a claim about the aggregated votes cast (e.g. "Alice received more votes than Bob"). An auditor may wish to audit several claims: for example, whether the reported winner is correct or whether the margin of victory is as large as announced.

From a statistical point of view, efficient risk-limiting audits can be implemented as sequential hypothesis tests. Namely, one tests the null hypothesis H_0:

© Springer Nature Switzerland AG 2021
R. Krimmer et al. (Eds.): E-Vote-ID 2021, LNCS 12900, pp. 124–139, 2021.
https://doi.org/10.1007/978-3-030-86942-7_9

"the assertion $\mathcal{A}$ is false," versus the alternative H_1: "the assertion $\mathcal{A}$ is true". Imagine then observing a random sequence of voter-cast ballots $X_1, X_2, \ldots, X_N$, where N is the total number of ballots. A sequential hypothesis test is represented by a sequence $(\phi_t)_{t=1}^{N}$ of binary-valued functions:

$$\phi_t := \phi(X_1, \ldots, X_t) \mapsto \{0, 1\},$$

where $\phi_t = 1$ represents rejecting H_0 (typically in favor of H_1), and $\phi_t = 0$ means that H_0 has not yet been rejected. The sequential test (and thus the RLA) stops as soon as $\phi_t = 1$ or once all N ballots are observed, whichever comes first. The "risk-limiting" property of RLAs states that if the assertion is false (in other words, if H_0 holds), then

$$\mathbb{P}_{H_0} \left(\exists t \in \{1, \ldots, N\} : \phi_t = 1 \right) \leq \alpha,$$

which is equivalent to type-I error control of the sequential test. Another way of interpreting the above statement is as follows: if the assertion is incorrect, then with probability at least $(1 - \alpha)$, $\phi_t = 0$ for every $t \in \{1, \ldots, N\}$ and hence all N ballots will be inspected, at which point the "true" outcome (which is the result of the full hand count) will be known with certainty.

1.1 SHANGRLA Reduces Election Auditing to Sequential Testing

Designing the sequential hypothesis test $(\phi_t)_{t=1}^{N}$ depends on the type of vote, the aggregation method, or the social choice function for the election, and thus past works have constructed a variety of tests. Some works have designed $(\phi_t)_{t=1}^{N}$ in the context of a particular type of election [6, 7, 9]. On the other hand, the "SHANGRLA" (Sets of Half-Average Nulls Generate RLAs) framework unifies many common election types including plurality elections, approval voting, ranked-choice voting, and more by reducing each of these to a simple hypothesis test of whether a finite collection of finite lists of bounded numbers has mean $\mu^\star$ at most $1/2$ [1, 13]. Let us give an illustrative example to show how SHANGRLA can be used in practice.

Suppose we have an election with two candidates, Alice and Bob. A ballot may contain a vote for Alice or for Bob, or it may contain no valid vote, e.g., because there was no selection or an overvote. It is reported that Alice and Bob received N_A and N_B votes respectively with $N_A > N_B$ and that there were a total of N_I invalid ballots for a total of $N = N_A + N_B + N_I$ voters. We encode votes for Alice as "1", votes for Bob as "0" and invalid votes as "1/2", to obtain a set of numbers $\{x_1, x_2, \ldots, x_N\}$. Crucially, Alice indeed received more votes than Bob if and only if $\mu^\star := \frac{1}{N} \sum_{i=1}^{N} x_i > 1/2$. In other words, *the report that Alice beat Bob can be translated into the assertion that $\mu^\star \in (1/2, 1]$.*

SHANGRLA proposes to audit an assertion by testing its complement: rejecting that "complementary null" is affirmative evidence that the assertion is indeed true. In other words, if one can ensure that $X_1, X_2, \ldots, X_N$ is a random permutation of $\{x_1, \ldots, x_N\}$ by sampling ballots without replacement (each ballot is chosen uniformly amongst remaining ballots), then we can concern ourselves with designing a hypothesis test $(\phi_t)_{t=1}^N$ to test the null $H_0 : \mu^\star \leq 1/2$ against the alternative $H_1 : \mu^\star > 1/2$.

One of the major benefits of SHANGRLA is the ability to reduce a wide range of election types to a testing problem of the above form. This permits the use of powerful statistical techniques which were designed specifically for such testing problems (but may not have been designed with RLAs in mind). Throughout this paper, we adopt the SHANGRLA framework, and while we return to the example of plurality elections for illustrative purposes, all of our methods can be applied to any election audit which has a SHANGRLA-like testing reduction [13].

1.2   Confidence Sequences

In the fixed-time (i.e. non-sequential) hypothesis testing regime, there is a well-known duality between hypothesis tests and confidence intervals for a parameter $\mu^\star$ of interest. We describe this briefly for $\mu^\star \in [0, 1]$ for simplicity. For each $\mu \in [0, 1]$, suppose that $\phi^\mu \equiv \phi^\mu(X_1, \ldots, X_n) \mapsto \{0, 1\}$ is a level-α nonsequential, fixed-sample test for the hypothesis $H_0 : \mu^\star = \mu$ versus $H_1 : \mu^\star \neq \mu$. Then, a nonsequential, fixed-sample $(1 - \alpha)$ confidence interval for $\mu^\star$ is given by the set of all $\mu \in [0, 1]$ for which ϕ^μ does not reject, that is $\{\mu \in [0, 1] : \phi^\mu = 0\}$.

As we discuss further in Sect. 2, an analogous duality holds for sequential hypothesis tests and time-uniform *confidence sequences* (here and throughout the paper, "time" is used to refer to the number of samples so far, and need not correspond to any particular units such as hours or seconds). We first give a brief preview of the results to come. Consider a family of sequential hypothesis tests $\{(\phi_t^\mu)_{t=1}^N\}_{\mu \in [0,1]}$, meaning that for each μ, $(\phi_t^\mu)_{t=1}^N$ is a sequential test for μ. Then, the set of all μ for which $\phi_t^\mu = 0$,

$$C_t := \{\mu \in [0, 1] : \phi_t^\mu = 0\}$$

forms a $(1 - \alpha)$ *confidence sequence* for $\mu^\star$, meaning that

$$\mathbb{P}(\exists t \in [N] : \mu^\star \notin C_t) \leq \alpha,$$

where $[N]$ is used to denote the set $\{1, 2, \ldots, N\}$. In other words, C_t will cover $\mu^\star$ at *every single* time t, except with some small probability $\leq \alpha$. Since C_t is typically an interval $[L_t, U_t]$, we call the lower endpoint $(L_t)_{t=1}^N$ as a lower confidence sequence (and similarly for upper).

In particular, given the sequential hypothesis testing problem that arises in SHANGRLA, we can cast the RLA as a sequential estimation problem that can be solved by developing confidence sequences (see Fig. 1).[1] As we will see in Sect. 2, our confidence sequences provide added flexibility and an intuitive visualizable interpretation for SHANGRLA-compatible election audits, without sacrificing any statistical efficiency.

---

[1] Code to reproduce all plots can be found at github.com/wannabesmith/RiLACS.

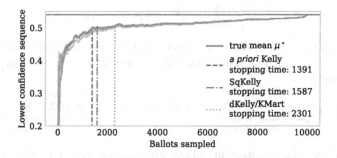

Fig. 1. 95% Lower confidence sequences for the margin of a plurality election between Alice and Bob for three different auditing methods. Votes for Alice are encoded by "1" and those for Bob are encoded by "0". The parameter of interest is then the average of these votes, which in this particular example is 54% (given by the horizontal grey line). The outcome is verified once the lower confidence sequence exceeds $1/2$. The time at which this happens is given by the vertical blue, green, and pink lines. (Color figure online)

1.3 Contributions and Outline

The contributions of this work are twofold. First, we introduce confidence sequences to the election auditing literature as intuitive and flexible ways of interpreting and visualizing risk-limiting audits. Second, we present algorithms for performing RLAs based on confidence sequences by deriving statistically and computationally efficient nonnegative martingales. At the risk of oversimplifying the issue, modern RLAs face a computational-statistical efficiency tradeoff. Methods such as BRAVO are easy to compute, but potentially less statistically efficient than the current state-of-the-art, KMart [13], but KMart can be prohibitively expensive to compute for large elections. The methods presented in this paper resolve this tradeoff: they typically match or outperform both BRAVO and KMart, while remaining practical to compute in large elections.

In Sect. 2, we show how confidence sequences generate risk-limiting audits, how they relate to more familiar RLAs based on sequentially valid p-values, and how they can be used to audit multiple contests. Section 3 derives novel confidence sequence-based RLAs and compares them to past RLA methods via simulation. Finally, Sect. 4 discusses how all of the aforementioned results apply to risk-limiting tallies for coercion-resistant voting schemes.

2 Confidence Sequences are Risk-Limiting

Consider an election consisting of N ballots. Following SHANGRLA [13], suppose that these can be transformed to a set of $[0, u]$-bounded real numbers $x_1, \ldots, x_N \in [0, u]$ with mean $\mu^\star := \frac{1}{N} \sum_{i=1}^{N} x_i$ for some known $u > 0$. Suppose that electoral assertions can be made purely in terms of $\mu^\star$. A classical $(1 - \alpha)$ confidence interval CI_n for $\mu^\star$ is an interval computed from data $X_1, X_2, \ldots, X_n$ with the guarantee that

$$\forall n \in [N], \ \mathbb{P}(\mu^\star \in \mathrm{CI}_n) \geq 1 - \alpha.$$

In contrast, a $(1 - \alpha)$ *confidence sequence* for $\mu^\star$ is a sequence of confidence sets, $C_1, C_2, \ldots, C_N$ which all simultaneously capture $\mu^\star$ with probability at least $(1 - \alpha)$. That is,

$$\underbrace{\mathbb{P}(\forall t \in [N], \ \mu^\star \in C_t) \geq 1 - \alpha,}_{\text{simultaneous coverage probability}} \quad \text{or equivalently} \quad \underbrace{\mathbb{P}(\exists t \in [N] : \mu^\star \notin C_t) \leq \alpha}_{\text{error probability}}.$$

The two probabilistic statements above are equivalent, but provide a different way of interpreting α and the corresponding guarantee.

If we have access to a $(1 - \alpha)$ confidence sequence for $\mu^\star$, we can audit any assertion about the election outcome made in terms of $\mu^\star$ with risk limit α. Here, we use $\mathcal{A} \subseteq [0, u]$ to denote an assertion. For example, SHANGRLA typically uses assertions of the form "$\mu^\star$ is greater than $1/2$", in which case $\mathcal{A} = (1/2, u]$.

Algorithm 1.1: Risk limiting audits via confidence sequences (RiLACS)

Input: Assertion $\mathcal{A} \subseteq [0, u]$, risk limit $\alpha \in (0, 1)$.
    for $t \in [N]$ **do**
        Randomly sample and remove X_t from the remaining ballots.
        Compute $C_t \equiv C(X_1, \ldots, X_t)$ at level α.
        if $\mathcal{A} \subseteq C_t$ **then**
            Certify the assertion $\mathcal{A}$ and stop if desired.
        end if
    end for

If the goal is to finish the audit as soon as possible above all else, then one can ignore the "if desired" condition. However, continued sampling can provide added assurance in $\mathcal{A}$, and maintains the risk limit at α. The following theorem summarizes the risk-limiting guarantee of the above algorithm.

Theorem 1. *Let $(C_t)_{t=1}^N$ be a $(1 - \alpha)$ confidence sequence for $\mu^\star$. Let $\mathcal{A} \subseteq [0, u]$ be an assertion about the electoral outcome (in terms of $\mu^\star$). The audit mechanism that certifies $\mathcal{A}$ as soon as $C_t \subseteq \mathcal{A}$ has risk limit α.*

Proof. We need to prove that if $\mu^\star \notin \mathcal{A}$, then $\mathbb{P}(\exists t \in [N] : C_t \subseteq \mathcal{A}) \leq \alpha$. First, notice that if $C_t \subseteq \mathcal{A}$, then we must have that $\mu^\star \notin C_t$ since $\mu^\star \notin \mathcal{A}$. Then,

$$\mathbb{P}(\exists t \in [N] : C_t \subseteq \mathcal{A}) \leq \mathbb{P}(\exists t \in [N] : \mu^\star \notin C_t)$$
$$\leq \alpha,$$

where the second inequality follows from the definition of a confidence sequence. This completes the proof. $\qquad\square$

Let us see how this theorem can be used in an example. Consider an election with two candidates, Alice and Bob, and a total of N cast ballots. Let

$\{x_1, \ldots, x_N\}$ be the list of numbers that result from encoding votes for Alice as 1, votes for Bob as 0, and ballots that do not contain a valid vote as $1/2$. Let $(C_t)_{t=1}^{N}$ be a $(1 - \alpha)$ confidence sequence for $\mu^\star := \frac{1}{N} \sum_{i=1}^{N} x_i$. If we wish to audit the assertion that "Alice beat Bob", then $u = 1$ and $\mathcal{A} = (1/2, 1]$. We can sequentially sample $X_1, X_2, \ldots, X_N$ without replacement, certifying the assertion once $C_t \subseteq \mathcal{A}$. By Theorem 1, this limits the risk to level α.

2.1   Relationship to Sequential Hypothesis Testing

The earliest work on RLAs did not use anytime p-values [10,11], but since about 2009, most RLA methods have used anytime p-values to conduct sequential hypothesis tests [3,7,8,12,13]. An anytime p-value is a sequence of p-values $(p_t)_{t=1}^{N}$ with the property that under some null hypothesis H_0,

$$\mathbb{P}_{H_0}(\exists t \in [N] : p_t \leq \alpha) \leq \alpha. \tag{1}$$

The anytime p-values $p_t \equiv p_t(\mu)$ are typically defined implicitly for each null hypothesis $H_0 : \mu^\star = \mu$ and yield a sequential hypothesis test $\phi_t^\mu := \mathbb{1}(p_t(\mu) \leq \alpha)$. As alluded to in Sect. 1.2, this immediately recovers a confidence sequence:

$$C_t := \{\mu \in [0, u] : \phi_t^\mu = 0\}.$$

Notice in Fig. 2 that the times at which nulls are rejected (or "stopping times") are the same for both confidence sequences and the associated p-values. Thus, nothing is lost by basing the RLA on confidence sequences rather than anytime p-values. Confidence sequences benefit from being visually intuitive and are arguably easier to interpret than anytime p-values.

For example, consider conducting an RLA for a simple two-candidate election between Alice and Bob with no invalid votes. Suppose that it is reported that Alice won, i.e., $\mu^\star := \frac{1}{N} \sum_{i=1}^{N} x_i > 1/2$ where $x_i = 1$ if the ith ballot is for Alice, 0 if for Bob, and $1/2$ if the ballot does not contain a valid vote for either candidate. A sequential RLA in the SHANGRLA framework would posit a null hypothesis $H_0 : \mu^\star \leq 1/2$ (the complement of the announced result: Bob actually won or the outcome is a tie), sample random ballots sequentially, and stop the audit (confirming the announced result) if and when H_0 is rejected at significance level α. If H_0 is not rejected before all ballots have been inspected, the true outcome is known.[2]

On the other hand, a ballot-polling RLA [6] based on confidence sequences proceeds by computing a lower $1 - \alpha$ confidence bound for the fraction $\mu^\star$ of votes for Alice. The audit stops, confirming the outcome, if and when this lower bound is larger than $1/2$. If that does not occur before the last ballot has been examined, the true outcome is known. In this formulation, there is no need to define a null hypothesis as the complement of the announced result and interpret

---

[2] At any point during the sampling, an election official can choose to abort the sampling and perform a full hand count for any reason. This cannot increase the risk limit: the chance of failing to correct an incorrect reported outcome does not increase.

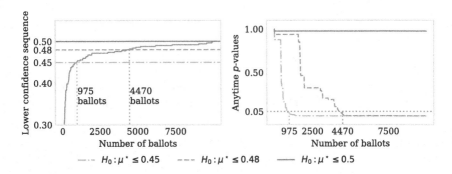

Fig. 2. The duality between anytime p-values and confidence sequences for three nulls: $H_0 : \mu^\star \leq \mu_0$ for $\mu_0 \in \{0.45, 0.48, 0.5\}$. The p-value for $H_0 : \mu^\star \leq 0.45$ (pink dash-dotted line) drops below 5% after 975 samples, exactly when the 95% *lower* confidence sequence exceeds 0.45. However, the p-value for $H_0 : \mu^\star \leq 0.5$ never reaches 0.05 and the 95% confidence sequence never excludes 0.5, the true value of $\mu^\star$. (Color figure online)

the resulting p-value, and so on. The approach also works for comparison audits using the "overstatement assorter" approach developed in [13], which transforms the problem into the same canonical form: testing whether the mean of any list in a collection of nonnegative, bounded lists is less than 1/2.

2.2   Auditing Multiple Contests

It is known that RLAs of multi-candidate, multi-winner elections can be reduced to several pairwise contests without adjusting for multiplicity [6]. This is accomplished by testing whether every single reported winner beat every single reported loser, and stopping once each of these tests rejects their respective nulls at level $\alpha \in (0, 1)$. For example, suppose it is reported that a set of candidates $\mathcal{W}$ beat a set of candidates $\mathcal{L}$ in a k-winner plurality contest with K candidates in all (that is, $|\mathcal{W}| = k$ and $|\mathcal{L}| = K - k$). For each reported winner $w \in \mathcal{W}$ and each reported loser $\ell \in \mathcal{L}$, encode votes for candidate w as "1", votes for ℓ as "0" and ballots with no valid vote in the contest or with a vote for any other candidate as "1/2" to obtain the population $\{x_1^{w,\ell}, \ldots, x_N^{w,\ell}\}$. Then as before, candidate w beat candidate ℓ if and only if $\mu_{w,\ell}^\star := \frac{1}{N} \sum_{i=1}^{N} x_i^{w,\ell} > 1/2$. In a two-candidate plurality election we would have proceeded by testing the null $H_0^{w,\ell} : \mu_{w,\ell}^\star \leq 1/2$ against the alternative $H_1^{w,\ell} : \mu_{w,\ell}^\star > 1/2$. To use the decomposition of a single winner or multi-winner plurality contest into a set of pairwise contests, we test each null $H_0^{w,\ell} : \mu_{w,\ell}^\star \leq 1/2$ for $w \in \mathcal{W}$ and $\ell \in \mathcal{L}$. The audit stops if and when *all* $k(K - k)$ *null hypotheses* are rejected. Crucially, if candidate $w \in \mathcal{W}$ did not win (i.e. $\mu_{w,\ell}^\star \leq 1/2$ for some $\ell \in \mathcal{L}$), then

$$\mathbb{P}(\text{reject all } H_{0,w,\ell} : w \in \mathcal{W}, \ell \in \mathcal{L}) \leq \min_{w \in \mathcal{W}, \ell \in \mathcal{L}} \mathbb{P}(\text{reject } H_{0,w,\ell}) \leq \alpha.$$

The same technique applies when auditing with confidence sequences. Let $\{(C_t^{w,\ell})_{t=1}^N\}$ be $(1 - \alpha)$ confidence sequences for $\{\mu_{w,\ell}^\star\}$, $w \in \mathcal{W}$, $\ell \in \mathcal{L}$. We verify the electoral outcome of every contest once $C_t^{w,\ell} \subseteq (1/2, u]$ for all $w \in \mathcal{W}$, $\ell \in \mathcal{L}$. Again, if $\mu_{w,\ell}^\star \leq 1/2$ for some $w \in \mathcal{W}$, and $\ell \in \mathcal{L}$, then

$$\mathbb{P}(\forall w \in \mathcal{W}, \forall \ell \in \mathcal{L}, \; C_t^{w,\ell} \subseteq (1/2, u]) \leq \min_{w \in \mathcal{W}, \ell \in \mathcal{L}} \mathbb{P}(C_t^{w,\ell} \subseteq (1/2, u]) \leq \alpha.$$

This technique can be generalized to handle audits of any number of contests from the same audit sample, as explained in [13]. For the sake of brevity, we omit the derivation, but it is a straightforward extension of the above.

3   Designing Powerful Confidence Sequences for RLAs

So far we have discussed how to conduct RLAs from confidence sequences for the parameter $\mu^\star$. In this section, we will discuss how to derive powerful confidence sequences for the purposes of conducting RLAs as efficiently as possible. For mathematical and notational convenience in the following derivations, we consider the case where $u = 1$. Note that nothing is lost in this setup since any population of $[0, u]$-bounded numbers can be scaled to the unit interval $[0, 1]$ by dividing each element by u (thereby scaling the population's mean as well).

As discussed in Sect. 2.1, we can construct confidence sequences by "inverting" sequential hypothesis tests. In particular, given a sequential hypothesis test $(\phi_t^\mu)_{t=1}^N$, the sequence of sets,

$$C_t := \{\mu \in [0, 1] : \phi_t^\mu = 0\}$$

forms a $(1-\alpha)$ confidence sequence for $\mu^\star$. Consequently, in order to develop powerful RLAs via confidence sequences, we can simply focus on carefully designing sequential tests $(\phi_t^\mu)_{t=1}^N$.[3]

To design sequential hypothesis tests, we start by finding *martingales* that translate to powerful tests. To this end, define $M_0(\mu) := 1$ and consider the following process for $t \in [N]$:

$$M_t(\mu) := \prod_{i=1}^t \left(1 + \lambda_i (X_i - \mathcal{C}_i(\mu))\right), \qquad (2)$$

where $\lambda_i \in \left[0, \frac{1}{\mathcal{C}_i(\mu)}\right]$ is a tuning parameter depending only on $X_1, \ldots, X_{i-1}$, and

$$\mathcal{C}_i(\mu) := \frac{N\mu - \sum_{j=1}^{i-1} X_j}{N - i + 1}$$

---

[3] Notice that it is not always feasible to compute the set of all $\mu \in [0, 1]$ such that $\phi_t^\mu = 0$ since $[0, 1]$ is uncountably infinite. However, all confidence sequences we will derive in this section are intervals (i.e. convex), and thus we can find the endpoints using a simple grid search or standard root-finding algorithms.

is the conditional mean of $X_i \mid X_1, \ldots, X_{i-1}$ if the mean of $\{x_1, \ldots, x_N\}$ were μ.

Following [15, Section 6], the process $(M_t(\mu^\star))_{t=0}^N$ is a nonnegative martingale starting at one. Formally, this means that $M_0(\mu^\star) = 1$, $M_t(\mu^\star) \geq 0$, and

$$\mathbb{E}(M_t(\mu^*) \mid X_1, \ldots, X_{t-1}) = M_{t-1}(\mu^*)$$

for each $t \in [N]$. Importantly for our purposes, nonnegative martingales are unlikely to ever become very large. This fact is known as *Ville's inequality* [2,14], which serves as a generalization of Markov's inequality to nonnegative (super)martingales, and can be stated formally as

$$\mathbb{P}\left(\exists t \in [N] : M_t(\mu^\star) \geq 1/\alpha\right) \leq \alpha M_0(\mu^\star) = \alpha, \tag{3}$$

where $\alpha \in (0, 1)$, and the equality follows from the fact that $M_0(\mu^\star) = 1$. As alluded to in Sect. 2, $(M_t(\mu^\star))_{t=0}^N$ can be interpreted as the reciprocal of an anytime p-value:

$$\mathbb{P}\left(\exists t \in [N] : \frac{1}{M_t(\mu^\star)} \leq \alpha\right) \leq \alpha,$$

which matches the probabilistic guarantee in (1). As a direct consequence of Ville's inequality, if we define the test $\phi_t^\mu := \mathbb{1}(M_t(\mu) \geq 1/\alpha)$, then

$$\mathbb{P}(\exists t \in [N] : \phi_t^{\mu^\star} = 1) \leq \alpha,$$

and thus $(\phi_t^\mu)_{t=1}^N$ is a level-α sequential hypothesis test. We can then invert $(\phi_t^\mu)_{t=1}^N$ and apply Theorem 1 to obtain confidence sequence-based RLAs with risk limit α.

3.1   Designing Martingales and Tests from Reported Vote Totals

So far, we have found a process $(M_t(\mu))_{t=0}^N$ that is a nonnegative martingale when $\mu = \mu^\star$, but what happens when $\mu \neq \mu^\star$? This is where the tuning parameters $(\lambda_t)_{t=1}^N$ come into the picture. Recall that an electoral assertion $\mathcal{A}$ is certified once $C_t \subseteq \mathcal{A}$. Therefore, to audit assertions quickly, we want C_t to be as tight as possible. Since C_t is defined as the set of $\mu \in [0, 1]$ such that $M_t(\mu) < 1/\alpha$, we can make C_t tight by making $M_t(\mu)$ as *large* as possible. To do so, we must carefully choose $(\lambda_t)_{t=1}^N$. This choice will depend on the type of election as well as the amount of information provided prior to the audit. First consider the case where reported vote totals are given (in addition to the announced winner).

For example, recall the election between Alice and Bob of Sect. 2, and suppose that $\{x_1, \ldots, x_N\}$ is the list of numbers encoding votes for Alice as 1, votes for Bob as 0, and ballots with no valid vote for either candidate as $1/2$. Recall that Alice beat Bob if and only if $\mu^\star := \frac{1}{N} \sum_{i=1}^N x_i > 1/2$, so we are interested in testing the null hypothesis $H_0 : \mu^\star \leq 1/2$ against the alternative $H_1 : \mu^\star > 1/2$. Suppose it is reported that Alice beat Bob with N_A' votes for Alice, N_B' for Bob,

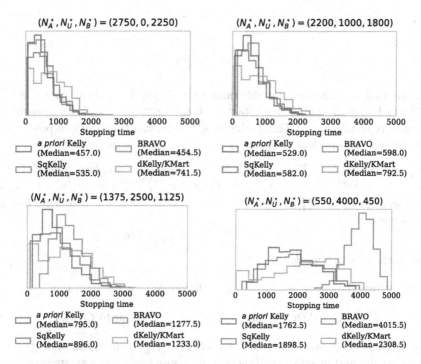

Fig. 3. Ballot-polling audit workload distributions under four possible outcomes of a two-candidate plurality election. Workload is defined as the number of distinct ballots examined before completing the audit. The first example considers an outcome where Alice and Bob received 2750 and 2250 votes respectively, and no ballots were invalid, for a margin of 0.1. The second, third, and fourth examples have the same margin, but with increasing numbers of invalid or "nuisance" ballots represented by $N_U^\star$. Notice that in the case with no nuisance ballots, *a priori* Kelly and BRAVO have an edge, while in the setting with many nuisance ballots, *a priori* Kelly vastly outperforms BRAVO. On the other hand, neither SqKelly nor dKelly require tuning based on the reported outcomes, but SqKelly outperforms dKelly in all four scenarios.

and N_U' nuisance votes (i.e. either invalid or for another party). If the reported outcome is *correct*, then for any fixed λ, we know the exact value of

$$\prod_{i=1}^{N}(1 + \lambda(x_i - 1/2)), \tag{4}$$

which is an inexact but reasonable proxy for $M_N(1/2)$, the final value of the process $(M_t(1/2))_{t=0}^{N}$. We can then choose the value of λ' that maximizes (4). Some algebra reveals that the maximizer of (4) is given by

$$\lambda' := 2\frac{N_A' - N_B'}{N_A' + N_B'}. \tag{5}$$

We then truncate λ' to obtain

$$\lambda_t^{\mathrm{apK}} := \min\left\{\lambda', \frac{1}{\mathcal{C}_t(\mu^\star)}\right\}, \tag{6}$$

ensuring that it lies in the allowable range $[0, 1/\mathcal{C}_t(\mu)]$. We call this choice of λ_t^{apK} *a priori* **Kelly** due to its connections to Kelly's criterion [5,15] for maximizing products of the form (4). This choice of λ_t^{apK} also has the desirable property of yielding convex confidence sequences, which we summarize below.

Proposition 1. *Let* $X_1, \ldots, X_N$ *be a sequential random sample from* $\{x_1, \ldots, x_N\}$ *with* $\mu^\star := \frac{1}{N}\sum_{i=1}^{N} x_i$. *Consider* $(\lambda_t^{\mathrm{apK}})_{t=1}^{N}$ *from (6) and define the process* $M_t(\mu) := \prod_{i=1}^{t}(1 + \lambda_i^{\mathrm{apK}}(X_i - \mathcal{C}_i(\mu)))$ *for any* $\mu \in [0,1]$. *Then the confidence set*

$$C_t^{\mathrm{apK}} := \{\mu \in [0,1] : M_t(\mu) < 1/\alpha\}$$

is an interval with probability one.

Proof. Notice that since $\lambda' \geq 0$, $\mathcal{C}_t(\mu) \geq 0$, and $X_i \geq 0$, we have that

$$\lambda_t^{\mathrm{apK}}(X_i - \mathcal{C}_t(\mu)) = \min\{\lambda' X_i, X_i/\mathcal{C}_t(\mu)\} - \min\{\lambda'\mathcal{C}_t(\mu), 1\}$$

is a nonincreasing function of μ for each $t \in [N]$. Consequently, $M_t(\mu)$ is a nonincreasing and quasiconvex function of μ, so its sublevel sets are convex. □

Note that *any* sequence $(\lambda_t)_{t=1}^{N}$ such that $\lambda_t \in [0, 1/\mathcal{C}_t(\mu)]$ would have yielded a valid nonnegative martingale, but we chose that which maximizes (4) so that the resulting hypothesis test $\phi_t := \mathbb{1}(M_t(1/2) > 1/\alpha)$ is powerful. In situations more complex than two-candidate plurality contests, the maximizer of (4) can still be found efficiently via standard root-finding algorithms. All of these methods are implemented in our Python package.[4]

While audits based on *a priori* Kelly display excellent empirical performance (see Fig. 3), their efficiency may be hurt when vote totals are erroneously reported. Small errors in reported vote totals seem to have minor adverse effects on stopping times (and in some cases can be slightly beneficial), but larger errors can significantly affect stopping time distributions (see Fig. 4). If we wish to audit the reported winner of an election but prefer not to rely on (or do not have access to) exact reported vote totals, we need an alternative to *a priori* Kelly. In the following section, we describe a family of such alternatives.

3.2   Designing Martingales and Tests Without Vote Totals

If the exact vote totals are not known, but we still wish to audit an assertion (e.g. that Alice beat Bob), we need to design a slightly different martingale that does not depend on maximizing (4) directly. Instead of finding an optimal λ', we will take $D \geq 2$ points evenly-spaced on the allowable range $[0, 1/\mathcal{C}_t(\mu)]$

---

[4] github.com/wannabesmith/RiLACS.

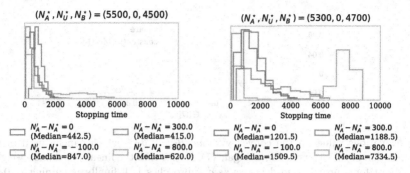

$(N_A^\star, N_U^\star, N_B^\star) = (5500, 0, 4500)$

$(N_A^\star, N_U^\star, N_B^\star) = (5300, 0, 4700)$

Stopping time   Stopping time

- $N_A' - N_A^\star = 0$ (Median=442.5)
- $N_A' - N_A^\star = 300.0$ (Median=415.0)
- $N_A' - N_A^\star = -100.0$ (Median=847.0)
- $N_A' - N_A^\star = 800.0$ (Median=620.0)

- $N_A' - N_A^\star = 0$ (Median=1201.5)
- $N_A' - N_A^\star = 300.0$ (Median=1188.5)
- $N_A' - N_A^\star = -100.0$ (Median=1509.5)
- $N_A' - N_A^\star = 800.0$ (Median=7334.5)

Fig. 4. Stopping times for *a priori* Kelly under various degrees of error in reported outcomes. In the above legends, $N_A^\star$ refers to the *true* number of votes for Alice, while N_A' refers to the incorrectly reported number of votes. Notice that empirical performance is relatively strong for $N_A' - N_A^\star \in \{0, 300\}$ but is adversely affected when $N_A' - N_A^\star \in \{-100, 800\}$, especially in the right-hand side plot with a narrower margin.

and "hedge our bets" among all of these. Making this more precise, note that a convex combination of martingales (with respect to the same filtration) is itself a martingale [15], and thus for any $(\theta_1, \ldots, \theta_D)$ such that $\theta_d \geq 0$ and $\sum_{d=1}^{D} \theta_d = 1$, we have that

$$M_t^D(\mu^\star) := \sum_{d=1}^{D} \theta_d \prod_{i=1}^{t} \left(1 + \frac{d}{(D+1)\mathcal{C}_i(\mu^\star)}(X_i - \mathcal{C}_i(\mu^\star))\right) \qquad (7)$$

forms a nonnegative martingale starting at one. Notice that we no longer have to depend on the reported vote totals to begin an audit. Furthermore, confidence sequences generated using sublevel sets of $M_t^D(\mu)$ are intervals with probability one [15, Proposition 4]. Nevertheless, choosing $(\theta_1, \ldots, \theta_D)$ is a nontrivial task. A natural—but as we will see, suboptimal—choice is to set $\theta_d = 1/D$ for each $d \in [D]$. Previous works [15] call this **dKelly** (for "diversified Kelly"), a name we adopt here. In fact, this choice of $(\theta_1, \ldots, \theta_D)$ gives an arbitrarily close and computationally efficient approximation to the *Kaplan martingale* (**KMart**) [13] which can otherwise be prohibitively expensive to compute for large N.

Better choices of $(\theta_d)_{d=1}^{D}$ exist for the types of elections one might encounter in practice. Recall that near-optimal values of λ are given by (5). However, setting $\theta_d = 1/D$ for each $d \in [D]$ implicitly treats all $d/((D+1)\mathcal{C}_i(\mu^\star))$ as equally reasonable values of λ. Elections with large values of $\mu^\star$ (e.g. closer to 1) are "easier" to audit, and the interesting or "difficult" regime is when $\mu^\star$ is close to (but strictly larger than) $1/2$. Therefore, we recommend designing $(\theta_1, \ldots, \theta_D)$ so that $(M_t^D(1/2))_{t=0}^{N}$ upweights optimal values of λ for margins close to 0, and downweights those for margins close to 1. Consider the following concrete examples. First, we have the truncated-square weights,

$$\theta_d^{\text{square}} := \frac{\gamma_d^{\text{square}}}{\sum_{d=1}^{D} \gamma_d^{\text{square}}}, \quad \text{where } \gamma_d^{\text{square}} := (1/3 - x)^2 \mathbb{1}_{d \leq 1/3}.$$

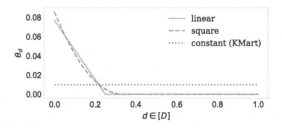

Fig. 5. Various values of the convex weights $(\theta_1, \ldots, \theta_D)$, which can be used in the construction of the diversified martingale (7). Notice that the linear and square weights are largest for d near 0, and decrease as d approaches $1/4$, finally remaining at 0 for all large d. Smaller values of d are upweighted since they correspond to those values of λ in $M_t^D(\mu^\star)$ that are optimal for smaller (i.e. interesting) electoral margins. This is in contrast to the constant weight function, which sets $\theta_d = 1/D$ for each $d \in [D]$. We find that square weights perform well in practice (see Fig. 3) but these can be tuned and tailored based on prior knowledge and the particular problem at hand.

and we normalize by $\sum_d \gamma_d^{\text{square}}$ to ensure that $\sum_d \theta_d = 1$. Another sensible choice is given by the truncated-linear weights, where we simply replace γ_d^{square} by $\gamma_d^{\text{linear}} := \max\{0, 1 - 2d\}$. These values of θ_d^{linear} and θ_d^{square} are large for $d \approx 0$ and small for $d \gg 0$, and hence the summands in the martingale given by (7) are upweighted for implicit values of λ which are optimal for "interesting" margins close to 0, and downweighted for simple margins much larger than 0 (see Fig. 5).

When M_t^D is combined with θ_d^{square}, we refer to the resulting martingales and confidence sequences as **SqKelly**. We compare their empirical workload against that of *a priori* Kelly, dKelly, and BRAVO in Fig. 3. A hybrid approach is also possible: suppose we want to use reported outcomes or prior knowledge alongside these convex-weighted martingales. We can simply choose $(\theta_1, \ldots, \theta_D)$ so that M_t^D upweights values in a neighborhood of λ' (or some other value chosen based on prior knowledge[5]).

4 Risk-Limiting Tallies via Confidence Sequences

Rather than audit an already-announced electoral outcome, it may be of interest to determine (for the purposes of making a first announcement) the election winner with high probability, without counting all N ballots. Such procedures are known as risk-limiting tallies (RLTs), which were developed for coercion-resistant, end-to-end verifiable voting schemes [4]. For example, suppose a voter is being coerced to vote for Bob. If the final vote tally reveals that Bob received few or no votes, then the coercer will suspect that the voter did not comply

---

[5] The use of the word "prior" here should not be interpreted in a Bayesian sense. No matter what values of $(\theta_1, \ldots, \theta_D)$ are chosen, the resulting tests and confidence sequences have *frequentist* risk-limiting guarantees.

with instructions. RLTs provide a way to mitigate this issue by providing high-probability guarantees that the reported winner truly won, leaving a large proportion of votes shrouded. In such cases, the voter is guaranteed plausible deniability, as they can claim to the coercer that their ballot is simply among the unrevealed ones.

While the motivations for RLTs are quite different from those for RLAs, the underlying techniques are similar. The same is true for confidence sequence-based RLTs. All methods introduced in this paper can be applied to RLTs (with the exception of "a priori Kelly" since it depends on the reported outcome) but with two-sided power. Consider the martingales we discussed in Sect. 3.2,

$$M_t^D(\mu^\star) := \sum_{d=1}^{D} \theta_d \prod_{i=1}^{t} \left(1 + \frac{d}{(D+1)\mathcal{C}_i(\mu^\star)} (X_i - \mathcal{C}_i(\mu^\star)) \right), \qquad (8)$$

where $(\theta_1, \ldots, \theta_D)$ are convex weights. Recall that our confidence sequences at a given time t were defined as those $\mu \in [0,1]$ for which $M_t^D(\mu) < 1/\alpha$. In other words, a given value μ is only excluded from the confidence set if $M_t^D(\mu)$ is large. However, notice that $M_t^D(\mu)$ will become large if the conditional mean $\mathcal{C}_t(\mu^\star) \equiv \mathbb{E}(X_t \mid X_1, \ldots, X_{t-1})$ is larger than the null conditional mean $\mathcal{C}_t(\mu)$, but the same cannot be said if $\mathcal{C}_t(\mu^\star) < \mathcal{C}_t(\mu)$. As a consequence, the resulting confidence sequences are all one-sided *lower* confidence sequences. To ensure that our bounds have non-trivial two-sided power, we can simply combine (8) with a martingale that also grows when $\mathcal{C}_t(\mu^\star) < \mathcal{C}_t(\mu)$ (Fig. 6).

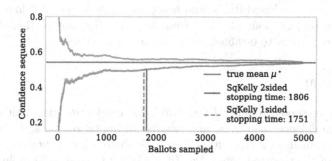

Fig. 6. Confidence sequence-based risk-limiting tally for a two-candidate election. Unlike RLAs, RLTs require two-sided confidence sequences so that the true winner can be determined (with high probability) without access to an announced result. Notice that testing the same null $H_0 : \mu^\star \leq 0.5$ is less efficient in an RLT than in an RLA. This is a necessary sacrifice for having nontrivial power against other alternatives.

Proposition 2. *For nonnegative vectors* $(\theta_1^+, \ldots, \theta_D^+)$ *and* $(\theta_1^-, \ldots, \theta_D^-)$ *that each sum to one, define the processes*

$$M_t^{D+}(\mu) := \sum_{d=1}^{D} \theta_d^+ \prod_{i=1}^{t} \left(1 + \frac{d}{(D+1)\mathcal{C}_i(\mu^\star)}(X_i - \mathcal{C}_i(\mu^\star)) \right),$$

$$M_t^{D-}(\mu) := \sum_{d=1}^{D} \theta_d^- \prod_{i=1}^{t} \left(1 - \frac{d}{(D+1)(1-\mathcal{C}_i(\mu^\star))}(X_i - \mathcal{C}_i(\mu^\star)) \right).$$

Next, for $\beta \in [0,1]$, *define their mixture*

$$M_t^{D\pm}(\mu) := \beta M_t^{D+}(\mu) + (1-\beta)M_t^{D-}(\mu).$$

Then, $M_t^{D\pm}(\mu^\star)$ *is a nonnegative martingale starting at one. Consequently,*

$$\mathcal{C}_t^\pm := \{\mu \in [0,1] : M_t^{D\pm}(\mu) < 1/\alpha\}$$

forms a $(1-\alpha)$ *confidence sequence for* $\mu^\star$.

Proof. This follows immediately from the fact that both $M_t^{D+}(\mu^\star)$ and $M_t^{D-}(\mu^\star)$ are martingales with respect to the same filtration, and that convex combinations of such martingales are also martingales.   □

With this setup and notation in mind, M_t^D as defined in Sect. 3.2 is a special case of $M_t^{D\pm}$ with $\beta = 1$. As noted by [4], RLTs involving multiple assertions *do* require correction for multiple testing, unlike RLAs. The same is true for confidence sequence-based RLTs (and hence the tricks of Sect. 2.2 do not apply). It suffices to perform a simple Bonferroni correction by constructing $(1 - \alpha/K)$ confidence sequences to establish K simultaneous assertions.

5   Summary

This paper presented a general framework for conducting risk-limiting audits based on confidence sequences, and derived computationally and statistically efficient martingales for computing them. We showed how *a priori* Kelly takes advantage of the reported vote totals (if available) to stop ballot-polling audits significantly earlier than extant ballot-polling methods, and how alternative martingales such as SqKelly also provide strong empirical performance in the absence of reported outcomes. Finally, we demonstrated how a simple tweak to the aforementioned algorithms provides two-sided confidence sequences, which can be used to perform risk-limiting tallies. Confidence sequences and these martingales can be applied to ballot-level comparison audits and batch-level comparison audits as well, using "overstatement assorters" [13], which reduce comparison audits to the same canonical statistical problem: testing whether the mean of any list in a collection of non-negative bounded lists is at most $1/2$. We hope that this new perspective on RLAs and its associated software will aid in making election audits simpler, faster, and more transparent.

References

1. Blom, M., et al.: Assertion-based approaches to auditing complex elections, with application to party-list proportional elections. In: Krimmer, R., et al. (eds.) E-Vote-ID 2021, LNCS 12900, pp. 47–62. Springer, Cham (2021)
2. Howard, S.R., Ramdas, A., McAuliffe, J., Sekhon, J.: Time-uniform Chernoff bounds via nonnegative supermartingales. Probab. Surv. **17**, 257–317 (2020)
3. Huang, Z., Rivest, R.L., Stark, P.B., Teague, V.J., Vukcevic, D.: A unified evaluation of two-candidate ballot-polling election auditing methods. In: Krimmer, R., et al. (eds.) E-Vote-ID 2020. LNCS, vol. 12455, pp. 112–128. Springer, Cham (2020). https://doi.org/10.1007/978-3-030-60347-2_8
4. Jamroga, W., Roenne, P.B., Ryan, P.Y.A., Stark, P.B.: Risk-limiting tallies. In: Krimmer, R., et al. (eds.) E-Vote-ID 2019. LNCS, vol. 11759, pp. 183–199. Springer, Cham (2019). https://doi.org/10.1007/978-3-030-30625-0_12
5. Kelly, J., Jr.: A new interpretation of information rate. Bell Syst. Tech. J. **35**(4), 917–926 (1956)
6. Lindeman, M., Stark, P.B., Yates, V.S.: BRAVO: ballot-polling risk-limiting audits to verify outcomes. In: 2012 Electronic Voting Technology Workshop/Workshop on Trustworthy Elections (EVT/WOTE 2012). USENIX Association, Bellevue, August 2012. https://www.usenix.org/conference/evtwote12/workshop-program/presentation/lindeman
7. Ottoboni, K., Bernhard, M., Halderman, J.A., Rivest, R.L., Stark, P.B.: Bernoulli ballot polling: a manifest improvement for risk-limiting audits. In: Bracciali, A., Clark, J., Pintore, F., Rønne, P.B., Sala, M. (eds.) FC 2019. LNCS, vol. 11599, pp. 226–241. Springer, Cham (2020). https://doi.org/10.1007/978-3-030-43725-1_16
8. Ottoboni, K., Stark, P.B., Lindeman, M., McBurnett, N.: Risk-limiting audits by stratified union-intersection tests of elections (SUITE). In: Krimmer, R., et al. (eds.) E-Vote-ID 2018. LNCS, vol. 11143, pp. 174–188. Springer, Cham (2018). https://doi.org/10.1007/978-3-030-00419-4_12
9. Rivest, R.L.: ClipAudit: a simple risk-limiting post-election audit. arXiv preprint arXiv:1701.08312 (2017)
10. Stark, P.B.: Conservative statistical post-election audits. Ann. Appl. Stat. **2**(2), 550–581 (2008)
11. Stark, P.B.: CAST: canvass audits by sampling and testing. IEEE Trans. Inf. Forensics Secur. **4**(4), 708–717 (2009)
12. Stark, P.B.: Risk-limiting postelection audits: conservative p-values from common probability inequalities. IEEE Trans. Inf. Forensics Secur. **4**(4), 1005–1014 (2009)
13. Stark, P.B.: Sets of half-average nulls generate risk-limiting audits: SHANGRLA. In: Bernhard, M., et al. (eds.) FC 2020. LNCS, vol. 12063, pp. 319–336. Springer, Cham (2020). https://doi.org/10.1007/978-3-030-54455-3_23
14. Ville, J.: Etude critique de la notion de collectif. Bull. Amer. Math. Soc. **45**(11), 824 (1939)
15. Waudby-Smith, I., Ramdas, A.: Estimating means of bounded random variables by betting. arXiv preprint arXiv:2010.09686 (2021)

Vote Secrecy and Voter Feedback in Remote Voting – Can We Have Both?

Arne Koitmäe[1], Jan Willemson[2]([⊠])[iD], and Priit Vinkel[2][iD]

[1] State Electoral Office, Lossi plats 1a, Tallinn, Estonia
[2] Cybernetica, Narva mnt 20, Tartu, Estonia

Abstract. The principle of secrecy is one of the most important tools to guarantee a voting process without undue influence to the voter. However, the concepts of the secret ballot and secret vote have strong ties to voting in a controlled environment in the polling station, and remote voting methods like postal voting or Internet voting need to employ special measures and approaches to achieve similar results. At the same time, limited options of observing the tallying process remotely potentially undermines the trust in remote voting. This paper looks at possible ways of giving the voter some feedback and assurance in the integrity of their vote, at the same time adhering to the freedom of voting principle. The Estonian Internet voting system is used as a model case for evaluation of a possible feedback channel architecture.

Keywords: Voting feedback · Freedom of voting · Secrecy of vote · Internet voting · Remote voting

1 Introduction

Freedom of voting – the principle where the voter is able to cast his or her vote without undue influence – is one of the cornerstones of the democratic process. Secrecy of the vote is one of the most important tools to achieve this goal. However, the way we understand vote secrecy is closely related to the concept of traditional voting – the ballot is filled in privately in the voting booth, and then deposited into the ballot box. However, many voting methods also deviate from this scheme. One example is postal voting, where there is no control whether the ballot is filled in privately, and no solid guarantees can be given that the ballot sent through mail is not lost, opened, or tampered with.

In general, once the paper vote is cast in the ballot box (or the envelope with a ballot posted in mail) the voter has no way of verifying how their vote is processed and counted. Observation of voting and vote counting procedures are meant to ensure the integrity of the tally. While the voter's participation is recorded in the voter list and the data of the voter lists can be compared to the final tally, the path of the vote itself – anonymous ballot – is untraceable by the voter. This is usually not a problem if the trust towards the election management is high enough. However, it can be a problem if the trust is low,

R. Krimmer et al. (Eds.): E-Vote-ID 2021, LNCS 12900, pp. 140–154, 2021.
https://doi.org/10.1007/978-3-030-86942-7_10

especially if there are doubts about the elections being conducted in a free and fair way.

Internet voting (i-voting) provides new challenges when implementing ballot secrecy. A well-implemented i-voting system can use cryptography to guarantee that the ballot is sent and received as intended, with its integrity untouched. An observer or an auditor can make sure that all the votes cast are accounted for, that the votes included in the tally are the same as cast, and that the votes were tabulated correctly. However, voters themselves cannot fully verify i-voting results and people need to have absolute faith in the accuracy, honesty and security of the whole electoral system [38]. The path of their vote is something voters cannot trace or observe directly, and this can undermine the trust in the i-voting system. Trustworthiness of i-voting is more and more connected to additional confirmations given to the voter about the vote being handled correctly and processed as required by law.

However, the more information we give to the voter about their vote, the more the secrecy of the vote is undermined. In order to ensure freedom of the vote, it should not be possible to use this information against the voter. Secrecy of the vote should remain intact and voters should not find themselves in a weaker position against possible malefactors because their voting information is revealed.

Another problem in regards to i-voting and vote secrecy is the voting environment, which should ensure voter privacy. This cannot be guaranteed by election administration when the voter is voting from the location of their choice using a personal computer. Hence there are inherent risks present, like a possibility of malware tampering with the vote, or taking over the electronic identity used to authenticate the voter and sign the encrypted ballot. The worst-case scenario is that a malicious actor casts the vote using voter's electronic identity without the voter even knowing it. The observers and auditors cannot review how the vote was cast at the location of the voter. This presents a need for additional checks available to the voter. Merely the confirmation that the i-voting tally is verifiably correct doesn't address this concern. This concern is not limited to i-voting either.

Therefore it would be beneficial to give voters further confirmation about how their vote is handled with a goal to increase the trust in voting in general. Another issue to consider is that such measures should not make voting arrangements too complex for the voter, as not to restrict access to voting. In this paper we will examine whether this can be achieved without significantly weakening vote secrecy.

In order to have a more concrete treatment of the topic, we will be using Estonian Internet voting as the example case study throughout this paper. In the Parliamentary and European Parliament elections of 2019, the share of i-votes cast was 43.8% and 46,7% of participating voters, respectively [14]. Thus legitimacy of elections in Estonia very much hinges on the perceived trust of i-voting. Estonian i-voting system features both individual verification (introduced in 2013 [32]) and server-side auditing (introduced in 2017 [29]). Swiss and

Norwegian i-voting solutions have implemented individual and universal verification solutions as well. The Swiss Post e-voting solution uses verification of votes cast both individually by voters and universally by the electoral commission [17]. The Norwegian i-voting system used return codes for individual verification and server side auditing [26]. Individual verification is limited to confirming that the voter's vote was received as intended by the vote collecting service. Server-side auditing, on the other hand, allows to certify that the votes as a complete set have been tallied correctly. However, the popularity of i-voting in Estonia has initiated debate over 1) how freedom of vote and vote secrecy are guaranteed for Internet voting, and 2) what measures would increase general trust in the system [13]. Contributing to this discussion is the main motivation behind the current paper.

The paper is organised as follows. Section 2 presents a discussion on the concept of secret ballot that has been traditionally used to guarantee voting freedom. We also take a broader look at remote voting environments to understand how far is it reasonable to go with the vote secrecy requirement in this setting. Section 3 studies a possible additional feedback channel notifying the voter on the fact that a vote has been cast on their behalf. We analyse possible implementations of such a channel together with their impact on voting freedom. Finally, Sect. 4 presents some conclusions and sets directions for future work.

2   Concept of the Secret Ballot

2.1   Secrecy of the Vote

Vote secrecy hasn't always been a requirement when conducting elections. Before mid-19th century it was rather a standard to vote openly, e.g. via stating one's preference out loud, or using visually distinguishable ballot sheets. Of course this also encouraged various coercive practices. To counter these, voting by secret ballot was introduced, with Australia being one of the first countries where it was systematically implemented [22,41].

Today the requirement of vote secrecy has been stated in the highest level of international legislative acts. The United Nations International Covenant on Civil and Political Rights (UN CCPR) [3, Art 25], United Nations Universal Declaration of Human Rights [1, Art 21] as well as the European Convention of Human Rights (ECHR) [2, Art 3 of Prot I] state that voting shall be held by secret ballot. UN CCPR's General Comment 25 [4] adds that states should take measures to guarantee the requirement of the secrecy of the vote during elections, implying that voters should be protected from any form of coercion or compulsion to disclose how they intend to vote or how they voted, and from any unlawful or arbitrary interference with the voting process.

On electronic voting, Article 3.2 (iv) of the Council of Europe (CoE) Venice Commission's Code of Good Practice In Electoral Matters states that the (electronic) voters should be able to obtain a confirmation of their votes and to correct them, if necessary, respecting secret suffrage [6]. The CoE recommendation CM/Rec(2017)5 [12] on standards for e-voting makes several suggestions towards maintaining vote secrecy. Article 23 of the Appendix to CM/Rec(2017)5 states that an e-voting system shall not provide the voter with proof of the content of the vote cast for use by third parties. Article 24 states that e-voting shall ensure that the secrecy of previous choices recorded and erased by the voter before issuing his or her final vote is respected.

The Code of Good Practice in Electoral Matters elaborates on the concept of secret suffrage on the voter's side as well. It states that for the voter, secrecy of voting is not only a right, but a duty as well. It also requires that voting must be individual, and that the list of persons actually voting should not be published [6, Art 4]. In the explanatory report, the Venice Commission explains that the purpose of the secrecy of the ballot is to shield voters from pressures they might face if others learned how they had voted [6, Par 52]. Moreover, since abstention may indicate a political choice, list of persons voting should not be published [6, Par 54].

From the voter's point of view, perceived vote secrecy is not necessarily equal to formal vote secrecy interpreted and implemented by the Electoral Management Body (EMB). The voters must also believe that the election administration operates in a way that their choices are kept secret (psychologically secret ballot) [27]. I-voting adds another dimension here, since the voters must additionally believe that other voters respect privacy and secrecy of the vote. Additionally, voters might feel socially obligated to reveal their votes, or they can believe that other voters might do so (social secrecy of the ballot) [27].

In the jurisprudence of the model case of Estonia, the current thinking regarding secrecy and Internet voting is based on the teleological approach, meaning that constitutional principles should be understood through the problems these principles were meant to solve [24]. It was first noted in 2004 as the underlying motivation for the draft legislation allowing for Internet voting [24]. In addition to that, the second source of the current approach is the liberal idea of trusting the voter [24,36]. The principle of secrecy would protect an individual from any pressure or influence against her or his free expression of a political preference. Thus, the principle of secrecy is a means, not an end goal [24,37]. Influence resistance in the Estonian i-voting system is guaranteed by the possibility of re-voting, thus the principle of secrecy, the end goal, is actually achieved [36]. This approach has now been generally accepted and expanded on [35,37,38] as not just the reasoning behind the original draft legislation, but as the actual explanation to how Internet voting conforms to the principle of secret ballot.

There remains a question whether the second part of reasoning – that the voter should be trusted – is applicable to the principle of secrecy. Vote secrecy cannot be understood as just optional, i.e. it's not just up to the voter to decide [19], but remote internet voting requires rethinking of the privacy principle [36,37]. In support of a more traditional approach, Buchstein in 2004 (before the first i-enabled Estonian elections in 2005) argued for the sanctity of the secret ballot, while admitting that Drechsler's and Madise's interpretation and Estonian constitutional debate comes in as a possible starting point for a paradigmatic change [23]. There were also concerns that the transition towards voting more from home, the concept of election may change without a real discussion on how that may weaken the voters' consciousness of a secret and personal vote [40]. This paradigmatic change has occurred, to an extent, when considering i-voting initiatives in Estonia, Switzerland and Norway, but also the raise in popularity of postal voting in general. The aforementioned countries have developed their i-voting system in line with the international standards and recommendations, while monitoring the experiences of other countries [21]. The updated CoE recommendation on i-voting CM/Rec(2017), now at its second iteration, reflects this change as well.

In practice vote secrecy on voter's side has been difficult to enforce, as many voters do not care about secrecy or do want to make their choice known, because of the social secrecy of the ballot as described by Gerber *et al.* [27].

2.2   Secrecy of Participation in Voting

Additional consideration should be given to how the principle of secrecy relates to voter's participation in voting. The Venice Commission has explained that voter lists with information on who voted shouldn't be published and abstention is a from of political choice [6, Par 54].

At the same time, when we look at voting as a general process, full participation secrecy is impossible to implement as voting in the polling station is public by nature. In regards to social secrecy of the vote, voters are often encouraged to participate and make their participation known by election stakeholders. This can possibly lead to problems in maintaining vote secrecy as well. For example, in Sweden, where ballots are printed separately for each party, party activists hand out ballots in front of the polling place to their voters. If the voter takes just one ballot, the content of the ballot is then known to bystanders [25].

The act of voting and content of the ballot are not approached the same way by voters and election stakeholders. As a result, voter lists (at least individual data of a voter) do not really fall under the umbrella of maintaining vote secrecy. In the past, personalised data on Internet voters has even been studied by researchers [35].

As for our model case of the Estonian Internet voting system, the current regulations stipulate that all data on Internet voters shared for scientific purposes must be made anonymous (including voting logs) [8, Par 77-1 (2)]. As for polling station voter lists that have been traditionally on paper, access to them is limited to the voters (personal information only) and parties; candidates and their representatives must justify why they need access (e.g. in case of an elections dispute) [8, Par 23 (2)]. Additionally, the data can be used for scientific purposes. Thus the data concerning the voter is always available to the person without limitations, but the voter list data cannot be published or released to third parties except in cases stipulated by the law.

2.3 Challenges of Keeping Vote Secrecy While Increasing Voter Trust in the Modern Voting Environment

A modern voting environment can include several methods of voting that differ in how much direct control the EMB has over it. Voting in a polling station takes place in a standardized environment, under control of the polling station staff. At the same time, the ballot box voting arrangements at home, overseas or at hospitals can be less convenient for the voter. On the other side of the spectrum are off-site voting methods like postal voting and Internet voting, being conducted without any supervision of the election administration. The vote delivery channel (mail or Internet) is in such cases not controlled by the EMB either.

If we accept that:

1. maintaining vote secrecy is not just the task of the EMB, but also of the voter,
2. not all ballots are cast under the direct supervision of election administration,
3. vote secrecy is just means to achieve the principle goal of free elections,

voters should also have the appropriate tools to be able to achieve that goal.

There are already a few measures at the disposal of the voter (with the implementation details varying across jurisdictions), e.g.:

- The voter can vote on the election day at a polling station and then observe the election procedures up to the end of vote counting. This gives a certain level of confidence that the voter's personal ballot (among other ballots) was not tampered with. Here the voter has to trust their own observation.
- Voters can check their data in the voter list, which includes information on whether they have voted, and possibly also the voting method that was used (i.e. Internet voting, voting outside the territory of their municipality or constituency). However, if the voter must personally access the voter list (or request the information from the EMB) then this requires action on voter's part and the voters must also be aware of the possibility. Therefore it is unlikely to provide any statistically significant amount of verifiability to increase trust in elections in general.
- An Internet voter could verify that the vote cast was received and stored as intended. There are several ways to implement this. For example, in Estonia, a smart device application is used for verification [32], but it does not help in the case when the voter is unaware that someone has cast a vote on their behalf. Since this method requires action on the voter's side, it hasn't achieved wide usage. The share of i-votes verified by the voters has remained between 4–5% of all i-votes since 2014 [14]. It can be used to detect certain mass attacks against i-voting (e.g. when malware is trying to manipulate active voting sessions), but not all of them (e.g. when malware itself initiates the sessions without voter participation).
- In case of postal voting in Finland, the postal voter and the voting procedure have to be accompanied by two independent witnesses who could attest in writing that the freedom of vote and vote secrecy have been adhered to in this process [33,39].

None of these measures undermine vote secrecy, but the problem is that these methods are limited in scope and they presume significant extra actions from the voters.

In order to certify one's vote, there are also other methods that are either discouraged by EMBs or not supported by legislation.

- Voters can take a photo of their ballots in the polling booth, or screen capture their choices in the Internet voting app or verification app. The voter can also live broadcast their voting from the polling booth [20]. This provides some (although quite a weak form of) proof that the vote has been cast correctly. This also lets the voter publish the image of the ballot taking, thus conflicting the vote secrecy principle.
- Voters can also mark their paper ballots in a way that it would be recognizable during the vote counting. If the voter (or some other informed party) then observes the count, they can make notice whether and how their vote was counted [42]. This is also possible for Internet voting, for example modifying the choice on the ballot in a way that the i-vote will be counted as invalid. As an example, there have been actual cases of sending in invalid votes in case of Estonian i-voting [30,31].

The two above channels are violating the vote secrecy requirement, presenting proof of the contents of the ballot, thus making the voter more vulnerable to undue coercion. However, neither of the methods is something the EMB can directly block. In such cases it should be up to the legislation and EMB to determine if the act of vote is impermissible or the vote invalid.

In Finland, for example, the votes that contain extra markings on them are declared invalid by law [5, Par 85 (6)]. However, in Estonia, such a regulation does not exist. In fact the law stipulates that if the ballot is not filled correctly (e.g. the number of the candidate is not written on the correct spot), but the choice of the voter is otherwise understood (e.g. the name of the candidate was written on the ballot), the ballot is considered valid [8, Par 57 (6) 8)]. This presents an opportunity for the voters to get creative, enabling tracking of their votes. As for taking pictures of ballots (and publishing them), restricting these activities is even more complicated.

In the case of *stemfies* (ballot selfies), it is also apparent that the legislation and our general understanding of the secrecy have not kept up with the technological advancements [20]. It is unclear, whether and how such voter-initiated deviation from secrecy should be blocked and enforced by law, especially for remote voting. The consensus in this hasn't been reached yet. For example Sect. 56 (6) 5a of German Federal Electoral Regulations states that the Electoral Board must turn away any voter whom they find taking photos or videos in the voting booth [7]. At the same time, in the Netherlands taking ballot selfies is allowed, although not encouraged [11]. *Stemfies* can also spark debate about other human rights and freedoms. European Court of Human Rights has ruled [15] that forbidding to use a mobile app to publish voter's ballot was in conflict with the Art 10 (Freedom of Expression) of the European Convention on Human Rights [2].

In summary, to improve voter's control over how voting is handled, we should be looking for a solution that wouldn't interfere with vote secrecy, give voters a way to verify their vote was handled correctly, and that would be universal enough to achieve statistically significant amount of checks.

A possible way to achieve the latter goal is to require as little action from the voter as possible. As we saw above, one of the main attack vectors not detected by the current verification mechanisms is malware that casts votes without the voter knowing about it. A similar problem occurs if the voter's eID is taken over physically. To detect such attacks, the system can be augmented with a feedback channel that gets triggered every time a vote is cast on voter's behalf. Next we will be studying the options of establishing such a channel.

3   Establishing a Feedback Channel

3.1   Feedback on the Fact of Casting a Vote

When introducing a feedback channel, our goal is to give i-voters additional assurance that they have (or have not!) voted. On the other hand, we do not want to publish the proof in a way that it would render re-voting as a measure to maintain voting freedom inefficient.

Currently, the Estonian system allows to get feedback on several levels.

- Confirmation that the vote collecting service has received the i-vote and received it as intended. In Estonia this is currently implemented by the smart device verification app.
- Confirmation that the i-vote was included in the set of i-votes that are going to be tallied. Since the list of i-voters is created by the Internet voting system, a voter can check if their i-vote is included in this list, but this action is very inconvenient to the voters (see Sect. 2.3).
- Confirmation that the i-vote was amongst the i-votes tallied. Currently no feedback for the voter exists here, but the integrity of the i-vote set is verified by the EMB and auditors.
- Confirmation that the vote was counted as intended. Currently no feedback for the voter exists here, but the result can be verified by the tallying proof by the EMB, auditors and by anyone who has created an auditing application.

What is missing from this list is a passive method for getting information about the vote being received by the system. If such a feedback on voting participation only reveals the fact that the voter has voted at some point, then the clash with the principle of vote secrecy is minimal. It would, however, imply that the voter has not abstained from voting. In such a way, giving a notification that a person has i-voted would be similar to situation when someone would take a photo of a voter leaving a polling station.

Introducing a voting fact feedback channel would benefit the voter in two main ways:

1. the voter would get assurance that the vote has been received and stored; and
2. even if the voter did not vote, absence of the voting notification would confirm that no-one else has voted for them.

Both confirmations would be useful to both i-voters and paper ballot voters. The assurance for the voter that no-one has cast a vote on their behalf can hopefully increase trust in the elections, including Internet voting.

Recall, however, that the ability to withstand coercion attacks relies on the possibility to cast re-votes in the Estonian system. Thus, assurance about which vote was processed (tallied) would potentially weaken the position of the i-voter, since this would reveal whether the coerced vote was later changed or not.

In conclusion, the feedback notification should just acknowledge the fact of receiving a vote by the system, but not much else (including the exact time, or the information whether it was a re-vote or not; see Sect. 3.3 for further discussion). Such a confirmation would be the most in line with the current legislation, not requiring to rethink how vote secrecy should be understood and protected.

In Estonia, such a system would be relatively easy to implement, since from 2021, electronic voter lists will be deployed. Amongst other features, it would enable the possibility to give voters automatic feedback whether they have voted, since this information is entered in the electronic voter list in real time.

Electronic voter lists make it possible for all (i.e. both paper and electronic) voters to receive such notifications. This is a positive outcome, since equal treatment of paper ballot and Internet voters has been a source of disagreement in Estonia before [9].

3.2 Setting up the Feedback Channel and Automation

The method of giving feedback should be considered as well. The feedback channel should be set up in a way that the information is easily accessible only to the voter. At the same time, it should be universal enough so that as many voters as possible are able to get this confirmation. An example would be an e-mail or SMS sent to the voter. The message can contain just the notification on the fact of voting, or an access link requiring further identification (eID in Estonia's case).

The biggest advantage of using automated feedback is that it would notify the voters if their credentials have been used to cast the vote. So if the voter's electronic ID has been compromised and a vote has been cast on the voter's behalf, the voter would be notified immediately and would be able to take action.

In Estonia, one logical solution would be to use State Portal eesti.ee to store and send receipts, as already suggested in the 2020 study on feasibility of mobile voting [16]. This is accessible to every voter using eID, and every ID-card user gets automatically an e-mail address at eesti.ee. Eesti.ee also includes a mail forwarding service which residents can set up to forward this information their main e-mail address. Other government services and the Population Registry share the data about residents' contacts with eesti.ee portal, making the voter contact database fairly accurate and up-to-date [10].[1] An example of a current voting related service that uses eesti.ee portal is the possibility to order electronic voter cards instead of voter cards sent on paper by post.

Eesti.ee contact information enables to send messages to most of the voters, and the voters would get this information using their eID (recall that ID-cards in Estonia are mandatory). Hence, such a feedback method would be both relatively easy to implement and the message ("I voted") easy to understand. Since coercion-resistance measures can be difficult to implement or, indeed, difficult for the voters to understand [34], this is suitable as the next step towards giving voters more assurance about how their votes are handled. Using eesti.ee service as a gateway would also mitigate the problem that an attacker can send out fake notifications *en masse* [28].

3.3 Information Provided by the Feedback

As noted above, the Estonian re-voting scheme relies, amongst other features, on the element of uncertainty, assuming the malefactor has no way of knowing which was the last vote cast by the voter or whether the voter re-voted. This holds equally for both small- and large-scale coercion attacks (e.g. vote buying). Thus, it is important to give as much information as necessary and as little as possible in the feedback.

The electronic list of voters includes information on the date and time of voting, voting method used (including i-voting) and of course the fact of voting itself. Additionally, the voting system logs more data on the voter, including the age, the operating system used, IP-address etc. [18]. However, since we view the feedback channel as similar to checking voter's information in the list of voters, we restrict our interest to the types of information provided through this list only.

The minimal information included in the voting receipt would be the fact of voting, i.e. confirming that the person has been recorded as having cast a vote.

The method of voting used is another bit of information that is available in the list of voters, the most important distinction here being whether the voter voted over Internet or with a paper ballot. If we would provide this information, it could reveal when the person re-voted with a paper vote, thus weakening the coercion resistance property. On the other hand, this information would give the voter assurance that their (i-)vote has not been changed.

It is also possible to send another confirmation after the voting period has ended, confirming that the voter's i-vote was entered into the count. This differs from checking one's data in the list of voters, since that information can be retrieved only from the Internet voting system before the votes are anonymized.

---

[1] The COVID-19 pandemic had a positive side effect in this regard, forcing the government agencies to update people's contact information in order to send out vaccination calls. As of May 2021, 1,260,203 people in the Estonian Population Registry had a valid e-mail address, and 238,162 did not. This means that about 84% of Estonian residents can be reached by email.

Such information is unavailable at all for paper ballots, which become anonymous once inside the ballot box. This wouldn't reveal more information to the malefactor besides the method of voting, but would give the voter assurance that the i-vote was actually tallied (and not misplaced), which in turn would hopefully increase the trustworthiness of Internet voting to some extent.

Since our goal is to just give confirmation on participating in voting, precise date and time of the vote should not be necessary, although the benefit of giving the voter assurance that their last vote was the one tallied is significant. However, the precise time of the cast of vote might be construed as proof of casting a specific vote which would be advantageous to the malefactor.

3.4 Timing of the Feedback

If the feedback is given during the voting period, this would give the malefactor a slight advantage, enabling them to coerce the voter to cast the vote again. If we do not include the date and time of voting in the receipt, the advantage for the malefactor is insignificant, essentially amounting to knowing that the person has voted at some point. Revealing the method used to vote or, for example, the date of voting (without the exact time) gives some additional information, showing possibly that an i-voter has re-voted in the polling station.

If the voting receipt is given after the voting period, then this would give the malefactor even less advantage, since the voter cannot re-cast the vote any more.

However, the advantage of giving feedback during the voting period is that it enables the voter to either re-vote if necessary, or file a complaint with a chance that the complaint will be resolved during the voting period. Instant feedback would also notify the voter if a vote has been cast using their credentials, thus exposing malicious takeovers of voters' electronic ID. If the complaint is filed after the end of the voting period, the voter has essentially no recovery mechanisms available. Even if the National Election Committee and/or the Supreme Court accept that the electoral law has been violated, the voter cannot cast a new vote after the voting has ended. The existing individual vote verification mechanism can be easily extended so that it would also provide a partial integrity check [28].

4 Conclusions and Future Work

The debate on the secrecy of vote has often concentrated on the fact of secrecy of vote itself, as if the secrecy is the definitive measure to guarantee free and fair elections. This is certainly commendable, but one should not forget that the concept of secret ballot does not exist in a vacuum. "Old" Western countries take some justified pride in how the understanding of vote secrecy is ingrained in their society. However, this concept works well only for on-site voting, but the modern voting environment encompasses different popular voting solutions for off-site voting as well. We agree with the interpretation suggested by Madise *et al.* that vote secrecy is not the ultimate goal, rather than a necessary means to achieve free and fair elections. Vote secrecy is just one part of the equation. We need to maintain trust in the voting system by addressing other possible issues as well. Voters are more and more moving away from the polling places and off-site voting methods like postal voting, voting at home and i-voting gain more and more traction. It is inevitable that some conflict is built in here, but even so we must try to seek for a good balance in regards to vote secrecy and transparency.

One of the weak points is the voters' and observers' inability to observe and track the path of their ballot. In a way, i-voting has opened a Pandora's Box which made voters question voting methods and trustworthiness of elections in general. Whether aforementioned inability is real or perceived doesn't even matter, since trust is ultimately based on what people think, not what they are told by the election authority. Recent debates in Estonia (but also surely in many other countries) have shown the need to consider voter's trust in the system as a whole and to address these concerns. Therefore we propose to augment the system with a feedback channel allowing the voter to detect misuses of the voting credentials.

We recommend giving automatic feedback to voters on their voting: the method they used to vote as well as the day (but not the time) they voted. This would enable the voters to get assurance that their vote was cast and received as intended, that their vote was not changed later and, in case of abstention, no one voted using the voter's credentials. Making this feedback automatic (e.g. in Estonia through state portal eesti.ee) guarantees that most of the electorate will receive this notification, creating a new layer of verifiability for the system. The ballot count will still remain anonymous and a voter cannot link their vote to a counted vote, a necessary concession to support secrecy and coercion-resistance of the vote.

Establishing such an automated personal feedback channel to voters is not necessarily in conflict with the principle of secret suffrage when restricted just to the fact of voting. It is similar to a voter accessing one's data in the voter list, although the final verdict depends on the amount of data revealed. Determining a good balance between secrecy and transparency is a subject for further discussion. It would also seem that a feedback channel requires some amendments to the legislation, since it concerns processing voting data. Working out the exact nature of such amendments remains the subject for future research as well. We also hope that the debate over secrecy of the vote, what this entails and on how to handle this in a modern voting environment, will continue.

Acknowledgements. This paper has been supported by the Estonian Research Council under the grant number PRG920. The authors are grateful to the Estonian Information System Authority and State Electoral Office for their support to the research process.

References

1. Universal Declaration of Human Rights, united Nations (1948). https://www.un. org/en/about-us/universal-declaration-of-human-rights
2. European Convention on Human Rights, European Court of Human Rights (1950). https://www.echr.coe.int/documents/convention_eng.pdf
3. International Covenant on Civil and Political Rights, united Nations (1966). https://www.ohchr.org/en/professionalinterest/pages/ccpr.aspx
4. CCPR General Comment No. 25: Article 25 (Participation in Public Affairs and the Right to Vote), The Right to Participate in Public Affairs, Voting Rights and the Right of Equal Access to Public Service, united Nations Committee on Human Rights (1996). https://ccprcentre.org/page/view/general_comments/28883
5. Vaalilaki, last amended 1.01.2021, parliament of Finland (1998). https://finlex.fi/ fi/laki/ajantasa/1998/19980714
6. Code of Good Practice In Electoral Matters: Guidelines and Explanatory Report, European Commission for Democracy Through Law (Venice Commission) (2002). https://rm.coe.int/090000168092af01
7. Federal electoral regulations, bundestag (2002). https://www.bundeswahlleiter. de/en/dam/jcr/e146a529-fd3b-4131-9588-8242c283537a/bundeswahlordnung_ engl.pdf
8. Riigikogu Election Act, RT I 2002, 57, 355; RT I, 03.01.2020, 2, parliament of Estonia (2002). https://www.riigiteataja.ee/en/eli/514122020002/consolide
9. Constitutional judgment 3-4-1-13-05: Petition of the President of the Republic to declare the Local Government Council Election Act Amendment Act, passed by the Riigikogu on 28 June 2005, unconstitutional, supreme Court of Estonia (2005). https://www.riigikohus.ee/en/constitutional-judgment-3-4-1-13-05
10. Vabariigi Valitsuse määrus Eesti teabevärava eesti.ee haldamise, teabe kättesaadavaks tegemise, arendamise ning kasutamise nõuded ja kord, RT I, 25.03.2021, 5, government of Estonia (2013). https://www.riigiteataja.ee/akt/ 125032021005
11. ECLI:NL:RBDHA:2014:5657, Rechtbank Den Haag (RBDHA), court of the Hague, Netherlands (2014). https://e-justice.europa.eu/ecli/ECLI:NL:RBDHA:2014:5657
12. Recommendation CM/Rec(2017) 5 of the Committee of Ministers to member States on standards for e-voting, council of Europe Committee of Ministers (2017). https://rm.coe.int/090000168092af01
13. E-valimiste turvalisuse töörühma koondaruanne, Estonian Ministry of Economic Affairs and Communications, in Estonian (2019). https://www.mkm.ee/sites/ default/files/content-editors/e-valimiste_tooruhma_koondaruanne_12.12.2019_0. pdf
14. Statistics about Internet voting in Estonia (2019). https://www.valimised.ee/en/ archive/statistics-about-internet-voting-estonia
15. Case ECH-2020-1-002 Magyar Kétfarkú Kutya Párt v. Hungary, european Court of Human Rights (2020). http://www.codices.coe.int/NXT/gateway.dll/CODICES/ precis/eng/EUR/ECH/ECH-2020-1-002
16. Mobile voting feasibility study and risk analysis, report number T-184-5, Cyber- netica AS (2020). https://www.valimised.ee/sites/default/files/uploads/eng/2020_ m-voting-report.pdf
17. E-voting: Online voting and elections (2021). https://www.post.ch/en/business- solutions/e-voting

18. Vabariigi Valimiskomisjoni otsus "Tehnilised nõuded elektroonilise hääletamise üldpõhimõtete tagamiseks", RT III, 27.01.2021, 6, estonian National Electoral Committee (2021). https://www.riigiteataja.ee/akt/327012021006
19. Annus, T.: Riigiõigus. Juura, in Estonian (2006)
20. Benaloh, J.: Rethinking voter coercion: the realities imposed by technology. In: 2013 Electronic Voting Technology Workshop/Workshop on Trustworthy Elections, EVT/WOTE 2013, Washington, D.C., USA, 12–13 August 2013. USENIX Association (2013). https://www.usenix.org/conference/evtwote13/workshop-program/presentation/benaloh
21. Braun Binder, N., Krimmer, R., Wenda, G., Fischer, D.H.: International standards and ICT projects in public administration: introducing electronic voting in Norway, Estonia and Switzerland compared. Halduskultuur Estonian J. Adm. C. Digit. Gov. 19(2), 8–21 (2019)
22. Brent, P.: The Australian ballot: not the secret ballot. Aust. J. Polit. Sci. 41(1), 39–50 (2006)
23. Buchstein, H.: Online democracy, is it viable? Is it desirable? Internet Voting and Normative Democratic Theory. In: Kersting, N., Baldersheim, H. (eds.) Electronic Voting and Democracy: A Comparative Analysis, pp. 97–108. Palgrave Macmillan UK (2004)
24. Drechsler, W., Madise, Ü.: Electronic voting in Estonia. In: Kersting, N., Baldersheim, H. (eds.) Electronic Voting and Democracy: A Comparative Analysis, pp. 97–108. Palgrave Macmillan, UK (2004)
25. Elklit, J.: Is voting in Sweden secret? An illustration of the challenges in reaching electoral integrity. In: IPSA World Congress, University of Brisbane (2018)
26. Barrat i Esteve, J., Goldsmith, B., Turner, J.: Compliance with International Standards (2021). https://www.regjeringen.no/globalassets/upload/krd/prosjekter/e-valg/evaluering/topic4_assessment.pdf
27. Gerber, A.S., Huber, G.A., Doherty, D., Dowling, C.M.: Is there a secret ballot? Ballot secrecy perceptions and their implications for voting behaviour. Br. J. Polit. Sci. 43, 77–102 (2013)
28. Heiberg, S., Krips, K., Willemson, J.: Planning the next steps for Estonian internet voting. In: Proceedings of the E-Vote-ID 2020, p. 82 (2020)
29. Heiberg, S., Martens, T., Vinkel, P., Willemson, J.: Improving the verifiability of the Estonian internet voting scheme. In: Krimmer, R., et al. (eds.) E-Vote-ID 2016. LNCS, vol. 10141, pp. 92–107. Springer, Cham (2017). https://doi.org/10.1007/978-3-319-52240-1_6
30. Heiberg, S., Parsovs, A., Willemson, J.: Log Analysis of Estonian Internet Voting 2013–2015. Cryptology ePrint Archive, Report 2015/1211 (2015). https://eprint.iacr.org/2015/1211
31. Heiberg, S., Willemson, J.: Modeling threats of a voting method. In: Design, Development, and Use of Secure Electronic Voting Systems, pp. 128–148. IGI Global (2014)
32. Heiberg, S., Willemson, J.: Verifiable internet voting in Estonia. In: Proceedings of the 6th International Conference on Electronic Voting: Verifying the Vote, EVOTE 2014, Lochau/Bregenz, Austria, 29–31 October 2014, pp. 1–8. IEEE (2014). https://doi.org/10.1109/EVOTE.2014.7001135
33. Jääskeläinen, A.: The Finnish Election System: Overwiew (2020). Oikeusministeriö
34. Krips, K., Willemson, J.: On practical aspects of coercion-resistant remote voting systems. In: Krimmer, R., et al. (eds.) E-Vote-ID 2019. LNCS, vol. 11759, pp. 216–232. Springer, Cham (2019). https://doi.org/10.1007/978-3-030-30625-0_14

35. Madise, Ü., Martens, T.: E-voting in Estonia 2005. the first practice of country-wide binding internet voting in the world. In: Krimmer, R. (ed.) Electronic Voting 2006–2nd International Workshop, Co-organized by Council of Europe, ESF TED, IFIP WG 8.6 and E-Voting.CC, pp. 15–26. Gesellschaft für Informatik e.V., Bonn (2006)

36. Madise, Ü., Priit, V.: Constitutionality of remote internet voting: the Estonian perspective. Juridica Int'l **18**, 4 (2011)

37. Madise, Ü., Vinkel, P.: Internet voting in Estonia: from constitutional debate to evaluation of experience over six elections. In: Kerikmäe, T. (ed.) Regulating eTechnologies in the European Union, pp. 53–72. Springer, Cham (2014). https://doi.org/10.1007/978-3-319-08117-5_4

38. Madise, Ü., Vinkel, P.: A judicial approach to internet voting in Estonia. In: E-Voting Case Law, pp. 135–158. Routledge (2016)

39. Nemčok, M., Peltoniemi, J.: Distance and trust: an examination of the two opposing factors impacting adoption of postal voting among citizens living abroad. Polit. Behav. 1–25 (2021). https://link.springer.com/article/10.1007/s11109-021-09709-7

40. Vollan, K.: Voting in uncontrolled environment and the secrecy of the vote. In: Electronic Voting 2006–2nd International Workshop, Co-organized by Council of Europe, ESF TED, IFIP WG 8.6 and E-Voting. CC. Gesellschaft für Informatik eV (2006)

41. Wasley, P.: Back when everyone knew how you voted. Humanities **37**(4) (2016). https://www.neh.gov/humanities/2016/fall/feature/back-when-everyone-knew-how-you-voted

42. Willemson, J.: Bits or paper: which should get to carry your vote? J. Inf. Secur. Appl. **38**, 124–131 (2018). https://doi.org/10.1016/j.jisa.2017.11.007

"Just for the Sake of Transparency": Exploring Voter Mental Models of Verifiability

Marie-Laure Zollinger[1]([✉]), Ehsan Estaji[1], Peter Y.A. Ryan[1], and Karola Marky[2]

[1] University of Luxembourg, Esch-sur-Alzette, Luxembourg
{marie-laure.zollinger,ehsan.estaji,peter.ryan}@uni.lu
[2] University of Glasgow, Glasgow, UK
karola.marky@glasgow.ac.uk

Abstract. Verifiable voting schemes allow voters to verify their individual votes and the election outcome. The voting protocol Selene offers verification of plaintext votes while preserving privacy. Misconceptions of verification mechanisms might result in voters mistrust of the system or abstaining from using it. In this paper, we interviewed 24 participants and invited them to illustrate their mental models of Selene. The drawings demonstrated different levels of sophistication and four mental models: 1) technology understanding, 2) meaning of the verification phase, 3) security concerns, and 4) unnecessary steps. We highlight the misconceptions expressed regarding Internet voting technologies and the system design. Based on our findings, we conclude with recommendations for future implementations of Selene as well as for the design of Internet voting systems in general.

1 Introduction

Elections are the foundations of democracy. To improve access to elections, several countries introduced ways to conduct elections over the Internet (e.g., Estonia [12], or Switzerland [30]). To uphold democratic principles, voting researchers have proposed secure and robust systems ensuring the integrity of Internet elections. The goal is to satisfy two main security features among others: privacy and verifiability. Privacy, in particular vote-secrecy, is well-known as it is also mandated by the law in many countries. Verifiability comprises *individual verification* meaning that each voter can check that their vote has been correctly recorded, and *universal verification* meaning that the outcome of the election can be confirmed by any observer [4]. Verification mechanisms seek to provide assurance of the correct execution of an election and hence in the outcome.

Verifiability must provide convincing proof to any voter that their votes are correctly cast-as-intended, recorded-as-cast, and counted-as-recorded [4]. To achieve this, Internet voting schemes rely on cryptography, often at the expense

© Springer Nature Switzerland AG 2021
R. Krimmer et al. (Eds.): E-Vote-ID 2021, LNCS 12900, pp. 155–170, 2021.
https://doi.org/10.1007/978-3-030-86942-7_11

of usability (cf. [2,19,20]). Research on voting has shown that voters are concerned by risks related to security [31,33] affecting their trust, especially as voters can consider verifiability mechanisms as privacy breaches [24,28], or question their necessity [2,19]. This might be due to the novelty of verification, which has been used in only a few real elections with high stakes, e.g., [12,30]. It might also be due to the complexity of the verification, requiring the voters to perform extra steps, understand complex mechanisms, or compare cryptographic data [5,7,8].

To counter this, the e-voting scheme Selene has been developed to minimize the voters' interaction with cryptography while providing individual and universal verifiability [26]. Selene's usability has already been demonstrated in studies with voters [11]. However, usability studies of Internet voting protocols have shown that mere usability is not sufficient in convincing voters about the correct processing of votes [2,13,19]. This might be because the voters' mental models do not align with the verification procedure.

Mental models are the internal representations that humans derive from interacting with a technology [25]. Mental models using the Selene protocol have been evaluated in a previous study [37]. In this paper, we investigate an improved implementation of the Selene protocol that builds on previous results. We evaluate voters' perceptions of the Selene e-voting protocol with 24 participants. To achieve that, after letting them interact with the app, we asked the participants to draw their understanding of voting and verifying using Selene.

Our Contributions. We explore the voters' understanding of the verification mechanism in the Selene Internet voting protocol. For that, we performed an analysis of the drawings and the answers and extracted four categories of mental models: 1) technology understanding, 2) meaning of the verification phase, 3) security concerns, and 4) unnecessary steps. We also classified the understanding of participants into levels of sophistication of their mental models. Finally, we discuss our findings and propose a list of recommendations applicable to Selene and to other Internet voting systems, focused on 1) education of voters on risks, 2) need for correctness and transparency, 3) integration of simple interactions with security features, and 4) design of several levels of verification.

Related Work. *Mental models* are internal representations that humans derive from the real world to interact with technology [14,25]. The level of sophistication of a mental model can differ amongst humans [9,14,15] and the mental models must be sound enough that users can effectively interact with a technology [16]. Generally, two types of mental models can be observed: functional and structural models [25]. Functional models mean that users know how to use a technology, but they do not how it works in detail. Structural models offer a more detailed understanding of how technology works. Once a mental model has been established, it is difficult to shift [32]. There are different ways to capture mental models, such as interviews (cf. [34]), sketching, or think-aloud techniques [15]. Related work in the domain of privacy has demonstrated that the combination of sketching and think-aloud is effective to capture the mental models [35].

Mental models have been investigated within the scope of security and privacy [1,3,15,36] indicating that misconceptions within mental models can lead users to engage in insecure behaviours, or in behaviours that do not match their intentions. Mental models within the scope of verifiable voting have also been investigated. Acemyan et al. [3] let voters draw their mental models after interacting with the three electronic voting schemes Helios, Prêt à Voter, and Scantegrity II. This study reveals that mental models are almost exclusively based on the voting process from their perspectives in all three protocols. Thus, voters expressed rather functional mental models that did not describe how the voting schemes worked. 75% of participants expressed to have recognized that their votes have been encrypted when using the Helios protocol. The usability of Helios [5] has been studied in many papers, such as [2,3,19]. Later investigations of Helios confirmed that the probabilistic nature does not align with voters' mental models, and because of that, voters considered verification to be unnecessary [19]. In a previous study of the Selene protocol, Zollinger et al. investigated mental models of the participants regarding technical properties that are required for security [37]. Their results show that voters are aware of potential security issues in Internet voting, but the presented verification mechanism did not convince them to mitigate these security issues. Our study takes into account this previous result.

Another line of research investigated perceptions of vote verification. As part of the trials to deploy online voting in Norway, participants failed to determine whether their votes had been submitted, although the scheme offers verification [13]. Using Helios, between 10 and 43% of participants were able to verify successfully [2,19]. Information provided to voters is crucial for the acceptance of verification [20].

In summary, research has shown that mental models have to be sound enough such that users can effectively interact with a technology. If voters have misconceptions, they might be unsuccessful in verifying their votes, consider it redundant, or question the security of the voting scheme. Adding to this body of research, we report a detailed investigation of mental models regarding the Selene Internet voting protocol.

2   The Selene Internet Voting Protocol

The app used for the user study is an implementation of the Internet voting protocol Selene [26]. Selene allows voters to identify their plaintext vote in the tally using a tracking number (or tracker) which is revealed to the voters *after* the election's outcome has been published. This is to provide coercion mitigation: letting voters identify another tracker to show to a coercer. However, this feature is not in the scope of the paper. Showing the voter the plaintext vote in the final tally should be more understandable than more conventional verifiable schemes that require the voter to check an encryption of the vote in the input to the tally.

2.1   Voter Experience and Protocol Setup

In this section, we summarize Selene's cryptographic setup[1].

Preliminaries: Each voter has a public/private key pair for use in the verification phase. The keys are generated and handled by the app; the voters do not have to interact with them. An election public key is generated with a corresponding private key. The public key is included in the app to avoid direct interaction with the voters.

Setup (Authorities): First, the election authorities generate a list of unique trackers. These trackers are encrypted with the public election key, secretly shuffled, and each of them is associated with a voter. A commitment to each tracker is created, sealing the relation between a tracker and a voter without revealing it. Each commitment can be opened only by its associated voter, using the voter's private key and a secret term delivered after the tally has been published.

Voting (Voters): To cast their votes voters log in to the voting app with credentials that they received before the election. After a welcome page, they select a candidate. Then, the app computes an encryption of their vote under the election public key and sends it to the election authority. The latter stores the encrypted votes next to the encrypted tracking number.

Tally (Authorities): When voting is over, the authorities extract the pairs of encrypted trackers and votes, which they shuffle and decrypt to obtain the pairs of plaintext trackers and votes which are then posted to the bulletin board.

Verifying (Voters): After the election, the secret value associated with the commitment is sent to the respective voter. The app combines the secret and the commitment and uses the voter's private key to reveal the tracker, without revealing the value to anyone else. We also highlighted one positive aspect regarding verification: the correctness of the records can be verified by anyone.

2.2   App Design

To increase security, the interfaces are split into two apps: one for voting and one for verifying. In case the voting app is compromised, it should not impact verifiability. This should also indicate to voters that their vote is not recorded by the voting app: when they check their vote, they retrieve a tracker and verify the associated vote.

Within the interfaces, we do not communicate all the information regarding the protocol. Instead, we stick to the interactions the voters perform: voting and verifying. In particular, the setup phase was not communicated in advance, and the tally is computed between the voting and the verification phases. Also, most security interactions that voters have with the protocol are related to encryption/decryption. In our app, the voter must explicitly push a button with the label "Encrypt", while the trackers are automatically decrypted. The information is shown to the user through a loading screen.

---

[1] A full cryptographic description of the protocol can be found in [26].

Finally, the possibility to chose another tracker in case of coercion is not provided in this version of the app since coercion mitigation was out of this investigation's scope.

3   Method

To evaluate the users' perceptions and understanding of the Selene Internet voting protocol, we conducted a user study with 24 participants.

Selene has been partially implemented as a demonstrator in the UK with a commercial partner [27]. For our study, we developed an interface where the voters can perform the required tasks: voting and verifying their vote. The interface design was informed by guidelines for Internet voting interface from the literature [20]. We also implemented a backend server where the authorities can set up elections, store votes, and compute the tally pairs (tracker, vote). The apps simulated an election for a past parliament for Germany to give a realistic scenario as recommended in [21,29]. Therefore, we used the ballots and results from the last election in the constituency where the study took place. The election had two contests, the first one had six candidates and the second one 20.

3.1   Procedure

Before interviewing the participants, they interacted with the Internet voting scheme. With this, we wanted to know whether the participants were able to verify their votes successfully. To capture this, we randomly manipulated one of the two contests for all participants. This means that the voting option next to the tracker did not correspond to the voter's choice. The procedure of our study was as follows.

We welcomed the participants by explaining that we are investigating an online voting protocol and that they are going to vote in an Internet (dummy) election followed by an interview. Then, we let them read the consent form and the study's data protection policy. Each participant provided demographics consisting of age, gender, education, and occupation. We also asked about previous voting experiences. The participants were introduced to the voting materials and devices consisting of a letter with sealed voting credentials (voter ID and password) as in a real election. Each participant received randomly chosen voting instructions, i.e. voting option for each ballot. This was to preserve the participants' vote privacy since we took screen-recordings [21]. Note that we explored additional user experience and usability aspects related to tracker-based protocols, that we elaborate in [22].

Each participant cast two votes since we wanted them to experience the voting scheme with and without a manipulated vote. In each round, the participants were asked to cast a vote matching the instructions. In the second round, we randomly manipulated one vote of a contest. When the participants reported completion, the examiner gave the following scenario: two weeks have passed[2]

---

[2] In Germany, where the study was conducted, this is the standard time frame between the end of the voting phase and the announcement of the outcome.

since the voting phase and the election results are now available. The participants were asked to use the verification app[3].

After the interaction with Selene was completed, we proceeded with the interview part. We explained that we would like them to draw their understanding of the following questions and that there are no wrong answers. The drawing area was recorded with a camera, and the participant's comments were audio-taped. We told the participants when we started the recording and proceeded with the semi-structured interview which was guided by the following main questions:

- Could you sketch how vote casting works according to your understanding?
- What to your understanding is the purpose of the tracking number?
- Why to your understanding is it necessary to see the list of all votes and not only your own one or is it not necessary at all?
- How to your understanding does the vote verification work?
- Why do you think voters are asked to verify?
- Consider an election, would you want information on how the vote verification works? Where or when would you like to receive this information?

In each question, the participant could integrate cards with pictures that we provided into their drawings. The cards had pictures of the following components: an icon representing the voter, a ballot, a ballot box, a smartphone, the icon of the app, an icon representing the Internet, an icon for encryption and a server. We provided the items to facilitate the drawing for the participants.

Participant were invited to ask questions, or to provide further feedback. We did not compensate individual participants but they could participate in a raffle for a voucher for online shopping in the value of about 100 Dollars.

3.2 Participants and Ethical Considerations

We recruited the 24 participants by mailing lists, social networks, and poster advertisements that did not mention verifiability. Fifteen participants identified as male, eight as female and one as other. The average age was 24.8 years (Min $= 19$, Max $= 40$, SD $= 5.37$). All participants reported daily Internet usage. The study followed the guidelines provided by the ethics commissions at the authors' institution and conforms to strict national law. In particular, our studies must limit the collection of personal data to preserve the privacy of participants. To anonymise the data, each participant received a randomly assigned identifier. Before the study, each participant signed a consent form that was recorded separately such that data cannot be linked to participants' identity. The following information were provided to the participants: goal and procedure of the study, risks associated with the participation, and how data storage and analysis is handled. Finally, it has a paragraph regarding data protection policy. The study was conducted before COVID-19.

---

[3] The emphasis was placed on the individual check of the tracking number. We did not explicitly ask the participants to recount the votes for universal verifiability.

3.3 Data Analysis

We transcribed the interviews and used a deductive coding methodology to categorize the data. The categories were discussed before starting the coding and emerged from the questions given to participants and the existing literature on the analysis of voters' perception. Then, two researchers coded the interviews independently. The agreement is given by Cohen's Kappa was calculated at 0.822, referring to an almost perfect agreement [10]. Then, the coders compared their findings and resolved disagreements. The drawings were categorized by two researchers, ordering them according accuracy and then relating them to the participants feedback about their experience.

3.4 Limitations

Although we took precautions and recruited participants beyond the university campus, some of our participants had background in computer science or were students. Consequently, our sample might not be representative. Our aim was to provide a explorative stepping stone for further investigations.

Furthermore, if technology-savvy voters already demonstrate understandability issues, those are likely to be exacerbated in a more general sample.

Another limitation is that the study was run in a lab hence a controlled environment [17,18], potentially leading to biased answers from the participants. However, for the voting area, it is hard to conduct experiments over real elections while preserving voters' privacy [21].

One feature of Selene, the coercion mitigation mechanism, was not in the scope of this study. Hence, we cannot draw conclusions about the voters' mental models regarding this feature. Finally, the results and conclusions are applicable to countries with similar cultures (Germany).

4 Results

In this section, we present the results of our study. Previous studies that investigated Selene demonstrated a good user experience but some misconceptions remain [11,37]. In this paper, we want to go further by asking the participants explicitly how they understand Selene and represent it in drawings to reveal their understanding of the verification mechanisms and their beliefs regarding Internet voting technologies. In the remainder of this section, we first present *levels of sophistication* before detailing the observed *mental models explicitly.*

4.1 Levels of Sophistication

Many participants had a good overview and provided a good explanation of how the system works according to their understanding. We classified the drawings in two types of mental models as described in [25]: 1) functional models and 2) structural models. The functional model describes the drawings in which the

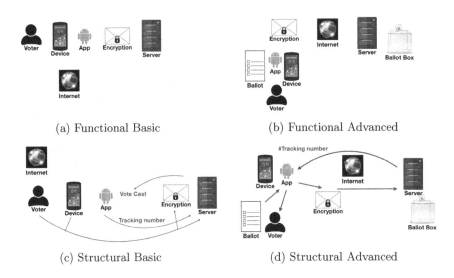

(a) Functional Basic   (b) Functional Advanced

(c) Structural Basic   (d) Structural Advanced

Fig. 1. Four levels of understanding.

participants used the provided components without linking those components together. The structural model describes the drawings depending on the use of components and their relations to each other.

We can deduce two levels of understanding inside those two main categories: basic and advanced. Figure 1 shows an example of drawing (reproduced) for every category mentioned below. We describe the four levels as follows:

1. **Functional basic** (one participant): some components are used but are not detailing the entire procedure. In Fig. 1a, P22 used some components, but the ballot and the ballot box are missing.
2. **Functional advanced** (seven participants): the components are used in a specific order to express the functional tasks that were performed. In Fig. 1b, P21 used all components and grouped them while explaining his experience.
3. **Structural basic** (nine participants): some components are used and related to each other. In Fig. 1c, P14 used some components and tried to relate them but misplaced or did not use all of them.
4. **Structural advanced** (seven participants): the components and their relations were correctly set. In Fig. 1d, P01 used all components and explained the correct structure and relations between all of them.

Regarding the vote manipulation, we counted 20 participants who clearly reported that they have seen a problem to the examiner.

Besides the general level of sophistication, the comments and drawings from the participants can be grouped into: 1) *technology understanding*, 2) *meaning of the verification phase*, 3) *security concerns* and 4) *unnecessary steps* which we detail in the following sections.

4.2   Technology Understanding

All participants gave their vision of how the voting system is designed and how they understood the technology behind it. As described in Sect. 3, we provided several components to participants. Some of them were related to a standard paper-based system (ballot, ballot box), and others were related to online technologies (Internet, app, device, encryption, server).

Overall Voting Technology. From the 24 participants, seven did not use the paper-based components in their drawings. All other components were used but sometimes misplaced. Six participants thought that encryption occurs on the server side, although the app mentioned that it is done locally. Three participants placed the ballot box in the smartphone instead of the server. For instance, participant P16 said: *"The smartphone is the ballot box and the app is a tool."*

Nineteen participants provided a good description of their experience and the technology in use. For example: *"The smartphone uses the app to apparently retrieve the data from the server of the electoral authorities and show the voter which vote he has cast based on this tracking number."* (P06); or *"The encrypted vote is then forwarded via the Internet and placed in the digital ballot box and added. And this ballot box is stored on a server where all election results are then uploaded. And where they can then be retrieved again by the voter after the election, for example by the verification app."* (P12).

Verification Phase. The procedure itself for individual verification was understood, but the overall process remained unclear. As described in Sect. 2, the app contains information about the tracking number in the verification phase, but does not provide details on how the connection between trackers and votes are made. Nevertheless, seven participants described how their vote was linked to their tracking number. For example, participant P19 said: *"It's probably generated from some data from my smartphone because it has to store it somehow because I didn't have to enter it anywhere".*

Only one participant (P17) misunderstood the content of the bulletin board and thought that it shows links to voters: *"We receive the list of, as far as I understood, all voters."*

4.3   Meaning of the Verification Phase

Besides technical details of verification, we asked the participants to explain the purpose of the tracking number and the bulletin board. Finally, we asked them why verification is required. We describe their answers based on comments about 1) *individual verifiability*, 2) *universal verifiability*, and 3) *general purpose*.

Individual Verifiability. 23 of 24 participants explained individual verification with the tracking numbers. Fifteen of them explicitly mentioned the *correctness* of recorded votes, others explained a comparison between the recorded vote and their vote intention. For example: *"Here is a list of numbers and votes and these will be sent to my smartphone and I can compare them with my tracking number to see if what I voted for finally reached the server."* (P04); or *"I as a voter I can check if I have voted correctly."* (P12).

Universal Verifiability. Participants expressed difficulties in explaining why they can see all votes instead of only their own. Eleven participants talked about recounting even if the app did not offer an intuitive way to do it, for example, P02 said: *"It wasn't possible with the app but theoretically I could use all the votes to check if everything is correct and of course I need all the votes for that."*. Two participants also mentioned that the bulletin board was necessary to find their own vote as the tracking number was stored locally on the phone. For instance, P09: *"I need them all at some point because I have to find my own."*

General Purpose. Three participants compared Selene's features to actual voting systems that do not allow them to verify. For instance, P01 said: *"It offers a way to see if the vote is present at all because in old systems that's not there at all"*. Four participants mentioned transparency as a goal, e.g.: *"[...] that we can offer the citizens a certain transparency."* (P16); or *"I do think it is necessary just for the sake of transparency."* (P23). Five participants also mentioned it as a confidence or trust feature, like P11 mentioned that it is *"to give a little more confidence."*

4.4   Security Concerns

All participants mentioned different security concerns and considerations during the interviews. With respect to the previous section about the meaning of the verification phase, the correctness of the result and the integrity of the elections were mentioned by 15 participants as a security concern, e.g., P07 said: *"There is a bit of certainty that it was done correctly"*.

All participants noticed the encryption of the votes. Three participants questioned the encryption of other parts, for instance, the encryption of the channel between the app and the server and encryption of the data on the server itself, e.g., P05: *"I didn't pay attention to it but I hope there was an encrypted connection to the infrastructure of the election office, via the Internet"*.

Sixteen participants mentioned that they wanted to have information regarding the verification phase in advance during the registration process for three different reasons: First, four said that it would help them decide whether they choose this app to cast their vote. Second, eleven mentioned that they would evaluate the reliability of the app, and third six said that it would provide more time to voters to understand how it works.

Nine participants questioned the implementation and said it had a direct impact on their trust. For example, some participants questioned the origin of the tracking number and whether it indeed shows their cast vote. For instance, P15 said: *"It was cryptic in the sense that I just received it from the server, I couldn't understand if this is really the vote I cast."*. Furthermore, three participants questioned the system by describing it in a skeptical way, e.g. P05: *"Hopefully the votes cast are stored there in encrypted form"*.

Attacks or bugs in the system were mentioned by nine participants, such as ballot rigging or possible manipulations: *"I would know theoretically whether they were manipulated or not"* (P20); *"The votes that were cast could also, as it was the case with me once, simply have been wrong somehow"* (P10).

Four participants mentioned anonymity as one of their concerns linked to the tracking number, e.g. P01: *"They are anonymous because nobody has any idea which tracking number the other person has."*

Concerns about dispute resolution were also mentioned by three participants, two of them noticed that they cannot prove how they voted afterwards so questioned how to prove a mistake, e.g. P19: *"Somehow nobody can prove that you have actually chosen something else."*

Only two participants mentioned the decryption of the tracking number in the app, and one of them questioned the origin of the keys in use in the app. Finally, two participants believed that from the bulletin board, one might figure out whom a specific voter voted for, hence breaking privacy.

4.5   Unnecessary Steps

Thirteen participants perceived some verification steps as unnecessary. In particular, the bulletin board was considered as useless. For example, P09 mentioned: *"If I already know what my tracker is, I honestly don't see the point of seeing all of them."* Even if participants mentioned recounting of votes as an option, they were not interested in doing it. For example, P06 said: *"You could say that it's about comparing this list of votes with the overall election results, of course. But then again, I do not see how the normal voter should actually do that with several million eligible voters or several million votes cast"*.

Even if most of the participants understood the purpose of individual verification, two were not convinced by the provided information and questioned the need of making the system verifiable. For instance, P03 mentioned that *"It also doesn't help me to check if this is really part of the final result or not."*

5   Discussion

5.1   Lessons Learned

In this section, we discuss observations from our interview study and its results.

Impact of Vote Manipulation. In our study, the participants executed the protocol twice. In the second round, the cast vote was modified, since vote manipulations are recommended to measure the execution of a given mental task [21,29]. In our case, this manipulation showed a possible source of errors in an Internet election to the participants. Twenty participants clearly reported it to the examiner, we cannot tell if the four remaining participants did not understand or lacked confidence to highlight the issue, as mentioned in [23]. In previous studies on the Selene protocol [11,37], such a threat was not shown to the participants and the participants had more difficulties explaining why verification is useful. Combined to the explanations provided in the app experiencing an incorrect vote had a positive impact on the understanding of the participants. Indeed, almost all of them had a good idea of the meaning of the verification phase, in particular, showing the correctness of the result. Of course, we cannot trigger such an attack and make voters experience errors in a real election, but it shows that being aware of the risks helps understanding the meaning to a given task.

Different Needs for the Users. Several participants expressed a need of learning more details about the setup and the origin of tracking numbers, or wanted to have additional proofs. The correct understanding of the available features was not enough to convince them. This had a negative impact on participants as it raised many questions and affected their trust in Selene. Several participants said that they would prefer to have information regarding the system before the elections to ensure their correct understanding and the reliability of the system. Selene can provide additional mathematical proofs, and it is specified in the original protocol that more verifiable data is available to the public.

More than half of the participants did not consider it necessary to access the complete list of votes, even if some of them explained the possibility of recounting the votes and the transparency that it provides. As mentioned in Sect. 2, one important security feature in the protocol design, not tested here, is the accessibility of the bulletin board in order to let a possibly coerced voter choose another tracking number. It has been highlighted in a previous study that this missing feature might help the voters to understand better the opportunity of accessing the complete list of votes [37].

Bada *et al.* [6] acknowledged that risk awareness and understanding are prerequisites to change security behaviours. However, they also highlighted that additional factors must be taken into considerations, in particular the adaptability to the audience and to its needs is encouraged.

Impact of the Security Communication. In the apps, security-related information was communicated on several screens. First, several loading screens between the direct interactions with the users showed the following information: authentication, encryption of votes, and decryption of the tracking numbers. Furthermore, before the vote encryption, the users were explicitly pushing a button indicating "Encrypt" to encrypt their vote. Finally, the anonymity of the trackers was explained inside the app before the verification. In two prior studies of Selene [11,37], the authors highlighted that the security, even if visible, remained unseen by the participants of their study. A possible reason for that could have been the lack of interactivity with the security features. In our study, using an "encryption button", we observed that all participants mentioned this feature. However, the drawings revealed that the location of the encryption computation sometimes remained unclear. This might be due to a lack of knowledge in security properties and software design but it did not have a negative impact on the participants. On the contrary, interacting with encryption had a positive impact on the security concerns of the participants, as it made them aware that a security feature is implemented. Similarly to previous studies, participants did not notice the decryption of tracking number, since it was mentioned only in the loading screen.

5.2   Recommendations

Based on our observations and the lessons learned above, we distill four recommendations to inform the design of future verifiable voting schemes, applicable to Selene but also other verifiable schemes.

1. **Provide information to support transparency.** The security concern regarding correctness was often mentioned during interviews when explaining the meaning of the verification phase. As discussed above, one reason might be the impact of the vote manipulation but we can also mention the verification app that gives several insights on verifiability to voters, among which the correctness of records was cited. On the other side, few participants mentioned transparency, but this did not justify the display of all votes for them. For future implementations, our first recommendation concerns the clear designation of each entity that a user might deal with and their purpose to ensure a complete understanding of the expected tasks.

2. **Provide education materials about risks.** The vote manipulation made participants aware of possible risks related to online voting and let them better understand the meaning of the verification phase. We highlighted that risk communication, control over verifiability procedures and easy security interactions can lead to a better understanding of the tasks one must perform. To be accepted, an Internet voting system needs to convince enough voters to perform those additional individual checks. It is recommended to provide voters with materials to educate themselves on possible risks related to Internet voting, and how to counter them. The Swiss Post voting protocol, for instance, provides such access to voters [30]. In addition, informative materials, such as TV spots or websites, could use an incorrect vote and show voters how it can be detected with a verification mechanism.

3. **Provide simple interactions with a security emphasis.** The interaction with the encryption button has shown to raise the awareness of participants regarding the security implementation. Other screens in the app where security was shown without interactivity were mentioned by participants only twice. This confirms the previous studies with this voting protocol [11,37] and related voting schemes [20]. Therefore, we recommend to communicate security through simple interactions whenever possible. Following the example of the encryption, naming the security tasks on a simple interaction like pushing a button is enough to raise the awareness of users.

4. **Provide different levels of verification.** Many participants understood the verification features but were not always convinced by them, while other participants considered certain information as unnecessary. Hence, we recommend organizing the verifiable data and information such that it is displayed only on demand. We can distinguish three levels of verifiable information: 1)

a minimal display, showing the individual vote to be verified only, 2) a full display, showing the individual vote and the entire bulletin board, and 3) a full access for experts, containing detailed specification on how to perform additional checks. This last level will let any expert (eligible to vote or not) verify more steps of the protocol.

6　Conclusion and Future Work

We investigated mental models of 24 participants using the Selene Internet voting protocol. We let them draw their understanding of voting and verification using Selene and we interviewed them. The mental models demonstrated different levels of sophistication, security concerns, and understanding. We also highlighted that the tracker used to verify their individual votes was not enough for all users; in contrast the full bulletin board given for universal verifiability was stressed as unnecessary. Furthermore, we found that direct interaction with security features had a positive impact on the awareness of a secure implementation. These findings helped us to understand the users' expectations in Internet voting applications, and highlight their need of transparency and correctness for elections, as well as more interactions with security features and more control on the process. Some features were not explored yet in this study and as future work, we will test their impact on the voters' understanding and trust in the system. Also, the mental models of voters with paper voting systems might differ and a comparison of voters' models with paper and internet voting schemes will be explored. Finally, having a misconception of how the system works might not prevent a voter to use it correctly. This is also an interesting future direction for our research.

Acknowledgements. This research was supported by the Luxembourg National Research Fund (FNR), under the joint INTER project SeVoTe (INTER/FNRS/ 15/11106658/SeVoTe) as well as the Deutsche Forschungsgemeinschaft (DFG, German Research Foundation) – 251805230/GRK 2050.

References

1. Abdi, N., Ramokapane, K.M., Such, J.M.: More than smart speakers: security and privacy perceptions of smart home personal assistants. In: Proceedings of the Symposium on Usable Privacy and Security, pp. 1–16. USENIX Association, Berkeley, CA, USA (2019)
2. Acemyan, C.Z., Kortum, P., Byrne, M.D., Wallach, D.S.: Usability of voter verifiable, end-to-end voting systems: baseline data for Helios, Prêt à Voter, and Scantegrity II. SENIX J. Elect. Technol. Syst. 2(3), 26–56 (2014)
3. Acemyan, C.Z., Kortum, P.T., Byrne, M.D., Wallach, D.S.: Users' mental models for three end-to-end voting systems: helios, prêt à voter, and scantegrity II. In: International Conference on Human Aspects of Information Security, Privacy, and Trust (2015)

4. Adida, B.: Advances in Cryptographic Voting Systems. Ph.D. thesis, Massachusetts Institute of Technology (2006)
5. Adida, B.: Helios: Web-based open-audit voting. In: Proceedings of the USENIX Security Symposium, pp. 335–348. USENIX Association, Berkeley, CA, USA (2008)
6. Bada, M., Sasse, A.M., Nurse, J.R.C.: Cyber security awareness campaigns: why do they fail to change behaviour? (2019)
7. Ben-Nun, J., et al.: A new implementation of a dual (paper and cryptographic) voting system. In: International Conference on Electronic Voting (2012)
8. Benaloh, J., et al.: Star-vote: a secure, transparent, auditable, and reliable voting system. CoRR (2012)
9. Borgman, C.L.: The user's mental model of an information retrieval system: an experiment on a prototype online catalog. Int. J. Man Mach. Stud. **24**(1), 47–64 (1986)
10. Cohen, J.: A coefficient of agreement for nominal scales. Educ. Psychol. Meas. **20**(1), 37–46 (1960)
11. Distler, V., Zollinger, M., Lallemand, C., Rønne, P.B., Ryan, P.Y.A., Koenig, V.: Security - visible, yet unseen? In: Proceedings of the CHI Conference on Human Factors in Computing Systems (2019)
12. Estonian national electoral committee (2019). https://www.valimised.ee/en/archive/statistics-about-internet-voting-estonia
13. Fuglerud, K.S., Røssvoll, T.H.: An evaluation of web-based voting usability and accessibility. Univ. Access Inf. Soc. **11**(4), 359–373 (2012). https://doi.org/10.1007/s10209-011-0253-9
14. Johnson-Laird, P.N.: Mental models: towards a cognitive science of language, inference, and consciousness. No. 6, Harvard University Press (1983)
15. Kang, R., Dabbish, L., Fruchter, N., Kiesler, S.: "My data just goes everywhere": user mental models of the internet and implications for privacy and security. In: Proceedings of the Symposium on Usable Privacy and Security, pp. 39–52. USENIX Association, Berkeley, CA, USA (2015)
16. Kulesza, T., Stumpf, S., Burnett, M., Yang, S., Kwan, I., Wong, W.: Too much, too little, or just right? Ways explanations impact end users' mental models. In: Proceedings of the IEEE Symposium on Visual Languages and Human Centric Computing, pp. 3–10 (September 2013). https://doi.org/10.1109/VLHCC.2013.6645235
17. Lallemand, C., Koenig, V.: Lab testing beyond usability: challenges and recommendations for assessing user experiences. J. Usability Stud. **12**(3), 133–154 (2017)
18. Levitt, S.D., List, J.A.: What do laboratory experiments tell us about the real world. J. Econ. Perspect., 153–174 (2007)
19. Marky, K., Kulyk, O., Renaud, K., Volkamer, M.: What did i really vote for? On the usability of verifiable e-voting schemes. In: Proceedings of the CHI Conference on Human Factors in Computing Systems, pp. 176:1–176:13. ACM, New York, NY, USA (2018). https://doi.org/10.1145/3173574.3173750
20. Marky, K., Zimmermann, V., Funk, M., Daubert, J., Bleck, K., Mühlhäuser, M.: Improving the usability and ux of the swiss internet voting interface. In: Proceedings of the CHI Conference on Human Factors in Computing Systems, pp. 640:1–640:13. ACM, New York, NY, USA (2020). https://doi.org/10.1145/3313831.3376769
21. Marky, K., Zollinger, M.L., Funk, M., Ryan, P.Y., Mühlhäuser, M.: How to assess the usability metrics of e-voting schemes. In: Financial Cryptography and Data Security, Workshop on Workshop on Advances in Secure Electronic Voting (2019)

22. Marky, K., Zollinger, M.L., Roenne, P.B., Ryan, P.Y., Grube, T., Kunze, K.: Investigating usability and user experience of individually verifiable internet voting schemes. ACM Trans. Comput. Hum. Interact. **28**(5) (2021). https://kaikunze. de/papers/pdf/marky2021investigating.pdf

23. Moher, E., Clark, J., Essex, A.: Diffusion of voter responsibility: potential failings in e2e voter receipt checking. USENIX J. Elect. Technol. Syst. (JETS) **1**(3), 1–17 (2014). https://www.usenix.org/jets/issues/0301/moher

24. Nestas, L., Hole, K.: Building and maintaining trust in internet voting. Computer **45**(5), 74–80 (2012). https://doi.org/10.1109/MC.2012.35

25. Norman, D.A.: Some observations on mental models. In: Mental models, pp. 15–22. Psychology Press (2014)

26. Ryan, P.Y.A., Rønne, P.B., Iovino, V.: Selene: voting with transparent verifiability and coercion-mitigation. In: Proceedings of the Financial Cryptography and Data Security (2016)

27. Sallal, M., et al.: VMV: augmenting an internet voting system with selene verifiability (2019)

28. Schneider, S., Llewellyn, M., Culnane, C., Heather, J., Srinivasan, S., Xia, Z.: Focus group views on prêt à voter 1.0. In: International Workshop on Requirements Engineering for Electronic Voting Systems (2011)

29. Selker, T., Rosenzweig, E., Pandolfo, A.: A methodology for testing voting systems. J. Usability Stud. **2**(1), 7–21 (2006). http://dl.acm.org/citation.cfm?id=2835536. 2835538

30. Serdült, U., Germann, M., Mendez, F., Portenier, A., Wellig, C.: Fifteen years of internet voting in switzerland [history, governance and use]. In: Proceedings of the Second International Conference on eDemocracy eGovernment (2015)

31. Serdült, U., Kryssanov, V.: Internet voting user rates and trust in Switzerland. In: Proceedings of the International Joint Conference on Electronic Voting, pp. 211–212 (2018). https://doi.org/10.5167/uzh-156867

32. Tullio, J., Dey, A.K., Chalecki, J., Fogarty, J.: How it works: a field study of non-technical users interacting with an intelligent system. In: Proceedings of the SIGCHI Conference on Human Factors in Computing Systems, pp. 31–40. Association for Computing Machinery, New York, NY, USA (2007). https://doi.org/10. 1145/1240624.1240630

33. Warkentin, M., Sharma, S., Gefen, D., Rose, G.M., Pavlou, P.: Social identity and trust in internet-based voting adoption. Gov. Inf. Q. **35**(2), 195–209 (2018)

34. Wash, R.: Folk models of home computer security. In: Proceedings of the Symposium on Usable Privacy and Security. Association for Computing Machinery, New York, NY, USA (2010). https://doi.org/10.1145/1837110.1837125

35. Zeng, E., Mare, S., Roesner, F.: End user security & privacy concerns with smart homes. In: Proceedings of the Symposium on Usable Privacy and Security, pp. 65–80. USENIX Association, Berkeley, CA, USA (2017)

36. Zimmermann, V., Gerber, P., Marky, K., Böck, L., Kirchbuchner, F.: Assessing users' privacy and security concerns of smart home technologies. i-com **18**(3), 197–216 (2019)

37. Zollinger, M., Distler, V., Rønne, P.B., Ryan, P.Y., Lallemand, C., Koenig, V.: User experience design for e-voting: how mental models align with security mechanisms. In: Proceedings of the Joint International Conference on Electronic Voting (2019)

Author Index

Printed in the United States
by Baker & Taylor Publisher Services

Printed in the United States
by Baker & Taylor Publisher Services